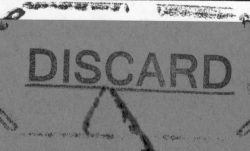

THE RAMAPO MOUNTAIN PEOPLE

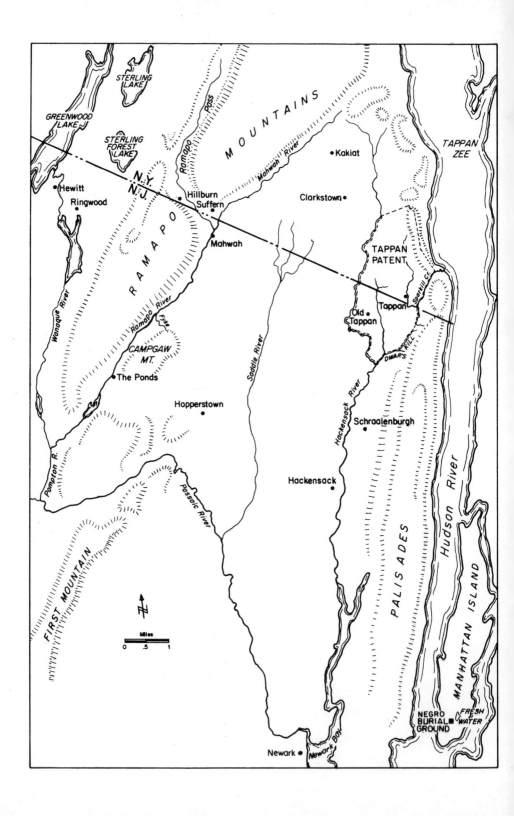

The Ramapo Mountain People

DAVID STEVEN COHEN

Photographs by Robert Goldstein

RUTGERS UNIVERSITY PRESS
New Brunswick, New Jersey

49490

Library of Congress Cataloging in Publication Data

Cohen, David Steven, 1943–
    The Ramapo Mountain people.

    Bibliography: p.
    1. Ramapo Mountain people.   I.   Title.
E184.R3C64   917.47'28   74-9581
ISBN 0-8135-0768-5

To the memory of my grandfather William Gottlieb
and
to my parents Molly and Lew Cohen

CONTENTS

TABLES

PREFACE

This book is about a group of people who have no name for themselves. They are known to many of their neighbors as the Jackson Whites, a name that is offensive to them. I call them the Ramapo Mountain People. They are found today principally in three communities where the Ramapos cross the border between southeastern New York and northern New Jersey.

The region consists of tree-covered ridges and hollows with streams running down from mountain lakes. Hiking paths such as the Cannon Ball Trail criss-cross the mountains. The Ramapos are not especially high; their rounded peaks reach no more than 800 feet above the bordering valleys—the Wanaque River Valley on the northwest and the Ramapo River Valley on the southeast. The Ramapos are divided by the Ramapo Pass, through which run the New York State Thruway, State Highway Route 17, and the Erie Railroad on their way to upstate New York. The mountains mark the northwestern edge of the metropolitan New York City suburbs.

The Ramapo Mountain People today are a relatively small group. They number only approximately 1,500 and live in Mahwah and Ringwood, New Jersey, and Hillburn, New York. Yet they are distinct from the surrounding society. Their racially mixed ancestry socially isolates them as a separate racial group. Marriage within the group over many generations has resulted in their being a separate kinship group. A few surnames predominate, the oldest being De Freese, Van Dunk, De Groat, and Mann.

I first became aware of the Ramapo Mountain People when I was a high school student in Westwood, New Jersey. John C. Storms, a newspaper editor in Park Ridge, New Jersey, who had written a booklet about these people, was invited by my sister Judy to lecture about them in a course she was taking at Fairleigh Dickinson University. Years later as a graduate student at the University of Pennsylvania, I was reminded of Mr. Storms's lecture. Rereading his booklet in light of graduate courses in folklore I had taken, I began to suspect that his account was more folklore than history. I decided to begin an inter- disciplinary study that would combine the concepts and methods of anthropology, sociology, folklore, and history.

I moved to the Ramapos to live for a year among the Mountain People and to study their culture at first hand. I did extensive genea- logical research. I began a study of the personal names in church records of marriages and baptisms, the names and properties described in deeds, wills, and inventories in county courthouses, the information contained in the manuscript federal and state censuses, and the col- lections of local libraries, historical societies, and the New York Public Library. I also consulted informants among the Mountain People about their ancestors and relatives. In time I was able to construct family trees of the early ancestors of the Ramapo Mountain People.

There are other racially mixed groups in the eastern United States: the Lumbees or Croatans in North Carolina, the Melungeons in eastern Tennessee, the Brass Ankles in South Carolina, the Redbones in western Louisiana, the Wesorts in Maryland, and the Moors and Nanticokes in Delaware. Because their histories were not recorded, many of these groups have legends about their origins. (See Appendix E for a survey of the scholarly literature about them.)

The Ramapo Mountain People who reside in the section of the mountains southwest of the Ramapo Pass use the term *colored* to describe their race. By this they mean nonwhite. They are sometimes confused with white mountaineers also called Jackson Whites who made splint baskets and lived in the northeastern section of the Ramapos near Ladentown, New York. Among the latter were families named Hogenkamp, Pitt, and Conklin. They were descendants of white settlers who moved into what is today Rockland County, New York, in the eighteenth century. There is no evidence of their having any racially mixed ancestry. Most of them were moved out of the Ramapos to make way for Harriman State Park. The colored Ramapo Mountain People consider these white mountaineers a separate group;

and, notwithstanding one or two marriages between these groups, their separateness is substantiated by my genealogical research.

In reflecting upon my experiences with the Ramapo Mountain People and the information I gathered about them, I found it necessary to decide which aspects of their culture should be included in this book. It is not a sociological study of poverty or housing conditions; not all the Mountain People live in poverty. It is not a study of genetics or health; that should be made by a scientist. Nor is it a study of the sexual behavior of the Mountain People; to be valid, such a study would have to be based on a statistical survey. I have concentrated on the three present-day settlements of the Mountain People. I have not included those Mountain People who have migrated from the Ramapo Mountains. I have emphasized those aspects of their culture that demonstrate the distinctive nature of their group (race and kinship), the relationship between their group and the surrounding society, and the relationship between their folklore and their history.

ACKNOWLEDGMENTS

I want to express my gratitude to the Ramapo Mountain People, who allowed me to live among them and to study them. My thanks to Wallace and Vivian De Groat and their family, with whom I lived during part of the field work. Howard Morgan, a man of great warmth and character, spent many afternoons providing genealogical information from his remarkable memory. The family of John and Madge Morgan, especially their son Wallace, welcomed me into their household and provided much information on the folklore of the Mountain People. Frank Milligan, a very talented story-teller, supplied many of the tall tales included in this book. Otto Mann, a Pentecostal minister and leader of the Stag Hill Civic League, was also very cooperative, as were Richard De Freese, Julia and Victor De Freese, Kitty De Freese, Peter and Mildred Galindez, Ed Morgan, Vince Morgan, Bob Milligan, Fred "Snoozy" Powell, Billy Van Dunk, and William "Pooch" Van Dunk.

Three professors at the University of Pennsylvania helped me during the early stages of my work: my advisor Ruben Reina, of the Anthropology Department, read my field notes, arranged monthly consultations, and gave me invaluable advice throughout the writing and revision of the dissertation. Kenneth Goldstein and Murray Murphey also read my dissertation and offered constructive criticism.

Photographer Robert Goldstein added another dimension to my study by his skill in capturing on film the spirit as well as the likenesses of the Ramapo Mountain People.

In his research on the history of blacks in Rockland County, New York, Professor Carl Nordstrom of Brooklyn College discovered genealogical material on the ancestors of the Ramapo Mountain People which he graciously made available to me.

Donald Sinclair, director of the Special Collections of the Rutgers University Library, steered me to important information on the Jersey Dutch dialect.

I am grateful for the help of Andrew Marshall, who had special insight into the problems of the Mountain People of the Ringwood Mine Area as director of HOW-TO, Inc.

The staffs of several libraries and institutions were helpful in my research: the Manuscript Section of the New York Public Library, the New-York Historical Society, the Archives of the New Jersey State Library, the Special Collections of the Rutgers University Library, the New Jersey Historical Society, the New Jersey section of the Newark Public Library, the Bergen County Historical Society collection of the Johnson Free Public Library, the Nyack Public Library, the Suffern Free Library, the Ridgewood Public Library, the Vineland Training School, and the offices of deeds and probate of Bergen and Rockland counties.

Other people who assisted me are Karen Baldwin, my brother Ronald Cohen, Charles Cummings, Jeff Darling, Eleanor and John Dater, Professor Warren Kimball, Professor Theodore Kury, Charles Kaufman, Adrian Leiby, Anne Lutz, Karen Post, Reverend Myron Miller, Robert Morris, David Rodriguez, Helen Reed, Jan Rubin, Harold Sherwood, James Ransom, Dr. Kenn Stryker-Rodda, George G. Shelps, Cecil and Mae Smith, Dr. James Veith, Reverend Sylvester Van Oort, Professor Peter Wacker, Gardner Watts, and Lewis West.

Linda Prentice helped read proofs. Charlotte Carlson prepared the maps, Roberta Blaché the index.

Finally, I am grateful to the New Jersey Historical Commission for its grant which made possible the aerial photographs of the Ramapo region.

THE RAMAPO MOUNTAIN PEOPLE

"Do you think it's right to rake up the past?"

"I don't feel that I know what you mean by raking it up. How can we get at it unless we dig a little? The present has such a rough way of treading it down."

"Oh I like the past, but I don't like critics," my hostess declared with her hard complacency.

"Neither do I, but I like their discoveries."

"Aren't they mostly lies?"

"The lies are what they sometimes discover," I said, smiling at the quiet impertinence of this. "They often lay bare the truth."

"The truth is God's, it isn't man's; we had better leave it alone. Who can judge of it?—who can say?"

From *The Aspern Papers*
by Henry James

1 THE ORIGIN OF THE JACKSON WHITES— HISTORY OR LEGEND?

In 1936 a small-town New Jersey newspaper editor named John C. Storms wrote and published a booklet entitled *The Origin of the Jackson-Whites of the Ramapo Mountains*. In it Storms said the Tuscarora Indians "represent the first real influx into the mountains, and constituted the first element in the race of people that grew up there, and has become known as the Jackson Whites."

Originally the Ramapo Mountain region was a favorite resort of the Hagingashackie (Hackensack). Indians, part of the Leni Lenipe family of the Iroquois [in fact, they were part of the Algonquin, not the Iroquois, language group]. . . . These aborigines had practically all disappeared by the end of the seventeenth century. However, a few remained together with a scattered population that had sought the security of the mountains to evade their brother white man, his laws and customs. Thus it was sort of No Man's Land.

The first real influx of a permanent population in the Ramapo Mountains was in 1714. This was a remnant of the Tuscarora Indians. . . .[1]

Storms described how the Tuscarora originally lived in North Carolina and their defeat by white settlers in a war that lasted from 1711 to 1713.

From time to time, thereafter the natives wandered away, principally northward, their spirit completely broken by the chastisement that they had received. . . .

Arrived at the Ramapos a stop was made for a time; perhaps it was because there were to be found congenial spirits among the remaining Hagingashackies and the wild renegades who were hiding there. But the ultimate object was to unite theirs with the powerful Five Nations that ruled the country to the northward. . . .

However, the women, children, old men and a few others elected to remain for the present at least, in the Ramapos. The Hovenkopf (so called by the Dutch, for "High Head") . . . seemed to offer a place of comparative security for the wanderers. It is probable that the original intention was for those who were left behind to eventually follow their kinsmen further north. It is known that to this day there are occasional visits paid to this region by representatives of the tribes from the central part of New York State. They seek certain places and conduct ritual services, probably in relation to some who are buried there.[2]

"It was in Germany that the second element of this race was recruited," Storms continued, referring to the Hessian mercenaries who fought for the British during the Revolutionary War.

Reaching America under duress, placed in the forefront at every important battle in which they were engaged, beaten by their officers with the broadside of swords if they attempted to retreat, made to do the menial labor of their British companions, their fate was a particularly cruel one. With no interest in the outcome of the military struggle, unfamiliar with the theory of "liberty" for which the Americans were fighting, it is not to be wondered at that they proved unfaithful, and deserted the army at every opportunity.

In the fighting that took place in the vicinity of New York City, from the camps scattered throughout this region, and at the marches across New Jersey, these men, known by the general name of Hessians, fled to the nearest place of safety—the Ramapo Mountains.

There was no possibility of escape, no opportunity to return to their native land, so they made for themselves homes in their retreat, mated with those they found already there, and reared families.[3]

The third strain in the ancestry of the Mountain People, according to Storms, consisted of English and West Indian women brought as prostitutes for the British soldiers occupying New York City during the Revolution.

The British War Office had a problem on its hands—keeping New York City loyal to the Crown as a Tory city, while keeping thousands of its soldiers in the military camp that General Clinton had established there. . . .

But there was a way out of the difficulty, a way that had long been in vogue by warring European nations, in fact, by England herself. A little judicious questioning and a man was found who would accept the undertaking. The man's name was Jackson—history has not preserved for us anything more about him than this, not even his given name. We do not know whether he was a resident of London or not, though presumably he was, as he was known to the War Office located there.

A contract was entered into that Jackson was to secure thirty-five hundred young women whom England felt it could very well dispense with, and transport them to America to become the intimate property of the army quartered in New York City, thus relieving the tension now felt that at any moment these same soldiers might take to themselves such of the residents as temporarily pleased their fancy.

The government was to furnish transportation for the victims of this plot, and on their arrival at New York City would provide for them in its own way. . . . For his services the man was to be paid in English gold; the best information that is now obtainable is that it was to be two pounds for each female.

Jackson set his agents at the task of recruiting from the inmates of brothels of London, Liverpool, Southhampton and other English cities along the sea coast. . . . If a young woman or matron chanced to be on her way home from her occupation, or on the street on an honest mission she fared the same fate as the inmates of the houses of ill fame, and many a respectable working girl or young housewife was shanghaied, and carried off to a life of shame across the sea.

Jackson loaded his human cargo into vessels in the harbors, forced them below decks and battened down the hatches to prevent escape, even from suicide by leaping overboard. Every available vessel that was seaworthy was in use to transport soldiers and supplies for the army, none could be spared except the merest hulks. Twenty of these Jackson used. All set sail for America, but on the way across the ocean a violent storm arose. Some of the vessels became separated from the others. At last, one by one they reached New York—nineteen of them. Somewhere one had foundered in mid ocean, carrying down to a more merciful fate fifty women and the entire crew. . . .

Accordingly, one vessel was dispatched to the West Indies, most accessible British possession, loaded with negresses collected in the same manner as the others had been, and brought to New York.

. . . Lispenards Meadows [a low, swampy, salt meadow on the west side of Manhattan near the present entrance to the Holland Tunnel] had been secured as quarters for the anticipated "guests," and was being duly prepared. . . .[4]

Storms described the stockade built for the women. He then discussed the hasty evacuation of "ten thousand" British soldiers and Tories in 1783, when the Americans reoccupied the city.

Suddenly someone remembered the hundreds of English women imprisoned at Lispenard's Meadow. . . . A hurried order was given, a messenger rode pell mell to the Meadows, unbarred and threw open the big gate of the stockade, and hurried back to escape from the city with his companions.

Out of the stockade gate poured the motley throngs of women, after several years of confinement in their noisome quarters. Soon the party separated; about five hundred of the women decided to go northward, and wandered up along the shore of the Hudson River until they reached open country in the vicinity of the present town of Hoosick Falls [New York], one hundred and fifty miles from their former prison. There they remained, a diminishing group until about forty years ago, when they finally disappeared entirely, the last of the race having died.

By far the larger portion of the human stream that flowed out of Lispenard's Meadows on that eventful Evacuation Day of 1783, by some unknown means, reached the western shore of the Hudson. . . . The horde has been estimated at about three thousand or slightly more. . . . To the company was added a few soldiers who preferred to cast in their lot with the refugees, having formed a quasi-attachment for some member of it. Tories, too, who had been unable to secure passage to the Canadian ports considered their bodily safety rather than their social standing. . . . Then, too, the confusion of departure afforded an added opportunity for a number of Hessians to make their escape. . . .

Then followed another memorable trek. Across the Hackensack Meadows, up the Saddle River valley, these derelicts made their way on foot. . . . Pillaging of orchards and deliberate raids on fields and gardens provoked the farmers, who drove the wanderers on with hard words and often with harder blows, all of which was retaliated. No one wanted these unfortunates. . . .

At last, with Oakland past, the crowd entered the Ramapo Pass and soon found itself in a country that, while wild and inhospitable in character, yet offered the boon of peace; there was no one to drive them away. Here the colony scattered, finding shelters in the woods and among the rocks. Here the individual members found companionship of peaceful Indians, escaped outlaws, Hessians, runaway slaves—there was ample companionship, and it was readily accepted.[5]

Storms said the name Jackson Whites appeared in a New York Tory newspaper published during the Revolution under several titles—*Riv-*

ington's New York Gazetteer, Rivington's Loyal Gazette, and the
Loyal Gazette.

In these columns occur references of visits paid by various companies of
soldiers to "Jackson's Whites," and sometimes to "Jackson's Blacks." These
sly hints are made in a jocular vein, seem to carry no stigma, reproach, or
violation of military discipline. The term "Whites" and "Blacks" following
Jackson's name quite clearly show to which group of inmates of the stockade the visitor's attention was paid.[6]

The fourth strain in the ancestry, according to Storms, consisted
of escaped slaves who took refuge in the mountains.

The story of negro slavery in America is too well known to need any
explanation here. The Dutch settlers kept these bondsmen as servants principally, and the bondage was not particularly hard in most cases. Still, it
frequently happened that these escaped slaves would seek their own freedom, and the most accessible place and most secure was the fastness of the
Ramapos. . . .
These people carried with them names of former masters, white ac-
quaintances, or those that they had adopted. Thus we sometimes find family
names among them that are borne by prominent and socially acceptable
white persons.[7]

Many people have accepted this account as history, believing what
they have been told or what they have read. Some amateur historians
and students have tried to test the historical accuracy of the Storms
account by checking it against documented historical knowledge.[8] The
results have been inconclusive. The account does contain some accurate
historical information, but there is no evidence that this information is
related to the origins of the Ramapo Mountain People.
The Tuscarora Indians did migrate north after the war in North
Carolina, and they became the sixth nation of the Iroquois Confederacy.
The migration was gradual, over a ninety-year period, and straggling
bands settled temporarily along the way. But historical documents indicate that the main route of Tuscarora migration was along the Susquehanna River Valley of Pennsylvania.* The Tuscarora settled tempor-

* Pennsylvania place-names are one index to the route. The Tuscarora Mountains are located south of the Juniata River. One writer mentions that "early traders to the Ohio, in following the dividing water-shed between the Potomac and

arily along the Juniata River (northwest of Harrisburg), along the
Susquehanna at Wyoming, Pennsylvania (near present-day Wilkes-
Barre), at Oquaga (near Binghamton, New York), and between Syracuse and Lake Oneida, New York.[9] Scattered bands may have drifted
outside this main route of migration, but there is no reliable historical
evidence that the Tuscarora came as far east as the Ramapo Mountains.

Dr. James Veith, an amateur archeologist from Suffern, New York,
told me that he has found no southern Iroquois (Tuscarora) pottery
in the Ramapo Pass area. But he warned against putting too much stock
in this fact because he feels that by 1713 the Tuscarora were probably
using copper and iron pots and other trade articles. Nevertheless, there
is no known archeological evidence that the Tuscarora came through
the Ramapo Pass.

Juniata, came to the 'Tuscarora Path,' the well-defined route used by that tribe in
their migration northward, and which led to their settlement in the valley beyond.
The first is known as Path Valley to this day, and the region where they had their
headquarters is still Tuscarora Valley, thus illustrating how language adheres to
the soil when the lips that spoke it are resolved into dust." (Abraham L. Guss, "The
Tuscarora Indians," in *History of . . . the Susquehanna and Juniata Valleys . . .* ,
eds. Franklin Ellis and A. N. Hungerford [Philadelphia: Everts, Peck, & Richards,
1886], 1:40.)

In 1720 Governor Spottswood of Virginia wrote to the governor of New
York: "In the years 1712 and 1713 they [the Five Nations] were actually in these
parts assisting the Tuscarouroes . . . and they have at this very day the chief
murderers, with the greatest part of that nation, seated under their protection
near Susquehannah river . . ." [Ibid.]

"John O'Neal wrote a letter to the Governor [of Pennsylvania] from Carlisle,
[Pennsylvania] May 27, 1753, in which he remarks,—'A large number of Delaware, Shawanese and Tuscaroras continue in this vicinity—the greater number
having gone to the west.'" [Ibid., p. 43.]

"On December 16, 1766, one hundred and sixty Tuscaroras from Carolina
arrived at Sir William Johnson's, in New York, who, while on their way, at
Paxtang, in Pennsylvania, were robbed of their horses and other goods to the value
of fifty-five pounds. In a diary kept at the Moravian mission at Friedenshutten
(Wyalusing), during the year 1767, we find these entries: 'January 25th—two feet
of snow fell last night. The Tuscaroras were so alarmed, not being accustomed to
snow, that they all left their huts down by the river and came up to us.' In February mention is made of several Tuscaroras coming to the mission to stay there,
who had planted, the summer previous, at the mouth of Tuscarora Creek, in
Wyoming County. 'In May seventy-five Tuscaroras came from Carolina.' . . .
In November, 1770, Sir William Johnson says: 'The Tuscaroras, since the last of
them came from the southward to join the rest, may now number about two
hundred and fifty.'" [Ibid., p. 44.]

Hessian mercenaries did fight on the British side during the Revolutionary War, and one historian estimated that 5,000 Hessians deserted during the war. Of this number, 236 deserted on the march across New Jersey in the summer of 1778.[10]

The Continental Congress encouraged enemy desertion with repeated offers of free land and exemption from military service to any deserter. One proclamation, dated April 1778, promised fifty acres of land to every soldier who deserted and eight hundred acres of woodland, four oxen, one bull, two cows, and four sows to any officer who brought forty men with him. Deserters were not obliged to serve in the American army, but any officer who was willing to do so would receive a higher rank than he had in the Hessian regiment.[11]

The alleged Hessian strain in the ancestry of the Mountain People is supposed to explain the most frequent surnames—De Freese, Van Dunk, De Groat, and Mann. But none of these names—which are Dutch, not German—appear on a list of marriages of Hessian soldiers from two regiments who participated in the campaign in the New York area.[12] Nor do any appear on a list of Hessian officers under Generals Howe, Clinton, and Carleton.[13]

Five investigators have searched the pages of *Rivington's Loyal Gazette*, but no references to Jackson's Whites have been found. One investigator, Anne Lutz, mentioned her negative results to Storms. He responded that he had not seen the references but that if they weren't there, someone must have torn them out.

Furthermore, there is no documentary evidence that either the sea captain named Jackson or the prostitutes ever existed.

The Dutch farmers in northern New Jersey and southeastern New York did own slaves. Contemporary New Jersey newspapers contained numerous advertisements for the return of escaped slaves.[14] But the assertion that these escaped slaves took refuge in the Ramapo Mountains remains unproven.

John C. Storms had a reputation for taking liberties with his stories. As Mrs. Etta Tice Terhune, an old-time resident of Park Ridge, New Jersey, told me in 1968,

Johnny Cip [Storms] was one that—ah, made everything flowery. You know, he wrote something about my grandfather in one of his pieces in the *Local*, a long time ago, and I objected, so I told him. So he says, "Well, Etta, you know, we have to make it flowery for people to read." So that was the kind of things that he wrote. . . . When he wrote anything, he had to make it flowery for people to read. That was Johnny Cip.*

Storms was not the historian he apparently wanted to be; he was a storyteller. Unfortunately many people believed his story was factual history.

In the fall of 1968 I met Lewis West of Midvale, New Jersey, whose father had been manager of the Abram S. Hewitt estate in Ringwood, New Jersey. Mr. West grew up among the Mountain People. He told me that he first heard the account of their origin when he was a boy in the 1920s.

West: I've heard that during the Revolutionary War, the British were fighting the colonists here and they had a division of Hessian soldiers who were going to revolt, due to the fact that they wanted women. This English seacaptain named Jackson was given the job to get women for the soldiers. He got prostitutes from England. In addition, he and his son convinced other young women that there was a better future and a better life in the colonies. Evidently, they went into the slums of England to get these women.

I don't know how many boats he had or how many women he had aboard each boat. Coming across the ocean they ran into a severe storm. Some of the women were washed overboard. Others, realizing Jackson's scheme, jumped overboard. After the storm, Jackson realized that he had lost so many women, and he was afraid of the consequences of not delivering the women. So he went to the West Indies and he and his crew actually kidnaped at gunpoint most any colored female. I want to point out that the colored women were *forced* to come to the colonies. They were victims. The white women came voluntarily, even though some of them were fooled into it.

So he brought the colored females and the white females that were left to the colonies and they had affairs with the Hessians and naturally there were offspring. Now, according to the story, the names Van Dunk, De Groat, De Freese, Morgan, and Milligan are Hessian names that were passed

---

* Except where noted, transcripts of tape-recorded interviews are presented as they were spoken. Since oral expression differs significantly from written expression, the reader will sometimes find these passages difficult to read.

down, but I don't know myself whether these are Hessian names. These people were known as half-breeds, so they mingled with the Lenni Lenapi Indians and that's how the three races came in there.

Cohen: Why are they called "Jackson Whites?"

West: Because Jackson was supposed to bring white prostitutes. The soldiers, who were expecting white women, sarcastically referred to the colored women as "Jackson's whites." It is as if I sent you for a Stillson wrench and you brought back a monkey wrench. I would then say you don't know what a Stillson wrench is.

Cohen: Can you tell me where you heard this explanation?

West: No, I can't say exactly where I got it. I heard it from different people.

Cohen: Was it from old-timers long ago?

West: Yes, from old-timers. I was very inquisitive as a youngster. It was in the early nineteen twenties when I first heard the story. I was about ten years old at the time. Of course, I didn't know what some of the words meant when I first heard the story, but I heard it many times.

Cohen: Was it told by both colored and white people?

West: I've heard it discussed by white people. I've heard it discussed by colored. And I've heard it discussed mixed.*

In answer to a question, West said that he had never read or previously heard about Storms's book. West's testimony suggests that this account of the origins of the Jackson Whites was in oral tradition more than ten years before Storms wrote his book. Storms evidently had recorded a folk legend.

Considering the Storms account as folklore cast it in a completely different light. Folk legends may not be factually true; however, they convey attitudes about the people who tell them and the people they are told about. Folklore often contains projections of group stereotypes.[15]

Tracing the development of the folk legend through written sources, I found that the legend apparently originated in parts over a fifty-year period between 1870 and 1920.† The earliest written reference to the Ramapo Mountain People I found was an article titled "A

---

* This text is not a tape transcript. Mr. West prefered that I take notes and that we revise the text so that the meaning would be clear. An attempt was made to use Mr. West's style of expression, and the final text was approved by him.

† These dates are approximate because each new part of the legend was probably in oral tradition for several years before it appeared in print.

Community of Outcasts" in *Appleton's Journal of Literature, Science, and Art,* for March 23, 1872.

In relation to this particular people, there are half a dozen legends current, all possessing more or less romance and attractiveness; but the most favored one is, for a rarity, the most reasonable.

The people will tell you that this stain upon their fair country was first put there by fugitive slaves, more than a hundred years ago.

There were gradually added to these fugitives of other descriptions, and the general antagonism to the world made each individual endure the others. They buried themselves deep in the fastnesses and gorges of the mountains, and reared children, wilder and more savage than themselves.[16]

According to David Cole's history of Rockland County, New York (1884), the Mountain People had a different version of their origin at that time. Cole noted

the fact that in the mountains in the western part of Ramapo at a very early date a large number of negroes were to be found. Whence they came we cannot tell. Tradition among them speaks of a "good Mr. Rutherford [Walter Rutherford, a large landowner in northern New Jersey after the Revolutionary War] who allowed people to settle on his land where they chose." In all probability they found it for their safety in those days when the "Negro had no rights which the white man was bound to respect," to dwell apart by themselves in these mountains.[17]

The first written reference to Hessian soldiers and Indians in this area appears in J. M. Van Valen's history of Bergen County, New Jersey, published in 1900.

The Ramapo Indians sometimes visited the settlements in the township of Franklin [no longer in existence in this locality]. They were known formerly as the Hackensack Indians, but are more properly described as the "Jackson Whites." They bear little resemblance to the Indians, yet as tradition gives it they are descendants of Hessians, Indians, and negroes, but know nothing of their ancestry, so ignorant have they become.[18]

The reference to "tradition" suggests that the author was aware he had collected a folk legend.

Arthur S. Tompkins's history of Rockland County, New York (1902), tells the story this way:

The Jackson Whites originated when the Indians were yet living in the lowlands along the Ramapo Mountains. The first race came by a union between the Indians and half breeds on one side, and colored laborers brought from the lower part of the county to work in the Ramapo factories on the other side. The colored people were either freed slaves ·or their children grown up, and many of the names to-day may be traced as identified with some of the old Holland pioneers of Orangetown, for the slaves in old times bore the surnames of their masters. Inter-marriage among these people has caused them to degenerate intellectually if not physically. The new prevailing race of genuine Jackson Whites is said by the best authority to have come from a number of white laborers brought from the same quarter of the county.[19]

This account is a mixture of folklore and historical guesswork. The parts about freed slaves and "a union between the Indians and half breeds" are traditional, but the part about colored laborers brought to work in the Ramapo factories is the contribution of the author.

The 1906/7 annual report of the secretary of the New Jersey Historical Society contains the following version:

The Secretary wrote that his understanding had been that they [the Jackson Whites] were a people of mixed Indian and negro blood, the Indian strain showing in their reticence, and the negro strain in their indolence and improvidence. They are supposed to be the offspring of former negro slaves, runaways, and free negroes, who sought refuge in the mountains where they could eke out a living by cutting hoop-poles and wood for charcoal, in the days of charcoal iron furnaces. They have been regarded as outcasts, and hence have been allowed to sink into a degraded state. . . .[20]

Here certain personality traits are associated with the different strains in the racial mixture. A black woman who married one of the Mountain People told me that her husband's laziness was a result of his Indian blood. She also attributed to his Indian blood the fact that he takes off from work when the hunting season begins.

The first mention in print that the Indian strain was specifically that of the Tuscarora appeared in an article published in 1911 by Frank Speck, an anthropologist at the University of Pennsylvania.

According to current tradition the [Jackson Whites] tribe, so-called, seems to have been founded by the blending of a few families of native

Algonquian Indians, probably Minisinks of the Delaware, with some of the Tuscarora who lingered for a rest in the Ramapo Valley on their way from Carolina in 1714 to join their colleagues, the Iroquois, in New York State. To this small nucleus became added from time to time runaway Negro slaves and perhaps freed men from the Dutch colonial plantations in the adjoining counties in New Jersey. Vagabond white men of all sorts also contributed a share to the community from the early days until now. The Jackson Whites may be regarded, therefore, as a type of triple race mixture.[21]

The unpublished study of the Mountain People completed in the same year by the Vineland Training School of Vineland, New Jersey, also mentions the Tuscarora.

These loose living descendants of slaves were gradually crowded back into the mountain districts where they lived from hand to mouth and where their numbers were from time to time recruited by whites whose tendencies were similar to their own. . . .

But how account for the Indian blood that shows itself so conspicuously among this race today? Undoubtedly a large part of it comes from Indians who were formerly held as slaves. . . .

The Indian blood found in the Jackson Whites whether it came down through individuals held as slaves or through isolated free Indians who intermarried with the emancipated negroes, is supposed to have belonged to a remnant of the Algonquin Tribe—to the Minsi, or Wolf Clan, who were natives of the Upper Delaware Valley in Pennsylvania, New Jersey, and New York. . . . There were also a few families of the Tuscarora Indians who remained in the Ramapo mountains after their tribe had made there a three years sojourn, from 1710 to 1713, on its way to join the five nations in New York State.[22]

Vince Morgan, one of the Mountain People from Mahwah, New Jersey, insists that the old-timers used to say that they were descended from Tuscarora Indians. This raises two questions. If this part of the legend is true, why weren't the Tuscarora specified in the legend until 1911? If it is not true, how did the Mountain People find out about the eighteenth-century migration of the Tuscarora Indians? It is possible that Frank Speck, who would have known about the Tuscarora migration, added this detail to the oral tradition.

The last part of the legend to get into print was the part about the prostitutes, which appeared in a 1923 edition of New York Walk Book.

Instead of farms we find now and then huts of "poor whites," or settlements of "Jackson Whites," a mixed race of whom there is a settlement at Halifax northwest of Darlington. Legend has it that the unattached followers of the British army were relegated to the wilderness and with Indians and negroes brought up a race of half-breeds.[23]

The date of this version corresponds with Lewis West's statement that he first heard the legend in the 1920s, when he was a boy.

In addition to the common four-part folk legend, there have been other explanations of the origin of the Mountain People, both in print and in oral tradition. Usually they associate the Mountain People with someone named Jackson.

A black woman from South Carolina who married one of the Mountain People gave me the following explanation:

Well, I heard that version from my brother-in-law. He said that the name "Jackson White" came directly from President Jackson. He said that President Jackson had had the underground railroad, and he had one station in Haverstraw, and one in some other section of Rockland County, and other sections, you know, including the South and here. And that he had put these Negro slaves and they had intermarried with people from this section—which was the Tuscarora Indians, that were run out of North Carolina by the white man—I imagine—North and South Carolina, by the white man—and they all got together, and that's how it all started.

This is a variant of the following version found in the 1923 edition of the *New York Walk Book*:

Another story is to the effect that negroes were brought here by the "Underground Railway" to hide and that they married into the low-grade whites about them. Near Hillburn is a large settlement of negroes, who seem to be full-bloods.[24]

Another version linking the Mountain People with President Andrew Jackson was given me by Harold Sherwood, a Spring Valley, New York, attorney and amateur historian. He said that a local physician named Degman had a theory that the name Jackson Whites came from the presidential campaign of 1824 or 1828, in which there was a tremendous increase in the number of people who voted. In those days,

Dr. Degman said, a colored person couldn't vote unless he proved his manumission, nor could "colored Indians" vote. Jackson's campaign managers got the Mountain People to vote for him, and hence the name Jackson's Whites. But, according to historian Lee Benson, "virulent hostility to free Negroes was part of the political stock in trade of the New York Jackson Party." It was the *Whig* Party in New York that pushed for a constitutional amendment providing equal suffrage for free blacks. The Democratic Party's opposition to this proposal was the basis for the party's support in Rockland County.[25]

A version collected by antiquarian Henry Charlton Beck in 1939 in central New Jersey linked the name Jackson Whites with General Thomas J. ("Stonewall") Jackson.

> Always "certain" that the Jackson Whites had some connection with one of the famous Jacksons, those who knew little and imagined much more divided themselves into camps, one connecting them with Andrew Jackson, another with General Stonewall. . . . [sic]
>
> The first made them out to be whites and Indians and others who ran off with negro slaves and servants of leading families of Hopewell, perhaps before it was Columbia, and Pennington, when it was Penny Town [in central Jersey], romantically taking to the hills and emerging only when there was necessity. The second avowed with equal certainty that other authorities had the wrong Jackson, that Georgia was too far away to have anything to do with New Jersey to provide connection with General James. These also attacked the conclusion that Colonel Jackson, of Montressor's Island, Stillwater or even Monmouth yielded deserters in such a cause.
>
> . . . Those who declare the Whites named for Stonewall have a campaign all figured out, the deserters hurrying from Virginia, to join those who, fleeing a Civil War prison back of Easton, Pennsylvania, crossed the Delaware to snatch comely servant girls south of the Sourlands.[26]

Beck was writing about a group of people living in Honey Hollow in the Sourlands north of Trenton. The fact that the name Jackson Whites was attached to those central Jersey people indicates that the use of the name had spread and was a general term of denigration by 1939.

Beck also collected in central Jersey a variant of the Storms's version of the legend.

> Jackson, the original Jackson, was neither general nor president by this variation, but the name of a sergeant who was in charge of a stockade where

camp-followers were confined for the British soldiery. There were perhaps as many sergeants as stockades but one always approached with a "Hello, Jackson!" as a barkeep might be addressed familiarly as "Hi-ya, Joe!" If one were a British officer, he rated a Jackson White. If he were just a common private, well. . . .[27]

Jackson becomes a British general in a version collected in 1940 by New York University graduate student Constance Crawford from Rev. William S. Briscoe of Valley Cottage, New York, a former missionary to the Mountain People.

The British General Jackson was given a certain sum of money to help destitute white families, and finding these people [the colored Mountain People] in dire need of help, he adopted the subterfuge of calling them whites and granted them supplies. . . . Other destitute women, other than the Whites, the Reds, the Blacks, the Yellows, possibly those from Spain, were in evidence, but that there was no money appropriated for their care. According to American custom, of the period, a loop hole was found in the law, which enabled him to take care of any color. There were Indian and other foreign elements. These women formed the female element of the clan. These women were picked up by the army and taken to wife, taking residence with the clan, the Jackson Whites being a clan rather than a tribe.[28]

Crawford also mentioned two other versions of the legend, but she failed to give her sources.

Some people contend that a man named Jackson was the leader of this mixed clan, and that the name came from him. . . .
   Still another version is an account of the Londoner, Jackson, who is said to have evacuated the 3,500 women from New York when the British left. Taking them in ships to the "slote," in what is now Rockland County, he is credited with leaving them there on the shore.[29]

This is obviously a variant on the Storms version.
   There is a version of the legend in E. Franklin Frazier's classic study, *The Negro Family in the United States*. In the chapter on racial islands, Frazier quoted one of his students, a woman about forty in 1939 who earned a bachelor's degree at Howard University, married, and returned to Hillburn, New York, to live.

More than a century ago some Boers were supposed to have been brought to this section by the English—possibly for the purpose of mining iron ore. As the story goes—among these Boers were four Johns—i.e., John De Groot, John Von Doonk, John De Vries and John Mann. Quite positive proof of this fact are the predominating names among the people at the present time; i.e., De Groat, Van Dunk, De Freese and Mann. After a time these people were visited by remnants of wandering tribes of Indians; i.e., Tuscaroras and Delawares who were traveling up from the South to join others of their tribe in central New York State. Still later were found, in this section, slaves maintained by a family of Sufferns. An amalgamation took place between these three classes of people. A slave named Jackson was believed to have been the first of his kind to mingle with the others and as a result we find a type of people with certain peculiarities called "Jackson Whites." [30]

Boers is the Dutch word for peasants or farmers. But here it is used to refer to German miners brought to the Ringwood iron mines. This account, like some others, appears to be a mixture of the folklore tradition and historical guesswork.

The Ramapo Mountain People have also attracted the attention of a number of noted journalists, writers, and poets. Albert Payson Terhune, the popular writer of dog stories from Pompton Lakes, New Jersey, made the Mountain People the villains in his book *Treasure* published in 1925. Pulitzer-prize-winning journalist Meyer Berger wrote an article published in the *New York Times Magazine* on March 24, 1935, in which he mistook the Jackson White legend for fact and associated it with the white mountaineers near Ladentown rather than the colored Mountain People. George Weller, also a winner of the Pulitzer prize for journalism, repeated the legend as fact in a piece for the *New Yorker* in 1938. William Carlos Williams referred to the Ramapo Mountain People, although not by name, in his poem "To Elsie" published in 1923.

In a prose section of his epic poem *Paterson*, published in 1947, Williams included another version of the legend.

If there was not beauty, there was a strangeness and a bold association of wild and cultured life grew up together in the Ramapos: two phases.
In the hills, where the brown trout slithered among the shallow stones, Ringwood—where the old Ryerson farm had been—among its velvet lawns,

TO ELSIE

The pure products of America
go crazy—
mountain folk from Kentucky

or the ribbed north end of
Jersey
with its isolate lakes and

valleys, its deaf-mutes, thieves
old names
and promiscuity between

devil-may-care men who have taken
to railroading
out of sheer lust of adventure—

and young slatterns, bathed
in filth
from Monday to Saturday

to be tricked out that night
with gauds
from imaginations which have no

peasant traditions to give them
character
but flutter and flaunt

sheer rags—succumbing without
emotion
save numbed terror

under some hedge of choke-cherry
or viburnum—
which they cannot express—

Unless it be that marriage
perhaps
with a dash of Indian blood

will throw up a girl so desolate
so hemmed around
with disease or murder

that she'll be rescued by an
agent—
reared by the state and

sent out at fifteen to work in
some hard pressed
house in the suburbs—

some doctor's family, some Elsie-
voluptuous water
expressed with broken

brain the truth about us—
her great
ungainly hips and flopping breasts

addressed to cheap
jewelry
and rich young men with fine eyes

as if the earth under our feet
were
an excrement of some sky

and we degraded prisoners
destined
to hunger until we eat filth

while the imagination strains
after deer
going by fields of goldenrod in

the stifling heat of September
Somehow
it seems to destroy us

It is only in isolate flocks that
something
is given off

No one
to witness
and adjust, no one to drive the car *

was ringed with forest trees, the butternut, and the elm, the white oak, the chestnut and the beech, the birches, the tupelo, the sweet-gum, the wild cherry and the hackleberry with its red tumbling fruit.

While in the forest clustered the ironworkers' cabins, the charcoal burners, the lime kiln workers—hidden from lovely Ringwood—where General Washington, gracing any poem, up from Pompton for rest after the traitors' hangings could be at ease—and the links were made for the great chain across the Hudson at West Point.

Violence broke out in Tennessee, a massacre by the Indians, hangings and exile—standing there on the scaffold waiting, sixty of them. The Tuscaroras, forced to leave their country, were invited by the Six Nations to join them in Upper New York. The bucks went on ahead but some of the women and the stragglers got no further than the valley-cleft near Suffern. They took to the mountains there where they were joined by Hessian deserters from the British Army, a number of albinos among them, escaped negro slaves and a lot of women and their brats released in New York City after the British had been forced to leave. They had them in a pen there— picked up in Liverpool and elsewhere by a man named Jackson under contract with the British Government to provide women for the soldiers in America.

The mixture ran in the woods and took the general name, Jackson's Whites. (There had been some blacks also, mixed in, some West Indian negresses, a ship-load, to replace the whites lost when their ship, one of six coming from England, had foundered in a storm at sea. He had to make it up somehow and that was the quickest and cheapest way.)

New Barbadoes Neck, the region was called.

Cromwell, in the middle of the seventeenth century, shipped some thousands of Irish women and children to the Barbadoes to be sold as slaves. Forced by their owners to mate with the others these unfortunates were succeeded by a few generations of Irish-speaking negroes and mulattoes. And it is commonly asserted to this day the natives of Barbadoes speak with an Irish brogue. [Actually New Barbadoes Neck, on the east bank of the Passaic River above Newark, was founded by English planters from Barbadoes, but there is no evidence that this region is related to the ancestry of the Ramapo Mountain People.] *

If the various versions of the legend do not satisfactorily explain the origin of the name Jackson Whites, where did the name originate? According to the study by the Vineland Training School, in 1911 the Mountain People maintained that the name had only recently come into

* William Carlos Williams, *Paterson*, Book I. Copyright 1946 by William Carlos Williams. Reprinted by permission of New Directions Publishing Corporation.

use.[31] The name does not appear in the 1872 article on the community of outcasts in *Appleton's Journal of Literature, Science, and Art.* The earliest known reference to the name in print has been located in the county newspaper, the *Rockland County Journal*, dated February 9, 1878.

At Court

The two Degroots, and Wm. Robinson, alias "Cock Robin," the "Jackson Whites," who broke into the office of Hutton Bro's, at Nanuet, and robbed the safe, some weeks since, were indicted for Burglary. Robinson plead guilty and the De Groots not guilty, to the charge.[32]

Anthropologist Frank Speck of the University of Pennsylvania wrote that "some claim that the term is the corruption of a contemptuous title, Jacks-and-whites." [33] The Vineland Training School study concurred with this hypothesis and explained the meaning of the phrase as follows:

Numerous traditions are afloat regarding the origin of the name Jackson White, the most reliable of these seem to be that the freed slaves were contemptuously termed "Jacks" when they began intermarrying with the white outcasts above alluded to, they were spoken of as "Jacks and Whites," which term in time was contracted into their present appellation, "Jackson-Whites." [34]

This usage of the word *jacks* to mean "freed slaves" does not appear in any of the standard dictionaries of slang, dialect, and cant, although some of the usages cited are suggestive.* But the term *free jacks* has

---

* *The American Dialect Dictionary* mentions *jack* as a verb, meaning "To make off speedily; run away quickly." It is probably a corruption of *jark it*. This usage probably dates from about 1870 and was obsolete by 1945. *Jack* was used as a noun to mean "a low prostitute" from about 1860 and was obsolete by 1940. The book *Life in Sing Sing* (1904) uses *jack* to mean a convict: " 'Jack,'—all convicts are Jack,—'do you smoke?' " In the 1930s and 40s jack was "a generic term for any tramp." In the central Pennsylvania mountains in 1930, *jack* was used to mean "a yokel." (Harold Wentworth, *American Dialect Dictionary* [New York: Thomas Y. Crowell Co., 1944], p. 325.)

The term *John* or *Jack* also is found in the mumming tradition in the West Indies associated with the *Jonkanoo* or *John Canoe* figure. "A *John Canoe* is a negro Jack Pudding, and these John Canoes wore white false faces, and enormous shocks of horse hair fastened to their wooly pates. Their character hovers some-

been collected as "a slang term for negroes" used in reference to another racially mixed group, the Redbones of southwestern Louisiana.[35] Since this usage has been verified in another part of the country, it may have been used in New York and New Jersey as well. Contractions similar to turning the phrase "jacks and whites" into Jackson Whites are common in folklore etymologies. When communication is oral, rather than written, often a familiar term will be substituted for an unfamiliar phrase.

The name Jackson Whites has always been considered offensive by the Mountain People. In 1911 it was not liked,[36] and it is not liked today. One apparent exception was recounted by one of the Mountain People from Hillburn, New York. He said that some of the light-skinned Mountain People in Mahwah, New Jersey, actually like the name because they like anything that includes the word *white*. I suspect, however, that this comment was prompted by antagonism between the Hillburn and Mahwah Mountain People. At any rate, few people admit to being a Jackson White. One of the Mountain People from Mahwah said to me with a curious logic that his people couldn't be the Jackson Whites "because there were Jackson's Whites and Jackson's Blacks and that makes mulatto." But, he said, his people were not mulattoes. The name always seems to be applied to someone else. People in Ringwood, New Jersey, say that the Jackson Whites are in Mahwah. People in Hillburn say that the Jackson Whites are the white mountaineers who used to live behind Ladentown, New York, in the northeast section of the Ramapo Mountains.

I asked several Mountain People why the name is so offensive to them. Some said they didn't like being characterized as one thing or another. One man said it makes them sound like a breed of cattle. One woman said it is the tone in which the name is usually spoken that is offensive, rather than the name itself. One can see why the name would be offensive by reason either of the original term *free jacks* or the derogatory legends allegedly explaining the name. But none of the Mountain People mentioned these reasons.

where between that of a harlequin and a clown." (Michael Scott's *Tom Cringle's Log* quoted in J. D. A. Widdowson, "Mummering and Janneying: Some Explanatory Notes," in *Christmas Mumming in Newfoundland*, ed. Herbert Halpert [Toronto: University of Toronto Press, 1969], p. 220.)

Inasmuch as none of these versions and variants of the legend have been historically substantiated, why do they appear with such persistence? Is it because people want to believe sensational stories? Perhaps there is another reason. There seems to be a tendency to identify a people in terms of where they came from. By the late nineteenth century, the origin of the Ramapo Mountain People lay beyond the memory of any living person, including the Mountain People themselves. Since the Mountain People had no tradition of written history, possibly the legend was created to fill this void. Possibly the stereotype of the Mountain People as outcasts, fugitives, and renegades was projected into the past to explain their origins. Because the stereotype is derogatory, the legend was almost certainly created by outsiders rather than by the Mountain People themselves. Repeated in newspaper and magazine articles and in local histories, the folk legend was mistaken for history, thereby reinforcing the stereotype by giving it the aura of historical veracity.

Although the legend probably originated among the white neighbors of the Mountain People and is based on a derogatory stereotype, some of the Mountain People, having no alternative explanation of their past, adopted their own version of the legend. John Morgan, a middle-aged resident of Ringwood who works as an operator of heavy equipment, tells the legend this way:

This is—this is an interesting community. Ah, this community is very historical. Ah, this dates back to Revolutionary War times. Now, there has been—ah, a lot of, ah, controversy over the race of these people. Ah, these people here are not pure Negro people. These people are a mixed blood of people. They are mostly Indian blood—most of the people here. Ah, they're a little different than even the people in Mahwah, because the people in Mahwah—ah, the so-called "Jackson White" people—they were mixed in with the Hessian soldiers, where these people—these people here were—were, ah, mixed up with Dutch. That's where the name Van Dunk, De Freese, ah, those names of that—ah—origin is Dutch, which you know. So—that's another thing that I would like cleared up as far as the—the newspapers are concerned, because they seem to think that these people are all Negroes, and we're all trash, and that's something I don't go for. I don't like that.

Morgan puts stress on the historical nature of the group. The Indian mixture is mentioned almost proudly as a factor that distinguishes the colored Mountain People from blacks. In fact, no mention is made of

any black mixture in the group's ancestry. No mention is made of
prostitutes or escaped slaves, and the Hessians are not said to be deserters. It is the Mahwah people, not the Ringwood people, who are the
Jackson Whites.

Another of the Mountain People, Otto Mann from Stag Hill in
Mahwah, supplied a second version. In his sixties, Brother Otto is a civic
leader and the minister in the Pentecostal church in Mahwah.

Otto Mann: Well, we've been told that, ah, that, ah—there was Hessians
that were brought over here from England, and they went up into the
mountains and—and, ah, married in with these—ah, mountain people, and
as far as I know, they—most of the people up there in the beginnings were
Indians, and these—ah, and before that there's always been a story that two
Dutchmen, likewise, went up there, and married amongst the people, because
I can remember as a child how some of them used to speak the Dutch
language.
Cohen: You said this was during the Revolutionary War?
Mann: Yeah, it was during the Revolutionary War that these soldiers, they.
—the story is that they deserted from the army and went into the mountains
and stayed there 'til the war was over, I suppose, and maybe some of them
lived the rest of their life around here and married and mingled in with the
rest of the people. 'Cause today, that's one of the things that happened all
over the United States, anyway.
Cohen: Was this something you read?
Mann: Well, I remember hearing the older people speak of these things.
And they could remember different ones.

Again the negative aspects of the legend are minimized. No mention is
made of escaped slaves or English and West Indian prostitutes. However, Hessian deserters are mentioned.

Generally, when the Mountain People are asked who they are,
they will respond that they are descendants of Tuscarora Indians and
Hessian soldiers. Sometimes it is admitted that the Hessians were
deserters. But one woman in Hillburn insists that these Hessians did
not desert; they simply remained in America after the war. Clearly,
the Mountain People's version of the legend reinforces their self-image,
reflecting their identification with Indians and whites and their denial
of any black ancestry.

2 COLORED PIONEERS IN NEW AMSTERDAM AND THE HACKENSACK RIVER VALLEY

The genealogical history of the Ramapo Mountain People dates from more than one hundred years prior to the time setting of the folk legend. It goes back to New Amsterdam when it was a small military and trading town occupying only the lower part of Manhattan Island. Its windmills, canals, step-gabled buildings, and Dutch-speaking inhabitants reflected the town's Dutch founding. As a part of New Netherland, which included all territory between the Fresh River (Connecticut River) and the South River (Delaware River), New Amsterdam was administered by the Dutch West India Company. But it was just one part of the joint-stock company's far-flung interests, which included slave depots in Angola on the west coast of Africa, the occupation of part of the coast of Brazil, and several islands in the Caribbean. The Dutch West India Company was engaged in a struggle with the Spaniards and Portuese for colonies and the slave trade.

The first written mention of slaves in New Amsterdam appeared in 1628, when Reverend Jonas Michaelius, the first dominie of the Dutch Reformed Church in New Amsterdam, wrote that "the Angola slaves are thievish, lazy, and useless trash." [1] When the patroon system was instituted in 1629, the Dutch West India Company promised to furnish each patroon "with twelve Black men and women out of the prizes in which Negroes shall be found (raids on Spanish slave ships) for the advancement of the colonies in New Netherland." [2] The company manumitted some of its slaves as early as 1643, when Governor Kieft and the council freed Manuel Gerrit and ten other slaves and their wives on the condition that each man pay the company yearly during their lives 30 skepels (22½ bushels) of grain and one fat hog.[3]

Many of these freed slaves in New Amsterdam were given title to land on the public road near a pond known as the Fresh Water on the outskirts of the town in the vicinity of present-day Chatham Square.[4] So many free black and mulatto landowners were given patents there that the area became known as the "Negroes' Land" in early deeds.[5] After the English took control of New Amsterdam in 1664 and renamed it New York, much of the Dutch character of the town remained, as did the free black settlement on its outskirts. Jasper Danckaerts described this neighborhood in October 1679:

We went from the city, following the Broadway. Upon both sides of this way were many habitations of negroes, mulattoes, and whites. These negroes were formerly the proper slaves of the [West India] company, but, in consequence of the frequent changes and conquests of the country, they have obtained their freedom and settled themselves down where they have thought proper, and thus on this road, where they have ground enough to live on with their families.[6]

Three of the colored * landowners living near the Fresh Water in the 1670s were John De Vries, Claes Emanuels, and Augustine Van Donck.

John De Vries was the son of the captain of the Dutch man-of-war *Blue Cock*—Johan de Fries, whose name means John from Friesland, a province of the Netherlands. This does not necessarily mean that the captain came from Friesland, only that his ancestors originated there.† Captain de Fries had fought with Petrus Stuyvesant in 1644 in his unsuccessful attempt to capture the West Indian island of Saint Martin from the Portuguese.[7] In May 1644, Captain de Fries had come to New

---

* Throughout this book I use the term *colored* to mean nonwhite. It is not a synonym for black, but includes Orientals, Indians, and racially-mixed people as well. It is in this sense that the Ramapo Mountain People refer to themselves as colored.

† Captain Johan de Fries should not be confused with David Pietersz De Vries, the Dutch patroon of Staten Island.

Amsterdam, bringing soldiers to fight the Indians. When they were in port captains of the company's ships were given a voice on the governor's council. In this capacity Captain de Fries had a seat on the council from July 1644 through April 1645.[8] In May 1645 the council called upon Captain de Fries and three others to be "adjuncts in the maintenance of order in light of the Indian problem." [9]

Captain de Fries was not one to conform to social conventions. According to the Council's Minutes, in 1646 he was in trouble with the civil authorities of New Amsterdam, which led to his being sent to Holland to stand trial.

Aug. 2. Judgment. Referring to Holland the case of Jan [Johan] de Fries, who is charged with having associated with the enemies of the government and calumniators of the chief magistracy, calling the director a liar in presence of the council, and attempting to strike him, assaulting councillor La Montagne, for all which he had been already cashiered; afterwards speaking disparagingly of the director, and declaring that he spat on any commission issued by him, addressing derisive papers to the court, and excepting to the judges; prisoner ordered to sail in the first ship, to justify his conduct. . . .[10]

Before he left New Amsterdam, Captain Johan de Fries issued an authorization to "Michiel Jansen to take care of, and justly treat, in his absence, his free Negroes and Brazilian women until the said Jan de Vries [Johan de Fries] shall otherwise order." [11] Also before he left, Captain de Fries fathered a son named Jan, who was baptized on August 25, 1647, in the Dutch Reformed Church of New Amsterdam.[12] The mother's name was Swartinne, derived from the Dutch word *zwaart*, which means black. She probably was one of the captain's "Brazilian women" and may have been Indian, black, or racially mixed; the Portuguese in Brazil had both black and Indian slaves.

When Captain Johan de Fries died, his mulatto son Jan and some of his former slaves inherited free status and property. Since Jan de Vries (hereafter called John De Vries II) was then only a child, his property was held in trust by Paulo de Angola and Clara Crioole, both former slaves of the captain. On March 8, 1651, they had to sell some of that property to settle a number of the captain's debts.

TABLE 1 THE DE FREESE FAMILY

Capt. Johan de Fries
Swartinne

John De Vries II (born 1647)
Ariaentje Dircks

Willem Pieterse
Marie De Vries (born 1682)

Dirck De Vries (born 1689, died young)

Marretje Becker
John De Vries III (born 1686)

Jacobus De Vries (born 169?)

Helena De Vries (born 1684)
Abraham Van Salee (born 1681) (see Mann family)

John De Vries IV (born 1719)
Catharina Gerreau

Hannah Van Horne
John De Freese V (born 1759)

Maria De Vries (born 1751)
Joseph Dowe

Catherine Dowers

At the provincial secretary's office appear Paulo de Angola, a negro, and Clara Crioole, a negress, both belonging to Capt. Johan de Vries [de Fries], deceased, who declare that they have amicably agreed regarding a "claim which Symon Joosten makes agst. said Capt. J de Vries, deceas'd, for 600 guilders, loaned money, to the effect that he, Paulo d'Angola, for himself and his two children and Clara Crioola, also, for the child of said Vries, a minor, for the said aforementioned claim, transport and convey a certain parcel of land situate on the east side of the Kolck of the Fresh-water, to them belonging according to the ground thereof . . . on this condition, however, that, if the aforesaid 600 guilders be paid for Capt. de Vries in Patria [Holland] to Abraham Jansen, as attorney, he Symon Joosten shall be obliged to restore to the above-mentioned Paulo, Clara, or the child of Jan de Vries [Johan de Fries] as large and a like quantity of land as is now received for the aforesaid claim. In the meanwhile, he, S. Joosten may transfer the aforesaid land back to Mr. Augustyn Herrmans, with power to enter upon, and cultivate the same as he shall think proper." On March 31, Joosten conveyed the property to Herrmans "according to the ground belief dated the 14th July A° 1645, granted by . . . Kieft for the behoof of Paulo d'Angola, late the negro of Capt. Jan de Vries.[13]

John De Vries II married Ariaentje Dircks of Albany on December 10, 1679.[14] They lived *aen de Groote Kill* (on the Big Creek) on the outskirts of New York. John De Vries was a member of the New York Dutch Reformed Church,[15] and he and Ariaentje had four children baptized in that church: Marie, born in 1682; Helena, born in 1684; Johannes (John III), born in 1686; and Dirck, born in 1689 but died young.[16]

Living in the same neighborhood with John De Vries was Claes Emanuels, whose name means Nicolaus the son of Manuel.* Nicolaus

---

* According to the Dutch patronymic naming system, children took as a surname their father's Christian name plus the suffix *zoon* (often shortened to *z*), *sen, se,* or *s*. Some families had name changes in each generation until the surnames finally were fixed in the eighteenth century. Thus Manuel Van Angola's son was named Claes Emanuels. In the following generations the surname became Claessen, Mannels, and finally Mann. But even after surnames became fixed, spellings were not necessarily standardized. For example, prior to the standardized spelling of De Freese, it was found as de Fries, De Vries, and De Freaze. Van Dunk was spelled Van Donck or Van Donk previously. In the text of this book, wherever there is a reference to a specific document, I have used the spelling found in that document. Elsewhere I have adopted the standardized spellings of De Vries, Van Donck, and Emanuels for the eighteenth century and De Freese, Van Dunk, and Mann for the nineteenth century.

TABLE 2 THE MANN FAMILY

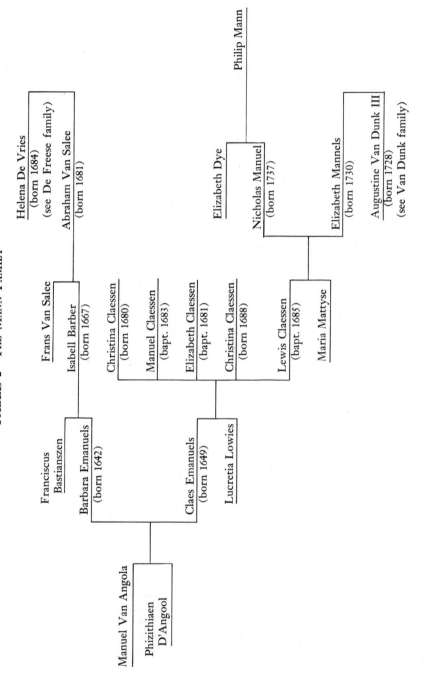

(Claes) was baptized on August 22, 1649, in the Dutch Reformed Church of New Amsterdam.[17] His father was Manuel Van Angola (Manuel from Angola). Manuel's name suggests that he may have been bought or captured from the Spaniards or Portuguese, perhaps in Brazil. Only the father's name appears in the baptismal entry, but in the records of the same church there is an entry for the marriage of Emanuel (Manuel) Van Angola, *neger*, and Phizithiaen D'Angool, on February 16, 1642.[18]

Claes Manuels (Emanuels) appears on a "Lyst van de negers" (List of the Negroes) who swore allegiance to the Prince of Orange in 1673 when the Dutch briefly reoccupied New York and renamed it New Orange.[19] On March 31, 1680, Claes Manuels, "Neger," married Lucretia Lovyse or Lowies, "Negrinne." Both were from Stuyvesant's Bouwery (farm).[20] They had five children baptized in the New York Dutch Reformed Church: Christyntie (Christina), born June 16, 1680, died young; Lysbeth (Elizabeth), born 1681; Emanuel (Manuel), born 1683; Lowys (Lewis), born 1685; and Christina, born 1688 but died before baptism.[21] Jan de Vries (John II) was a witness at the baptism of Claes Emanuels's first daughter named Christina.

The only evidence I could find pertaining to Augustine Van Donck * during this period was that a man named Augustine Sordonck

* There is no evidence that this colored Augustine Van Donck was related to Adriaen Van Der Donck (1620–circa 1655), one of the first lawyers in New Netherland and the patroon of Colen Donck, present-day Yonkers, New York. According to the genealogist of the Van Der Donck family, "He [Adriaen Van Der Donck] left his patroonship Colendonck to his wife and the property, after it had been patented anew to her and her second husband in their joint names in 1666, was immediately sold by them. These facts give strong evidence that van der Donck left no descendants." (William J. Hoffman, "An Armory of American Families of Dutch Descent: Van Der Donck-Van Bergen," *New York Genealogical and Biographical Record* 67, no. 4 [October 1936]: 339.)

"Prof. H. Kern, in *Nomina Geographica Neerlandica*, v. 2, p. 190–94, devotes an article to the meaning of the word *don(c)k*. He remarks that 'it seems a fact that several villages with names ending in donk are located in low land. It is also possible that in some instances it means settlement or hiding place.' *Navorscher* 39:230, 479 explains the meaning of the word in early Dutch as a slight elevation or hill in a depression or hollow. There are at least six small villages of that name in the Netherlands and the word don(c)k is found in a number of compound place names such as Baersdonck, Boerdonck, Meerendonk, Middeldonk, Meynendonk, Verspaendonck, Kelsdonck, also Gageldonck and Daesdonck, the last two (possibly a misspelling) resided between the Fresh Water and Harlem, his name appearing on the "lyst van de negers" compiled in 1673 by Governor Anthony Colvé.[22]

During the second half of the seventeenth century, settlement spread along the Hackensack, Passaic, and Raritan River Valleys west of the Hudson River. One of the first land transactions in the upper Hackensack River Valley was the Tappan Patent. On March 17, 1681 (1682 on the modern calendar), a group of people from the Bouwery Village on Manhattan Island purchased a tract of land from the Tappan Indians. The purchasers were represented by Jan Pietersen Haring, Adriaen Lambertsen Smidt, and Huybert Gerritsen Blauvelt, the Indians by their sachem Memsche, Towachkack (known as Jan Claes), Moccesin, Hanayahom, Corrunge, and Kerawak. The deed granted the land to Lady Elizabeth Carteret, one of the proprietors of East New Jersey, with the understanding that Lady Carteret would re-grant the land to the Dutchmen. But because the land was located along the disputed boundary between New York and East New Jersey, the patent was not granted back to the purchasers until March 17, 1686 (1687 new style), by Thomas Dongan, the governor of New York.[23]

The boundary of the Tappan Patent ran from the clove (gap) in the Palisades formed by Sparkill Creek at present-day Piermont, New York, southwest along Sparkill Creek across the present state boundary into New Jersey, then southwest along the Dwars Kill (creek) to its junction with the Hackensack River in present-day Harrington Park.

villages in the immediate vicinity of Breda, where Adriaen's family lived and where even today a Donck Street exists.

"It is evident that such place names have been the origin of the family names van der Don(c)k, van Don(c)k, Onderdonk, Don(c)k and others which are not uncommon in the Netherlands.

"Verdonck is really a contraction of van der Donck and Adriaen is called in the various documents both van der Donck and Verdonck (CDNY, 14:50, 73, etc.). Another American settler, Gysbert van der Donck, is also in some instances called Verdonck (RNA, 1:53).

"Very little was heretofore known about Adriaen van der Donck's ancestry and relatives. His family apparently became extinct in the Netherlands in the beginning of the 18th century." (Ibid., no. 3 [July 1936], pp. 229–30.)

It is possible that the handwritten *Ve* in Verdonck might have been mistaken for an *So* in the name Augustine Sordonck.

From there the boundary followed the Hackensack River north back
across the state line into New York to the Greenbush Swamp (present-
day Nyack Swamp). From there the boundary went east to the Palisades near present-day Nyack and then south along the Palisades back
to the clove in the Palisades, which gave access to the Hudson River.[24]

The purchasers of the Tappan Patent were mostly Dutch, although
the provinces of New York and East New Jersey had been under
English rule since 1664, except for the brief reoccupation by the Dutch
in 1673. Consequently, the land distribution was a modification of
the English open-field system. Each patentee received land in several
different locations so that both the good and bad land would be
equally divided. Lots of fifty morgen (one morgen equals approximately
two acres) were laid out along the east bank of the Hackensack
River, and meadows in two locations were distributed so that each
shareholder received six morgen of meadow land. One lot was set
aside for the Dutch Reformed Church and another lot for a courthouse. But rather than everyone having a house lot in a town under
the open-field system, the settlers in the Tappan Patent built their
houses on lots throughout the patent. Some people lived in the northern
end of the patent at present-day Orangeburg and Blauvelt, New York;
others settled at Tappan village (present-day Tappan, New York *);
and still others built their houses in what is now Bergen County, New
Jersey.[25]

Among the original shareholders in the Tappan Patent were Claes
Manuel (Emanuels) and John De Vries II. Claes Manuel purchased one
share, John De Vries II two shares, one for himself and one for his infant son John III. Of the ten families owning the sixteen shares in the
land patent, only one other family besides the De Vrieses purchased
two shares, and only two families owned three shares. The five other
families in the original distribution owned one share each. As each
share consisted of approximately 56 morgen (112 acres), the De Vries
family owned 112 morgen (224 acres) and the Emanuels family 56
morgen (112 acres).[26] In terms of seventeenth-century American

* When the boundary between New York and New Jersey was finally run in
1772, part of the Tappan Patent lay in New York and part in New Jersey. Thus,
today there are two towns with similar names: Tappan, New York, and Old
Tappan, New Jersey.

TABLE 3 NUMBER OF SHARES OWNED BY THE ORIGINAL FAMILIES
OF THE TAPPAN PATENT (1687)

Family head:	Shares
Jan Pietersen Haring of the Bowery, N.Y.	3
Adriaen Lambertsen Smidt of the Bowery, N.Y.	3
Blauvelt brothers (Huybert Gerritsen and Johannes Gerritsen) of the Bowery, N.Y.	2
John De Vries of the Bowery, N.Y.	2
Claus Manuel of the Bowery, N.Y.	1
Gerret Steynmetts of Ahasymus, N.J.	1
John Stratmaker of "Hobogen," N.J.	1
Staats De Groat of Bergen, N.J.	1
Ide Van Vorst of Ahasymus, N.J.	1
Cornelius Claessen Cuyper of Ahasymus, N.J.	1

Source: George Budke, "The History of Tappan Patent," *The Rockland Record* . . . edited by George H. Budke (Nyack, N.Y.:Rockland County Society of the State of New York, 1931), 2:35, 40.

colonial society, these landholdings represented middle-class economic status.

Both John De Vries and Claes Manuel (Emanuels) took the oath of allegiance to James II in Orange County, New York,* in 1687.[27] John De Vries was also listed in the 1702 census of Orange County.[28] Augustine Van Donck came to the Hackensack Valley by 1712, when he was listed as a resident of Orange Towne in the census of Orange County.[29]

These free, colored landowners can rightly be described as pioneers. They were among the first non-Indian settlers in the upper Hackensack River Valley. Culturally, they were Dutch. They had Dutch names, spoke the Dutch language, lived in Dutch colonial farmhouses, and were members of the Dutch Reformed Church. They were as Dutch as the Flemish, Walloons, and French Huguenots who have been grouped together under the name of Jersey Dutch.

Throughout the eighteenth century, the descendants of these colored pioneers owned farms in the upper Hackensack River Valley. In each generation their landholdings were diminished by the division of inheritances and by sales of portions of their land. Yet the size of

* Part of the Tappan Patent was located in what became Orange County, New York. Rockland County was not formed from Orange County until 1789.

the remaining holdings indicate the landowners had a lower-middle-class economic status.

By 1704, when formal releases were signed confirming each patentee in his share of land, John De Vries II had died and his eldest son John III had temporarily inherited his father's share—evidently in trust for his mother, brother, and sisters—in addition to the share purchased for him at the time of the original patent.[30] John De Vreese (De Vries III) was confirmed in his allotment of seven parcels of land: 25 morgen bounded on the north by the highway and on the south by the "cross kill" (river or creek) that runs into the Hackensack River, 30 morgen lying "over the Dwarse Kill" ranging from the "rhoad" to the Hackensack River, 75 morgen bounded on the east "by a small creek or run that runs into the Hackensack Kill," 50 morgen "lying in the range with the lotts that reaches the Greenbush [swamp]," 25 morgen along the "Tapane Kill" on the north side of the "Creeple bush" and bounded on the south by the path and on the east by the undivided lands, 25 morgen near the property of Barbary De Groat (widow of Staats De Groat) and John Ward, and 8 morgen in four lots of meadow land— a total of 238 morgen or approximately 476 acres.[31]

On November 2, 1704, John De Vries (III) sold 25 morgen "together with privileges in the woods for pasturage and cutting wood and timber soe long as any woods of Tapane's General Patent lyes common and undivided . . ." to John Ward;[32] and on May 2, 1706, he sold 50 morgen for 45 pounds to Daniel De Clerk of Orange Town.[33] He sold for 15 pounds a "full undivided sixteenth parte of all such land and privileges which . . . lyes common and undivided" to Thunes Van Houghton on April 29, 1708.[34]

The original share owned by the deceased John De Vries II was later divided between his widow, his daughters Maria (Marie) and Lenna (Helena), and his sons John III and Jacobus, the latter born in the 1690s and baptized in the Tappan Dutch Reformed Church. In 1715, they sold 20 acres on the Hackensack River to Jacob Vleeraboom for 26 pounds.[35] On May 14, 1716, Johannis De Vries (John III) and his mother sold 50 morgen of land and 50 morgen of rights to the undivided lands for 130 pounds to Francis Abrahamse, who married the niece of Claes Emanuels.[36] On May 1, 1717, Johannes De Vreese (John De Vries III) and Jacobus De Vreese (De Vries) conveyed to Daniel

De Klerck 50 morgen of undivided land near the Greenbush (swamp) that had been sold to him by their deceased father,[37] and in October of that year, John (III) sold 32 acres to Reneere Minardtse for 95 pounds.[38]

A deed dated December 24, 1723, confirmed Jacobus Devreese (De Vries), "blackeymore . . . , yeoman," in his possession of two parcels of land consisting of 80 acres and 41 acres respectively. The first plot was "at a place called the Stoney Point [New York]" and was bounded on the north by the lands of his brother Johannes De Vreese (John De Vries III), on the west by the Hackensack River, on the east by Abraham Blauvelt and the King's Road, and on the north by Abraham Van Salee, who had married Helena, the sister of John III and Jacobus.[39] "Cobus Defroest" (Jacobus De Vries) sold 20 morgen to Abraham Van Celea (Van Salee) and Lenah (Helena) for 30 pounds on February 16, 1730.[40]

In a deed dated April 16, 1725, Johannes De Vries (John III) leased to Heinrich Gessner, a millwright from Westchester, New York, 56 acres "at a place called Stony Point." The deed mentions a "dwelling house and grist-mill lately erected." Gessner paid De Vries 5 shillings plus "the rent of one pepper corn at or upon the four and twentieth day of June." [41] The following day Johannes (John) released Gessner from the lease for 160 pounds.[42] Possibly Gessner thereby purchased the mill.

In the next generation the De Vries family began to spread out. On July 19, 1750, Johannes De Vries (John IV) married Catharina Gerreau; both were from Tappan.[43] After their marriage, they moved northwest to Clarkstown, New York. His wife joined the Clarkstown Dutch Reformed Church in 1752, and their children were baptized in that church.[44] A 1787 tax list for Clarkstown indicates that Johannes (John IV) owned real estate assessed at 270 pounds and personal estate valued at 68 pounds 10 shillings.[45] It is estimated that the typical northern subsistence farm at that time consisted of 100 pounds of personal property and over 300 pounds of real property.[46]

A similar pattern of inheritance and land sales was followed by the descendants of Claes Emanuels. Claes had died by 1704, when the formal releases were signed. His surviving children, who took their father's name plus *sen* in accordance with the Dutch patronymic naming system, inherited his original share in the Tappan Patent.[47] As Manuel, Lewis, and Elizabeth Claussen (Claessen), they were confirmed in their allotment of seven parcels of land: 25 morgen bordering on the lands of John De Vrees (De Vries III) and "ranging from the meadows to the Hackensack Creek," 25 morgen "at a place called commonly the Durra Takes," 3 morgen "lying next to John De Vreese" (De Vries III) on the west side and the "Rhoad" on the north side, 10 morgen on the Dwarse (Dwars) Kill and bounded on the southwest by John De Vrees (De Vries III), a 2-morgen lot "at the Ringboom," 50 morgen near the Greenbush Swamp, and two lots of meadow containing about four morgen each—a total of 123 morgen or approximately 246 acres.[48]

Lewis Clausen (Claessen), whose occupation was "labourer," sold one half of the Claessen family rights to lots and undivided lands of the Tappan Patent to Frederick Symonson of Bushwick in Kings County, New York, for 30 pounds on April 29, 1707.[49] On May 1, 1708, he sold a 25-morgen lot to Jacob Vleeraboom for 30 pounds.[50] And on May 21, 1708, he sold 10 morgen to Garret Huybertse for 11 pounds 10 shillings.[51]

On May 19, 1730, Louwies Claesien (Lewis Claessen) married Maria Mattyse from Hackensack in the Hackensack Dutch Reformed Church.[52] A daughter named Elisabeth (Mannels) was born on November 3, 1730.[53] Although there is no baptism record to prove it, Lewis and Maria Claessen may have had a son also. A 1760 militia list for Orange County, New York, includes a man named Nicholas Manuel, who was born in Tappan, East Jersey, in 1737. His trade was listed as weaver and his race mulatto.[54] The Schraalenburgh, New Jersey, Dutch Reformed Church shows a marriage on June 25, 1758, between Lisabet (Elizabeth) Dye and Claes Emmanuel (Nicholas Manuel).[55]

Less information is available about the Van Donck family. The wife of Augustine Van Donck was named Fietje (maiden name unknown), and they had at least three daughters and two sons.

Their daughter Elizabeth Van Donk (Van Donck) married Casparus Haal on January 26, 1728, in the Hackensack Dutch Reformed Church.[56] Casparus and Elizabeth had a son named Jan who was born on April 14, 1728, and baptized in the Tappan Dutch Reformed Church.[57] The witnesses were Ariaentie De Vries (the wife of John

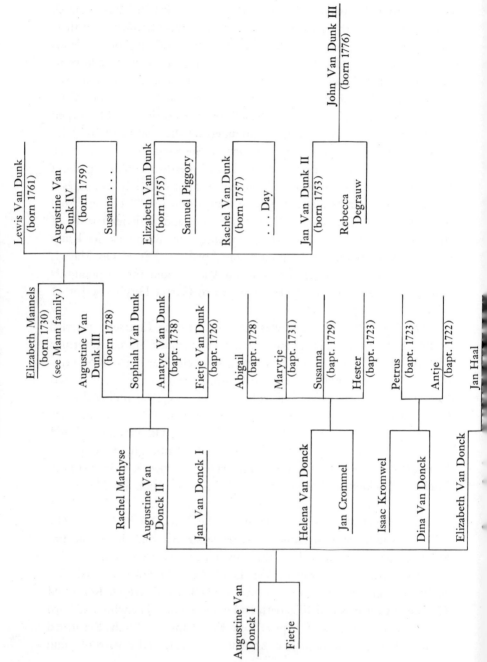

TABLE 4 THE VAN DUNK FAMILY

De Vries II) and Jan Van Donck. This Jan Van Donck may have been the son of Augustine and Fietje Van Donck; there is no more information about him.

The second daughter of Augustine and Fietje was Dina Van Donk (Donck), who married Isaac Kromwel.* Their third daughter, Helena or Lena Van Dunk, married Jan Crommel.† The relationship between Jan Crommel and Isaac Kromwel is not known, but it is possible that they were related, even brothers, in which case this was the first example of two brothers marrying two sisters in the genealogical history of the Mountain People.

There was one son of Augustine and Fietje Van Donck for whom there is a baptismal record. An entry in the Tappan Dutch Reformed Church records dated January 15, 1717, reads: "The 26th of June. Baptized the son of Agustyn Van Donck, named Aguystynes."[58] Augustine II was probably baptized as an adult, because on April 28, 1726, he married Rachel Mathyse in the Hackensack Dutch Reformed Church.[59] Rachel may have been the sister of Maria Mattyse, who married Louwies Claesien (Lewis Claessen).

In 1744 Augustine Van Donck II paid Willhemus Croom 80 pounds for 12 acres of land located along the disputed boundary be-

* On May 13, 1722, their daughter Antje was baptized in the New York Dutch Reformed Church, and on Sept. 18, 1723, their son Petrus was baptized in the same church. ("Records of the Reformed Dutch Church of New York," 2:434, 444.)

† On Oct. 15, 1723, two Crommel daughters named Hester and Abigail were baptized in the Tappan Dutch Reformed Church. ("Baptisms at Tappan," p. 8.)

In 1729 the following entry was made in the records of the New York City Lutheran Church: "31 Aug., in our church in Nieuw York, *Susanna*, ½ year old, of Jan *Crommel* (Cromwel?—written over, originally Crommel [?]) a mulatto at Hakkinsack, & Lena. P: Jora and her newly wedded husband Abraham Matthyssen, all free and baptized negroes." ("Baptisms in the Lutheran Church, New York City, From 1725," *New York Genealogical and Biographical Record* 97, no. 3 [July 1966]:168–69.)

In 1731, the minister from the same church baptized another daughter: "On the way, on the river called de Bullen, eod., *Marytje*, b. last Apr., of Jan *Cromwel* (written over) a baptized negro, & Lena, a baptized negress. G: Marytje Pieterse, widow, of New York, and Augustyn van Dunk, in whose places stood the grandparents, baptized negroes of the neighborhood." (Ibid., p. 229.) Marytje (Marie) Pieterse was the daughter of John De Vries II. She married Willem Pieterse. The abbreviation "G" for *getuygen* sometimes indicates godparents, sometimes witnesses, in these records.

tween New York and New Jersey. The deed contained the following clause:

in case it should so happen that at any time or times thereafter all or any part of the land and premises granted shall be cut-off or taken away by any division line that may hereafter be settled and run between the Provinces of New York and New Jersey . . . then the said Willhemus Croom . . . shall and will pay back, refund, and satisfy unto the said Augustine Van Donk . . . all such sum and sums of money as shall be in proportion to the number or quantity of acres that may so happen to be cut-off or taken away. . . .[60]

It has been estimated that the average small farm in New Jersey in the eighteenth century was about 80 acres. This would have made the Van Donck farm smaller than average. In the nearby town of Franklin in Bergen County, only one person in ten was landless. But Franklin was atypical, because it has been estimated that about 30 percent of the male population of New Jersey was landless.[61] Thus the economic status of Augustine Van Donck II might be described as lower middle class.

Augustine and Rachel Van Donck had four children: Fietje, Anatye, Sophiah, and Augustine III. On April 6, 1753, in the Tappan Dutch Reformed Church, Augustine III married Elizabeth Mannels, the daughter of Lewis and Marytie Claesen (Maria Claessen).[62] This marriage represents the first intermarriage between the families that were to become the core of the Ramapo Mountain People. Since Augustine's mother Rachel Mathyse and Elizabeth's mother Maria Mattyse may have been sisters, this may also represent the first first-cousin marriage among the ancestors of the Mountain People. A son named Jan Van Donk (Donck) was born on August 4, 1753. At Jan's baptism in the Tappan Dutch Reformed Church, Nicolaas Mannelse (Nicholas Manuel), Elizabeth's brother, was one of the witnesses.[63]

Augustine Van Donck II survived his son Augustine III. When Augustine II died, he divided his land between his widow and surviving children and grandchildren. In his will dated June 4, 1774, Augustine Van Dunk (Donck) II bequeathed the southwest fourth of his farm to his wife Rachel to have for her lifetime, and the remaining three fourths also to her, but only to have "during the time she shall continue

[his] widow" (i.e., as long as she did not remarry). After the death or remarriage of his wife, the northwest quarter of his farm was to be equally divided between his grandchildren John (Jan), Augustine IV, Lewis, and Rachel (children of his deceased son Augustine III), the northeast quarter was to go to his daughter Sophia (Sophiah), and the southeast quarter to his daughter Annaitje (Anatye). After the death of his wife, the southwest part of his farm was to go to his grandsons Augustine and Lewis.[64] This will shows a desire on Augustine's part to keep the farm within the family.

The land deeds indicate that the Van Dunk homestead was located on the banks of the Hackensack River near the main road in present-day River Vale, New Jersey.

There were also colored De Groots living in the Hackensack River Valley in the eighteenth century. On March 17, 1768, Jacobus De Groot married Janetje Dee in the Schraalenburgh Dutch Reformed Church (present-day Bergenfield, New Jersey). They are listed as "Aethiopes" (blacks).[65] Janetje was the daughter of Salomon and Susanne De from "Ackinsack [Hackensack]." Jacobus was the son of Joost De Groot * and Ariyaentye Sloove from Tappan. Jacobus and Janetje De Groot had two daughters who were baptized in the Hackensack Dutch Reformed Church: Susanna, born on May 3, 1771, and Ariaentye, baptized on May 21, 1769.† [66] They may have had other children who were not baptized.

One of the facts to emerge from the historical records is that a few of these colored pioneers owned slaves. The will of Jacobus De Vreese (De Vries) dated June 12, 1772, mentions his "negro wench, Bet., not to be sold without her consent." [67] The 1790 federal census lists John De Frieze (De Vries) as a white family head residing in Haverstraw, New York, and owning six slaves.[68] In the 1800 census, Catharine De Fres (De Vries) is listed as a free white family head residing in

---

* This colored Joost De Groot should not be confused with the white Joost De Groot, who was the son of Staats De Groat, one of the original shareholders in the Tappan Patent. The white Joost De Groot married Maritie Cornelise Banta in 1712. He died in 1748. (Theodore M. Banta, *A Frisian Family: The Banta Genealogy* . . . [New York: 1893], p. 22.) The colored Joost De Groot and his wife were still having children in the 1750s.

† Salomon and Susanna Dee (De) were the witnesses at the baptism of Susanna. Joost De Groot and his wife were the witnesses at the baptism of Ariaentye.

Clarkstown and owning two slaves.[69] The genealogies show that John and Catharine were members of the colored De Vries family. They seem to have been passing as white.

The only documentary evidence of the legendary Indian ancestry of the Ramapo Mountain People indicates that a John De Fries, who does not appear in the genealogies, in signing up for the Orange County militia in 1760, listed his race as "Indian." His age was twenty-five, his place of birth Tappan, and his trade variously listed as labourer, shoe-maker, and cordwainer.[70] This does not necessarily mean he was an Indian. He might have been trying to avoid the unfavorable attitude most whites had toward free blacks and mulattoes. On the other hand, he might have been the offspring of an interracial union.

Some historians believe that marriages between Indians and blacks were fairly common in New Jersey.

Of the New Jersey Indians it is said that "throughout the colonial history of the state, there were few marriages of white men and Indian women. Those that were contracted were looked upon in the light of miscegenation. For this reason the unions between Indians and Negroes were commonly so frequent indeed as to have left permanent impress upon the feature of many families of the Negroes of present day." [71]

But if there was early Indian ancestry, it would probably have been the Lenni-Lenape or Delaware Indians indigenous to the region rather than the Tuscarora, as the folk legend has it.[72] Also it probably could not have involved more than one or two individuals or there would have been more documentary evidence.

3 THE MIGRATION TO THE RAMAPO MOUNTAINS

Shortly after 1800 the ancestors of the Ramapo Mountain People began to sell their farms in the Hackensack River Valley and move to the Ramapo Mountains to the northwest. Because of the absence of diaries and other documents, the reasons for this migration are not known. Possibly it was motivated by the inferior legal and social status of free blacks, despite the middle-class economic status of the colored pioneers. A 1714 New Jersey statute expressed the prevailing white attitude toward free blacks in the eighteenth century: "it is found by Experience, that Free Negroes are an idle, slothful People. . . ." [1] Slavery still existed in New York and New Jersey,* and blacks were legally presumed to be slaves unless they could prove their free status.†

On March 14, 1798, the New Jersey legislature passed "An Act Respecting Slaves," which restricted the rights of free blacks to travel across county or state boundaries.

And be it enacted, That no free negro or mulatto, of or belonging to any other State in the union, shall be permitted to travel or reside in this State, without a certificate from two justices of the peace of such other State, that such negro or mulatto was set free, or deemed and taken to be free in that State. . . .

* New York didn't abolish slavery until 1827. New Jersey passed a law in 1804 providing for the gradual abolition of slavery.

† New Jersey Supreme Court Justice Ryerson stated in 1836 that "It was once the doctrine of this court that every colored person was presumed a slave until the contrary was shown." (Quoted in William Alexander Linn, "Slavery in Bergen County, New Jersey," *Papers and Proceedings of the Bergen County Historical Society* 4 [1907–8]:32.)

And be it enacted, That no free negro or mulatto, of or belonging to this State, shall be permitted to travel or remain in any county in this State, other than in the county where his or her place of residence may lawfully be, without a certificate from two justices of the peace of the county, in which he or she belonged, or from the clerk of the county, under the seal of the court, certifying that such negro or mulatto was set free, or deemed and taken to be free in such county.[2]

One would imagine that these restrictions were especially awkward for the colored pioneers of the Hackensack River Valley because they resided near the state boundary and had relatives in both New York and New Jersey.

Possibly the migration was motivated by the fact that the pattern of inheritance among these colored pioneers in the Hackensack River Valley was to divide their land between all their offspring, rather than willing it intact to the oldest son. As a result, in later generations the landholdings got progressively smaller until new land was needed for farming.*

On December 20, 1803, Augustine Van Dunk IV sold 2 acres in the Hackensack River Valley to James Demarest for $56.[3] Anntie (Anatye) Van Dunk sold eight acres to Henry Cole for 96 pounds on November 9, 1803.[4] On May 3, 1804, Augustine Van Dunk again sold more than 10 acres to James Demarest for $325.[5] And the last parcel of the old Van Dunk homestead, consisting of more than 18 acres, was sold by Annauchy (Anatye) Van Dunk to James Demarest on June 13, 1825, for $550.[6]

The De Freese family also moved from the Hackensack River Valley around 1806, when there was an intrafamily slander suit brought against Johannes Defreeze (John De Freese V) and his wife Hannah by their niece Catherine Dowers. According to Catherine's charge, Hannah

in the presence and hearing of divers other good and worthy Citizens of the said State reported, asserted, published, and declared in substance that

---

* Scholars have suggested that a similar pattern of inheritance created a land shortage in Puritan New England which necessitated expansion into new towns. (Kenneth Lockridge, "Land, Population and the Evolution of New England Society 1630–1790," *Past and Present* 39 [April 1968]:62–80; Philip Greven, Jr., *Four Generations: Population, Land, and Family in Colonial Andover, Massachusetts* [Ithaca: Cornell University Press, 1970], pp. 130ff.)

the said Catherine was a whore and that she had been delivered of a bastard child and that she had murdered the said child by means of speaking and publishing of which said several false, scandalous, and defamatory words and the reporting, propagating and publishing the slander aforesaid, the said Catherine has fallen into great scandal and disgrace and hath sustained damage to two thousand dollars and thereof she brings suit.[7]

To avoid prosecution, John and Hannah De Freese and their family moved to New York City.

About the same time colored Van Dunks, De Groats, Manns, and De Freeses began to show up in the Ramapo Mountains. Gaps in the genealogical records and the fact that the federal censuses for 1790–1830 are missing prevent establishing positively the exact relationship between many of these colored families in the mountains and the earlier colored families in the Hackensack River Valley. But in one case, the record is clear. In 1800 John Van Donk (Van Dunk III), the grandson of Augustine Van Dunk III and Elizabeth Mannels, was living in the town of Warwick in Orange County, New York.[8] By 1830 he had moved to Pompton Township, New Jersey, where the Ringwood iron mines were located.[9]

When the Mountain People first came to the Ramapo Mountains, they settled in the hollows and on the ridges southwest of the Ramapo Pass. Many of them purchased land and established mountain farms. The first to buy land was James De Groot (De Groat), who on January 18, 1805, bought more than fifteen acres of mountain land "lying and being within the Romopock Tract" * from Richard P. Wanmaker for $237.50.[10] In 1825 James De Grote (De Groat) and Robert Lowder bought more than ten acres from Garret W. Hopper for $100.00. It was described as

beginning at a large split rock in the Ramapough mountains marked with the letters G. H. [probably for Garret Hopper] lying about two miles northward from the said Garret W. Hopper dwelling house and about one chain distant on the northwest side of a small brook which flows out of a

* The "Romopock" (or "Ramapock" or Ramapo) Tract included 42,500 acres of land between the Saddle River and the Ramapo Mountains granted in November 1709 by Peter Sonmans, agent for the East Jersey proprietors, to a land syndicate headed by Peter Fauconier from New York City. (Edward Franklin Pierson, *The Ramapo Pass*, ed. H. Pierson Mapes [Ramapo, N.Y.: privately printed typescript, 1955, written in 1915], p. 31.)

. . . [green?] swamp and running through a place called . . . [Shongun?] clove into the Ramapough River. . . .[11]

From this description, James De Groat's farm appears to have been located in the vicinity of Green Mountain Valley, which was named Havemeyer's Hollow on later maps. In 1846 James De Groat bought another fifty-eight acres of mountain land from Mary Rutherford.[12] By 1850 his landholdings were valued at $700.[13]

An inventory compiled in 1860 after the death of James De Groat lists his personal property as follows:

A true and perfect inventory and appraisement of the personal property of James Degroat late of the county of Bergen, deceased, made by Susan Degroat, executrix, and Henry R. Wanmaker, and Michael E. Taylor, two disinterested freeholders this twelfth day of March in the year one thousand eight hundred and sixty.

	$ cts.
one yoke of oxen	100.00
five cows	100.00
three calves	15.00
one wagon	8.00
one sleigh	1.50
one plow	1.50
a lot of sundry articles	2.00
two beds & bedding	10.00
one stove and contents	1.50
a lot of crockery	3.00
one clock	.75
table and chairs	2.00
a lot of sundries	1.50
cash	10.00
	$256.75

	her		
Susan	X	De Groat	Executrix
	mark		

Henry R. Wanmaker
Michael E. Tayler   Appraisers [14]

In his will, James De Groat deeded his lands to his wife and four sons.

Philip Mann * was listed in the 1810 federal census as living in the Town of Ramapo, near the Ramapo Mountains in New York state.[15] In 1820 he was still living there, and his employment was listed as agriculture.[16] A list of employees in John Suffern's ledger indicates that Philip Man (Mann) worked in Suffern's ironworks in the Ramapo Pass in 1826.[17] But prior to 1850 he moved into the New Jersey section of the Ramapos. In 1850 he owned $500 worth of real estate,[18] and he added thirty-four acres to his holdings in 1862 at a price of $100.[19] In 1864, Philip Man sold land to James S. Wanmaker [20] and Elliot Man.[21]

By 1830 there was already a sizable population of colored Mountain People in the Ramapos. The 1830 federal census, the earliest available for New Jersey and the first census to list race, provides a good overview of the population distribution. Most of the Mountain People lived in what was then Franklin Township in the New Jersey section of the mountains southwest of the Ramapo Pass. Among them were the following free "negro" heads of families (the size of their families in parentheses): Richard Degroot (4), Joseph Degroot (7), William Degroot (5), Ellen Degroot (3), James Degroot (9), Elias Mann (9), Peter Mann (7), Juliana Mann (7), and Peter Debruse (probably De Frise) (4).

Residing at the Ramapo Pass in the Town of Ramapo, New York state, were John Man (3) and Philip Mayne (probably Mann) (11). Some Mountain People were already living in Pompton Township, New Jersey, in the Wanaque River Valley on the northwest side of the Ramapo Mountains: Samuel Vandonk (3), John Vandonk (3), and Morgan Lewis (probably Lewis Morgan) (3).† Still in the Hackensack

---

* Possibly Philip Mann was the son of Nicholas and Elizabeth Manuel. With Philip, the family surname became fixed as Mann.

† Other free colored family heads with the same surnames but different residences listed in the 1830 federal census were Joseph De Groat of Augusta in Oneida County, N.Y. (Carter Godwin Woodson, *Free Negro Heads of Families in the United States in 1830* [Washington, D.C.: Association for the Study of Negro Life and History, 1925], p. 100); Richard De Groat, John Degroat, James De Groat in the town of Onondaga in Onondaga, N.Y. (ibid., p. 101); Nicholas De Grote of Castelton in Richmond County, N.Y. (ibid., p. 105); Thomas De Groat in Elizabeth Township, Essex County, New Jersey (ibid., p. 77); and Lewis De Groat of New Haven County, Conn. (ibid., p. 5). It has not been established whether the colored De Groats migrated to the Ramapos from upstate New York or *vice versa*.

River Valley in Harrington Township, New Jersey, was a colored James De Groot with a family of six.[22]

Several new surnames were added to the Mountain People through marriage in the nineteenth century. One of these was the colored Suffern family. The Mountain People maintain that the colored Sufferns are related to the white Sufferns descended from Judge John Suffern, who settled at the entrance to the Ramapo Pass in 1773. The white Sufferns argue that the colored Sufferns are descended from John Suffern's slaves. The first reference to the colored Sufferns is in the record of the group baptism in the Zion Lutheran Church of Saddle River, New Jersey, on February 13, 1820, of the children of William and Hannah Suffern, identified as colored: Nicholas, born in 1812; Mary, born in 1814; Charles, born in 1816; and Sarah, born in 1819.[23] Who was this colored William Suffern? The white Judge John Suffern had a son named William, born in 1783,[24] but he married Martha Bertholf in 1804.[25] Their son James became a justice of the peace, a member of the New York state assembly, and a lieutenant colonel in the state militia.[26] The United States census indicates that John Suffern owned three slaves in 1790.[27] One of his slaves was named Kate. She is mentioned by name in John Suffern's will in 1836: "I also give her [his wife Elizabeth] my black girl Kate, she performing and fulfilling the requisitions of the Law in regard to her." [28] Kate was probably Kate Osborne, who was buried in the colored section of the Ramapo Reformed Church graveyard in Mahwah. Her tombstone inscription reads: "Kate Osborne / servant / deceased. a. 52 yrs. d. August 23, 1870." [29] Nearby is another tombstone inscribed: "Betsey Osborne / for 35 years a faithful servant in the family of John Suffern / d. May 10, 1857 a. 60 years." [30]

Other free colored family heads with different surnames residing in the same vicinity as the Mountain People were Henry Moore of Franklin Township, N.J. (ibid., p. 75); James Oliver, William Day, Richard Cisco, Francis Cisco, Nicholas Cisco, Samuel Moore, Samuel Pigenet, James Oliver and Nancy Sisco in Harrington Township, N.J. (ibid., p. 75); William Sisco of Saddle River Township, N.J. (ibid.); John Cisco, Mariah Pegra, William Jackson, Harry Pake, William Cisco, another William Cisco in Orangetown, Rockland County, N.Y. (ibid., p. 105); William Day, Samuel Sisco, Solomon Day, and another William Day in Onondaga town in Onondaga County, N.Y. (ibid., p. 101). Many of these colored families later married into the Mountain People.

"Uncle" Charlie De Freese

Wesley Van Dunk, husband

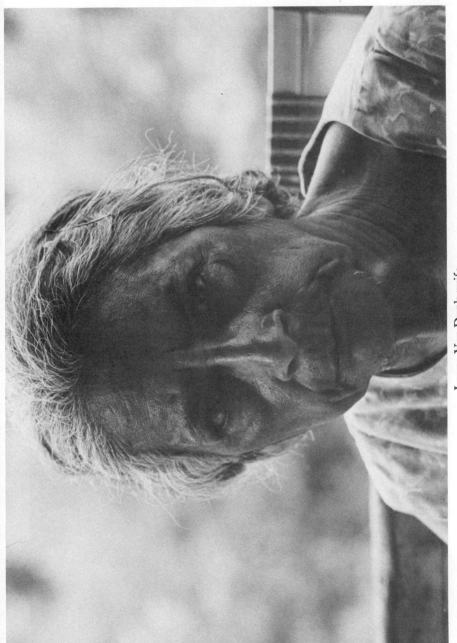

Leona Van Dunk, wife

Wally Morgan and his son Dwayne

Madge Morgan

Bob Milligan

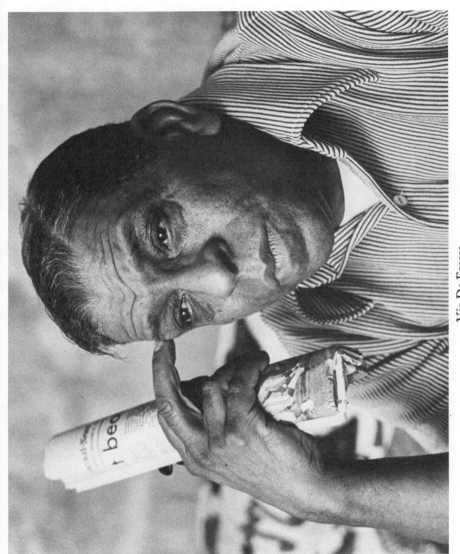

Vic De Freese

Myron Van Dunk

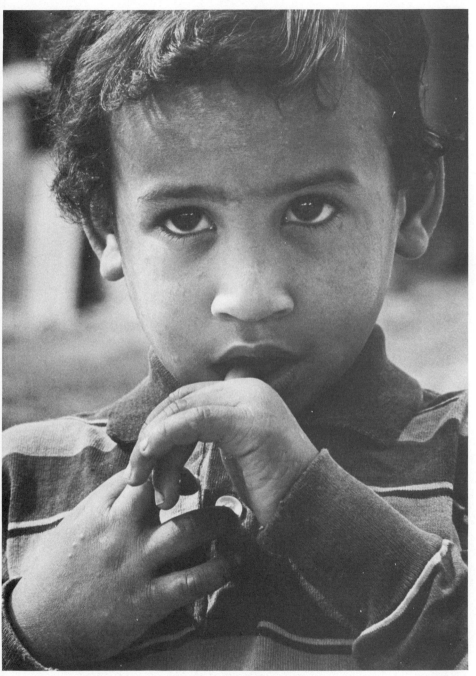

Gary Milligan, Jr.

Billy Van Dunk

Howard Morgan

Jack Van Dunk

Peter Galindez, Jr.

Mildred "Sis Alexander" Galindez

"Tracey" Powell

Alexandria Mae Galindez

Mary Galindez

Harriet "Aunt Meal" Van Dunk and her grandson John

The Vineland Training School's genealogical study of the Mountain People suggests that, not only the colored Sufferns, but also the colored Morgans, can be traced back to one of the slaves of the white Suffern family.

Rebecca Morgan, or "Granny Becky" as she is called at Hillburn, is probably the oldest living Jackson White. Born in 1814 of Indian-negro parents, most likely slaves, and married young, she had a large family and is a great, great grandmother . . .
Granny Becky married Richard Morgan, the son of a slave named Betsy Ritter. Betsy and her husband were owned by the Suffern family, who, after the couple had had two children, separated them and sold the man. Betsy afterwards had another child "by someone else." [This child was known as Peter Suffern and Granny Jane's (daughter of Granny Becky) family claim that old Judge Suffern himself was the father of it.] * 31

Possibly Betsy Ritter was the same person as Betsey Osborne, who is know to have been a servant of the Suffern family. Both Richard Morgan and Peter Suffurn (Suffern) were listed in the 1840 federal census as free Negroes.† Peter Suffurn was living with his family of six in the Wanaque River Valley and was working in agriculture. Richard Morgan was employed in mining in Ringwood.32 The 1850 federal census lists Richard Morgan, his wife Rebecca, and their family in Rockland County, New York. His place of birth is given as New York state.33 Peter Suffern shows up on a 1869 payroll for the Ringwood furnace.34 But this is not sufficient proof to substantiate the relationships described in the Vineland Training School's study.

Legend has it that the colored Jennings family, who married into the Mountain People in the late nineteenth century, are also the descendants of the slaves of local farmers. Local historian John Y. Dater wrote that H. O. Havemeyer, the owner of a farm along the Ramapo River in Mahwah, told him that

* The words in brackets are crossed out in the manuscript and marked "omit."
† A free, black family head named Lewis Morgan was living in the Ringwood area in 1830 (Woodson, p. 75). In the 1850 federal census his place of birth was given as New York state (U.S., Bureau of the Census, Seventh Census of the United States: 1850. New Jersey [manuscript], n.p.).

at the northwest end of the large field in front of the cow barns, along the
river bank [on his farm], there is a colored burial plot, where the slaves of
the owners of the various properties were buried. In this plot is the grave
of Sam Jennings, one of Hagerman's slaves.[35]

Henry Brazier Hagerman married the granddaughter of Andrew
Hopper, who is known to have owned slaves valued at $224.50 at the
time of his death in 1813.[36] The slaves owned by Hopper in 1813 had to
have been born prior to 1804, because New Jersey's gradual abolition
law passed in 1804 provided that any child born of slave parents after
that date would be free. But the child had to remain a servant of his or
her mother's owner until the child reached the age of twenty-five if
male and twenty-one if female.[37] According to Mrs. E. Oakes-Smith,
in the introduction to her book *The Salamander*, the former slaves of
the Hopper family remained as servants.

In the family of the Hoppers were 20 or 30 negroes, a fine, cheerful-
looking race, the remnants of the slavery which existed before the state
emancipation, free, yet clinging affectionately to the old family. It was
picturesque and amusing to see these indolently grouped about, for, in truth,
the smallest of their service is only exceeded by the greatness of indulgence
with which they are treated by their former owners; these dependents
scorn also all language but that in use in days gone by.[38]

Samuel Jennings, his wife Sarah, and his children William James, York,
Sally Maria, Joseph H., Samuel, Jr., Edward, and Richard are listed in
the New Jersey state census of 1865 [39] and the 1880 United States
census for New Jersey. The federal census indicates that Samuel
Jennings was born in 1816 in New Jersey.[40] Thus although Sam Jennings might have been the son of one of the Hopper's slaves, he probably was a free servant of the Hagerman family, rather than a slave.

Sam Jennings's children married into the Mountain People. William
James Jennings married Abbie De Groat in 1868.[41] York Jennings
married "Kate" De Groat. Sally Maria Jennings in 1869 married Richard Degroot, who owned the Halifax farm.[42] In 1892 Samuel Jennings,
Jr., married Eleanor Mann of Hillburn.[43]

"An Italian strain" married into the Mountain People in the late
nineteenth century, according to John C. Storms.

About 1870 the arrival of two brothers in this vicinity added to the mixture of blood and largely increased the population in a few years. These were James and Joseph Castaglionia, who had just arrived from Italy, and were the first persons of this nationality to settle in the vicinity. James married Delilah Sniffin, started as a blacksmith and horse trader, but later became a general contracter and padrone, acquiring considerable money and property.

Joseph settled on a farm near his brother, east of Montvale, New Jersey, and married Libby DeFriese. Both of these women inherited a longing for the free life of the mountains, being of Jackson-White descent; Libby had also a strain of Tuscarora blood. The offspring of these families naturally gravitated to the original homes of their mothers, and by settling in the mountains added a trace of Italian blood to the already much-crossed strains.

The original name of this family almost immediately became lost, and for it the shorter "Casalony" was substituted.[44]

Howard Morgan of Hillburn gave the following account of the entrance of the Castelony family into the group·

Way back in history there was—woodchopping used to be one of the industries around the mountains that the Mountain People followed. There was a person—I heard him spoke of as "the Dutchman"—that's all I knew about that—and he used to get this wood cut that he had to deliver. You see around that time Haverstraw was a brick town. They used wood for burning brick in Haverstraw. To get this wood out this man brought a group of Italians. Now the location of that wood job was . . . up the mountain from the Havemeyer estate. Up at this end of the mountain. It was called by the people "Maple Swamp." Now there was no facilities in that area to house those men, so they built shanties and lean-tos and whatnot and lived right there in the woods.

During that period, one man by the name of Joe Castelony met and married one of those mountain girls and she was always called "Lib" or "Lid"—whether that was Elizabeth I don't know whether she was a Mann or a DeFreese. Joe Castelony was the man who married this girl. When the rest of the Italians left here after the job was finished, he moved up on the back side of Hoevenkopf, built a new house, and raised a family. And that's where the name Castelony started . . . .

Joe had a brother Jim. I don't know too much about him. He lived down in Pearl River or some part of New Jersey. He had a mechanical organ or piano—not a steam caliopy, but something like that, and he used to come around this area once and a while.

Despite discrepancies on certain details, both these accounts are substantiated by documents. An 1868 deed in which Nelson Degroat sold
land to Richard De Groot mentions it as "adjoining the Italian company's lot. . . ."[45] This was probably the woodchoppers' camp in the
mountains. The records of the Ramapo Reformed Church show the
marriages on June 4, 1868, of James Castelyoni and Julia Conklin and
on June 6, 1868, of Joseph Castelyoni and Sarah Ann De Friest.[46] Joseph
Castleyonne and family settled in Hohokus Township, New Jersey,
where he was employed as a farm laborer.[47]

The Milligan family joined the Mountain People in Ringwood.
Silas Milligan, his wife Lavinia, and their family were living in Ringwood in 1865.[48] Silas was born in New York state in 1824.[49] Among
their children were Robert Milligan ("Uncle Rob," the strong man),
who married May ("Haddie") Van Dunk; Emilia ("Meal") Milligan,
who married George Van Dunk; Mary E. ("Mary Lib") Milligan,
who married Charlie Suffern; and Clara Milligan, who married George
Van Dunk. In 1897 Sarah Emma, the daughter of "Mary Lib" and
Charlie Suffern, married George E. Powell, thus accounting for the
introduction of the Powell surname among the Mountain People.[50]

One of the chief occupations of the Ramapo Mountain People
in the nineteenth century was farming. Richard De Groot was
a landowner in 1855, when he was listed in the New York state census
as a "person of color not taxed." His farm, known as Halifax, was
located on Monroe Ridge. His house was described as a log dwelling,
and he owned 60 acres of improved land, 150 acres of unimproved
land, 8 meat cattle, 4 working oxen, 7 milk cows, 2 horses, and 6 swine.
The cash value of his farm was estimated at $200, his stock at $600,
and his tools and implements at $30.[51] In 1868 he bought an additional
68 acres for $200 from Nelson Degroat, 60 acres for $66 from Susan
Degroat, the son and widow, respectively, of James Degroat, deceased,[52] and 11 acres for $175 from Elliot Man.[53]

Peter De Groat was another of these mountain farmers. He bought
approximately 56 acres for $224 from James Suffern in 1854. This land
was located "on the northeast side of a Pond lying on the north of the
Round Swamp, known by the name of Maple Swamp."[54] In the 1855

census Peter De Groat was listed as owning 45 acres of improved land, 13 acres of unimproved land, including 8 acres in meadow, 6½ acres in rye, ¾ acre in buckwheat, 4 acres in corn, and 1½ acres in potatoes. In addition, he owned four cows for milk, 3 cows for butter, two horses, and two swine. The cash value of his farm was estimated at $2,500, his stock at $300, and his tools and implements at $50. He also had another farm with 6 acres of improved and 5 acres of unimproved land valued at $550.[55]

Others who owned land in the mountains were Elias Van Dunk, John De Frease (De Freese), and John Mann. The descriptions of their land in the deeds indicate that their land bordered on one another. In the 1850 federal census, Elias Van Dunk * was listed as owning land valued at $500.[56] His land is mentioned in an 1868 deed as bordering the land sold to Richard De Groot by Nelson De Groot.[57] In 1850 John De Frease (De Freese) owned land worth $550.[58] In 1857 he bought an additional forty acres "along the state line" from Mary Rutherford.[59] John Dufries (De Freese) sold ten acres to Samuel and John Man (Mann) in 1865 for $160. This land was bounded on the north by the "York state line," on the west by his own land, on the south by John Van Dunk, and on the east by Philip Man and John Man.[60] John Mann owned $1,200 worth of land in 1850.[61] He sold some of this land to James S. Wanmaker in 1867.[62]

Not all the Mountain People owned farms. Some worked farms owned by absentee landlords. The "Gannor place" located in the mountains near Cranberry Lake, New Jersey, was worked by John and Etta Mann. Back in the Ramapos near Bald Mountain, Silas and Adie Mann worked the Davidson farm. The "Post place" was located near Mac-Millan Reservoir. Some of the Mountain People worked as farm helpers on the estates and farms in the Wanaque and Ramapo valleys. The Abram S. Hewitt estate in Ringwood (known as Ringwood Manor), the H. O. Havemeyer farm, and the A. B. Darling stables along the Ramapo River supplied work for some of the Mountain People in the late nineteenth century. Some of the Mountain People even worked as seasonal laborers on the farms in the Saddle River Valley and on Chest-

---

* He is listed as residing in Hohokus Township, which was formed from the northern part of Franklin Township in 1849 and included part of the southeastern side of the Ramapo Mountains.

nut Ridge to the southeast. Mrs. Etta Tice Terhune of Park Ridge, New Jersey, remembers them coming to work on her father's farm when she was a young girl.

There was a little house down the back. There were three rooms downstairs and an attic upstairs. Well, one family lived in the two rooms on one side of the house, and another family lived—well, it was just a man and his wife—in the one room, and they had the attic. . . . But, they—they stayed to themselves. And my father never made much friends with them.

He'd, ah—They're good workers. Very good workers. And they would pick berries. We had lots of berries. And they made plenty of money, and they didn't have to live the way they did. They didn't have any furniture. You'd never seen them move in, and you'd never seen them move out. They'd come, like on maybe Saturday, and they'd say, "Mr. Tice, we'd like to rent the little house." It was a dollar a week rent. No improvements, no light, no heat, nothing. So my father says, "You can lease in advance." Yes, well, they'd give him the dollar. No use to give them a receipt, because they couldn't read it. They'd just have to take your word for it. And we'd get up Monday morning, and used to see the smoke coming out of the chimney. You'd never seen them move in. And then it would get to be late in the fall, and Mom says, "Well, it's just about time for our friends to be moving out." And we'd get out and we'd look, and there'd be no smoke coming out of the chimney. And we'd know that they were gone.

In the 1850s, when Peter Cooper and Abram S. Hewitt reactivated the Ringwood iron mines and furnaces, many of the Mountain People migrated across the Ramapos to the Wanaque River Valley to find

TABLE 5   INCOME OF SAMUEL DE GROAT FOR THE YEAR 1869
AT THE RINGWOOD FURNACE

Date	Furnace	Wood Job	Teams	Coal Job	Store Trade
April	. . . . .	$ 2.40	. . . . .	. . . . .	$ 2.48
May	. . . . .	. . . . .	. . . . .	$45.11 [?]	. . . . .
July	$14.12	. . . . .	$ 8.25	17.87	17.21
August	. . . . .	. . . . .	. . . . .	26.69	26.69
September	31.63	. . . . .	. . . . .	. . . . .	17.35
October	. . . . .	. . . . .	38.00	. . . . .	25.05
November	. . . . .	. . . . .	. . . . .	37.50	23.43
December	. . . . .	15.50	6.00	. . . . .	11.44

Source: Compiled from payroll lists in the possession of Lewis West, Midvale, New Jersey.

TABLE 6 RAMAPO MOUNTAIN PEOPLE ON THE PAYROLL
FOR THE RINGWOOD FURNACE,
NOVEMBER 30, 1869

Name	Furnace	Coal Job	Teams	Store Trade
Moses De Groat	$45.00	.....	.....	$52.10
Richard De Groat	.....	.....	$13.50	8.63
Samuel Milligan	.....	$ 7.05	.....	7.05
John Morgan	77.50	.....	.....	66.19
Samuel Degroat	37.50	.....	.....	23.43
John De Groat	.....	27.85	.....	21.68
George Degroat	.....	17.18	.....	17.18
Moses Defrease	.....	47.69	.....	47.69
William Morgan	.....	47.65	.....	47.26
Peter Suffern	56.52	.....	.....	56.52
George Suffern	46.88	.....	.....	42.37
William Suffern	.....	14.74	.....	14.74
Edward Suffern	29.00	.....	.....	18.00
Martin Suffern	.....	32.29	.....	32.29
Thomas Dunk	.....	97.27	.....	97.86
Elias Dunk	34.37	.....	.....	17.18
Samuel Dunk	.....	.....	37.50	89.15

Source: Information taken from the original manuscript in the possession of Lewis West, Midvale, New Jersey.

employment. The payroll lists for the 1870s and 1880s show Mountain People working in the furnace, driving teams, and working coal jobs and wood jobs. Often the same man might work several different jobs in the course of the year. Most of their earnings were spent in the company store.

Coal jobs and wood jobs refer to the process of charcoal burning, since charcoal was the fuel in the furnace. Woodchoppers would be sent into the mountains to cut down trees, which were stacked in upright cone-shaped piles and covered with earth and damp leaves. Then these piles were set afire and allowed to burn for three to ten days. The burners would often camp near the burning pile in roughly built shelters in order to supervise these "firings." [63] While hiking in the Ramapo Mountains with a local guide in 1872, a reporter for *Appleton's Journal of Literature, Science, and Art* came across some of these charcoal burners.

The guide pointed to some black fragments on the ground. They seemed to have dropped from some bag or basket.

"Burners," said he, tersely.

A moment after, we breathed air which was impregnated with a peculiar odor. It was heavy and unpleasant. . . . Presently we emerged upon a little glade fifty feet across. In the centre was a huge, black, smouldering pile covered with earth, through which numberless jets of smoke were forcing themselves and rising straight into the air; a few feet above the heap they drew together and formed a broad white column . . . Upon the ground lay three men, with their arms stretched out and their faces turned upward. Every one was as black as dust and grime could make him. . . .

A boy came around from the farther side of the pile, dragging a broad wooden shovel after him. He began to beat the earth on the mound, smoothing and arranging it, meanwhile giving us the benefit of his glassy eyes between every stroke.

Suddenly a very tall man came out of the thick wood behind us, and walked straight up to where we were standing. . . .

The guide began to talk to him about charcoal, while I took the opportunity to look about. There was no house or habitation in sight. Upon the ground were scraps of bone, heaps of green wood, and some baskets. The trees in the neighborhood were stripped of their bark, and the ground at their feet was trampled. . . .

The man bargained with my companion in the most ungainly fashion. . . . He had negro blood in him, and the flavor of the plantation had accompanied his descent from a slave. . . . I agreed to purchase a basket of coal, to be delivered at the guide's house in the town below.

The man's languid spirit roused a little at this success. It made him vain. He fixed his eyes on his customer, and slowly swayed his head on his long neck, muttering in a half-stifled voice:

"It'll be dummed hot, boss!" [64]

Many of the Mountain People worked as miners until the mines were closed for the last time in the 1950s. There are still men in Ringwood who remember the days when the mines were working.

Frank Milligan: Now, you know, we put out seven hundred and fifty ton a shift. And we only had thirteen men, including the hoistman. And when those guys [the last managers of the mines] came in there, they had pretty near a hundred men, and remember, they was getting all the ore out of the settling pond. And they still had to rescreen that to get three hundred ton a day. And we were producing seven hundred ton a day. All these hotshots from Michigan, and they was gonna show us how to long-hole, and they didn't know nothing.

Russell Mann: I'll tell ya, they were paying top dollar at the time. They got more money than we got. We got—as a driller—we got a dollar seventy-three—that's top. Driller. Am I right or wrong, Frank? . . .
Frank: Well, you know, I started out the same as you. Right as a mucker. I worked right on through every job there. Foreman, testhole-driller, [garbled] driller, raise driller, drifter. I done every—every job in the mines. I ran slush, and I ran muck machines. I done it all. Every job in the mines. . . . Well, I started in the mines back January the fourth, nineteen forty-four. That's when I started . . . But, see, now, like my grandfather, he worked his whole life. Never did another job in his life. He started at eleven years old, driving mules in the mine, and he was running the hoist when he died at seventy-two years old.

Employment in iron-related industries also attracted Mountain People to the Ramapo Pass when the company town of Hillburn, New York, was founded in the 1870s by the Ramapo Wheel and Foundry Company, which made railroad wheels and brakeshoes. When a new foundry was built across the state line in Mahwah, New Jersey in 1902, the Mountain People followed their jobs.

A comparison of the occupations of the Mountain People in 1880 and 1915 reveals the change from agricultural to industrial employment. Of the Mountain People living in Hohokus Township (which included the New Jersey section of the mountains) in 1880, there were 6 farmers, 24 laborers, 1 coachman, 1 servant, and 1 worker in a lock factory. In Pompton Township, there were 15 laborers, 8 iron miners, 1 gardener, and 2 blacksmiths. In West Milford Township (Hewitt, New Jersey, the site of the Long Pond furnace), there were 7 laborers and 7 workers in the furnace. And in the Town of Ramapo (Hillburn), there were 7 laborers, 13 farm helpers, and 1 teamster.[65]
Of the Mountain People living in Hohokus Township (Mahwah) in 1915, there were 2 moulders, 8 laborers in the foundry, 15 farm laborers, 11 laborers, 1 coachman, 6 teamsters, 1 gardener's helper, 1 core maker in the foundry, 1 watchman, 1 mason, 1 chauffeur, 1 farmer, 1 electrician, and 1 blacksmith. In Pompton Township (Ringwood), there were 10 farm workers, 17 mine workers, 1 gardener, 3 team drivers, 1 blacksmith, 1 engineer, 1 caretaker of cattle, 1 fireman, and 1 laborer. In West Milford (Hewitt), there were 7 farm laborers, 3 team drivers, and 1 stable boss. And in Hillburn, there were 3 shop

laborers, 5 cranemen, 1 iron moulder helper, 1 machinist helper, 9 machinists, 1 machine oiler, 3 moulders, 1 coremaker, 6 foundry laborers, 1 frog builder, 1 foreman grinder, 1 outside foreman, 1 chipper, 2 machine laborers, 1 castings grinder, 1 machine worker, 1 farmer, 7 laborers, 2 firemen, 2 clergymen, 6 farm laborers, 4 coachmen, 4 house laborers, 1 contractor, 4 gardeners, 1 butler, 1 waiter, 2 highway laborers, 1 shipping clerk assistant, 1 stone mason, 1 laundryman, 1 station engineer, 1 woodchopper, 2 janitors, 1 accountant, 2 teamsters, and 1 laborer in the gas plant.[66]

Several of the Ramapo Mountain People served in the United States colored troops during the Civil War. Private Philip De Freese served in Company H, 33d Regiment; Henry Degrote was a corporal in Company C, 22d Regiment; Private John De Grote served in the cavalry; and Private William H. Jennings served in the 8th Regiment, Infantry. Private William De Groat, from Company H, 11th Regiment, died of inflammation of the bowels in an army camp near Falmouth, Virginia, in 1862. Private John Suffren, who was drafted, died in 1865 at the Corps D'Afrique Hospital in New Orleans. And Private William Van Dunk, who was hired as a substitute, died in 1865 at the U.S. Army General Hospital in New Orleans and was buried there.[67] James De Groat and Obadiah De Groat, both from Ramapo, served during "the Rebellion" in the 26th New York Volunteers.[68]

The arrival in the Ramapo Mountains of the colored pioneers from the Hackensack River Valley represents the beginning of the Ramapo Mountain People as a group with a distinct identity. While still in the Hackensack River Valley, the ancestors of the Mountain People had been essentially no different from free blacks. Once in the Ramapos, geographic isolation enabled them to consolidate a distinctive racial identity and an exclusive family and kinship system.

Yet isolation was never complete. Those who owned farms back in the mountains were the most isolated. By the midnineteenth century some of the Mountain People had migrated northwest across the Ramapos to the Wanaque River Valley to find employment in the iron mines and furnaces in Ringwood and Hewitt. Others began to work as agricultural laborers on the large valley farms in Ringwood and in Mahwah. When the company town of Hillburn was founded in the

Ramapo Pass, Mountain People moved there to work in the foundry. By the end of the century some of the Mountain People had migrated to the agricultural towns in Orange County, New York, the suburban towns in Bergen County, New Jersey, and the nearby cities of Paterson and Newark (see Appendix D). But the core of the Mountain People remained in the settlements at Mahwah, Ringwood, and Hillburn.

4 MAHWAH

The first settlement of the Mountain People in the Ramapo Mountains was in the section of the mountains overlooking the Ramapo Valley in what is today part of Mahwah, New Jersey. The name Mahwah is said to come from the Indian word *mawewi*, meaning meeting place or assembly. Some say the place is so named because it once was the site of an Indian encampment; others say it is "where streams, paths, or boundaries meet or come together." [1] This is where the Ramapo River emerges from the Ramapo Pass (at the present boundary between New Jersey and New York), is joined by the Mahwah River, and continues along the southeast side of the Ramapo Mountains. In the early eighteenth century the northern part of the Ramapo Valley was known as Ramapough (Ramapo). Where the valley narrows between the Ramapo Mountains and Campgaw Mountain was known as Yawpo or Yawpough.* The southern section of the valley widens at what was called The Ponds (present-day Oakland, New Jersey). [2]

The Ramapo Mountain People were not the first settlers in this region. When they migrated from the Hackensack River Valley to the Ramapo Mountains, they found German and Dutch farmers already settled in the valley below. The first European settler in the region had been a Dutchman named Lucas Kierstead. He built a trading post on the banks of the Ramapo River about one mile south of the present state boundary on land bought from the Indians in August 1700 by his sister Mrs. Blandina Kierstead Bayard. [3] In 1709, L. Kiestad (Lucas Kierstead), a New York City customs official named Peter Fauconier, and several associates—John Aboineau, John Barberie, Thomas Fresneau,

---

* This section was also called Tinker's Val, which may have been derived from the Dutch *Tenger Val* or "narrow valley."

Peter Bard, and E. Boudinot—bought 42,500 acres of land between the Saddle River and the Ramapo Mountains from an Indian sachem named Memereseum. Known as the Ramapock (Ramapo) Tract, this purchase included the northern part of the Ramapo Valley and part of the Saddle River Valley to the southeast. With the exception of the Dutchman Kierstead, this syndicate was made up of French Huguenots. As with the earlier Tappan Patent, the land was not directly purchased from the Indians. It was deeded to the East New Jersey Proprietors and then re-granted by their agent Peter Sonmans to the syndicate.[4] Kierstead had already settled on part of the land, but the others in the syndicate were land speculators who had no intention of settling there; they resold and leased parcels to others.*

German settlers were slow moving into the Ramapo Valley. Seventy-five-year-old Daniel Henion, in a deposition for the commission settling the New York-New Jersey boundary dispute in 1769, stated that he remembered Ramapough in 1710 when Lucas Kierstead was the only settler but that by 1719 Coenraads and Dederick Wanamaker were living at a place called The Island † about a mile northeast from Kierstead.[5] The Wanamaker family originated in the Palatinate region of Germany, but there were Wanamakers in Hoboken, New Jersey, as early as 1660. Coenraads and Dederick were probably related to John Wanamaker, who purchased a large tract of land at Ramapough from Fauconier and his associates.[6] Charles Clinton's 1739 survey of this region mentions "a house that belongs to Peter Vandemaka, a German." Clinton also noted that "the greater part of the tillable land in this Lot [number LXXV] is clear'd by the High Germans settled along the river as far as Ramapo by Mr. Falconer [Fauconier]."[7] The Lutheran German settlers in the valley built a log chapel at The Island

---

* In 1740 the Board of Proprietors of East Jersey contested the validity of the 1709 Ramapo land patent on the grounds that Sonmans did not have the authority to grant it. A lawsuit was initiated in the New Jersey Supreme Court. In 1742 the Proprietors reached an agreement with Mrs. Magdelene Fauconier Valleau, the daughter of Peter Fauconier, to buy her interest in the tract, but it was not until March 1753 that she released her claim. Some of the tenants refused to recognize the Board of Proprietors as their new landlords until years later. (William Roome, *The Early Days and Early Surveys of East New Jersey* [Butler, N.J.: Pequannock Valley Argus Steam Print, 1897], pp. 34–39.)

† The Island was a small ridge in the northern part of the Ramapo Valley along which present-day Island Road runs.

about 1720. It is mentioned by Clinton as "a little meeting house belonging to ye High Germans." [8]

Dutch settlers also moved into the Ramapo Valley during the colonial period. Sharing the log chapel with the German Lutherans, these Dutchmen in 1748 hired Domine Van Der Linde from the churches at Paramus and The Ponds to visit their church once a month. In 1795 they built The Island Dutch Reformed Church, later known as the Ramapo Reformed Church. The Lutherans, having trouble obtaining a minister, divided into two groups, some joining the Lutheran Church in Ramsey, New Jersey, and others going to the Lutheran Church in Airmont, New York. [9]

By the time of the Revolutionary War, three major roads converged at Ramapough near the entrance to the Ramapo Pass. The old King's Highway, later known as the Albany Post Road and the Orange Turnpike, ran south through the Ramapo Pass and turned northeast toward Kakiat, New York. Another road known as the Ramapo Valley Road or simply Valley Road (present Route 202) ran southwest down the Ramapo Valley toward The Ponds and Pompton, New Jersey. A third road ran southeast to Hopperstown and Paramus, New Jersey. According to maps made during the Revolution, the Wanamaker family owned land on the east side of the road to Paramus. [10] Along Valley Road were Joseph Baldwin, John Vanalen, Andrew Hopper, Samuel Bartholomew, Garret Garrison, Nicholas Romaine, Cornelius Bogart, Henry Vanalen, a gristmill, Bogart (first name omitted), and The Ponds Church. [11] John Suffern had settled at the entrance to the Ramapo Pass at a place he named New Antrim.

Ramapough was a strategic location during the Revolutionary War. The Ramapo Pass was the main access by land through the Ramapo Mountains to upstate New York. Washington stationed troops in the entrance to the pass, and he allegedly slept at both the Hopper and the Suffern houses. Along the top of the Ramapo Mountains, parallel to Valley Road, ran the Cannon Ball Road, which according to local legend was used to transport armaments secretly by the Continental Army. The Ramapo Mountains were the haunt of the outlaw Claudius Smith, who robbed from Tory and Whig alike during the war until he was hanged in Goshen, New York.

This was the scene into which the Ramapo Mountain People moved

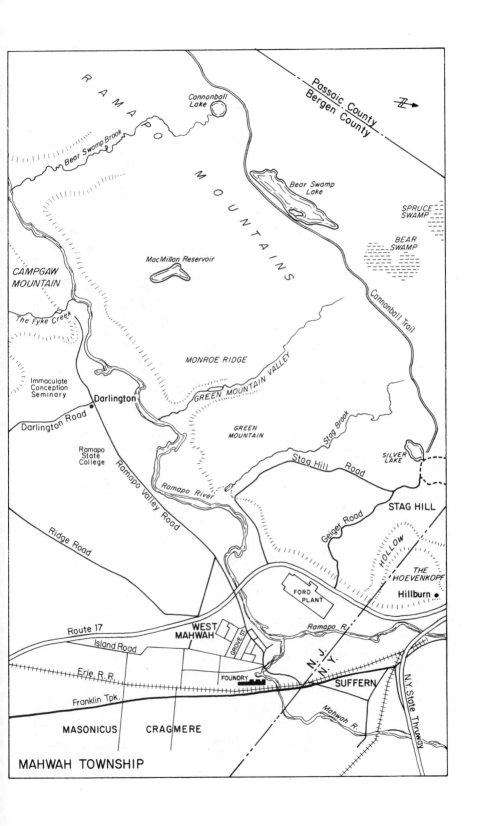

RAMAPO MOUNTAINS

Passaic County
Bergen County

Cannonball
Lake

Bear Swamp Brook

Bear Swamp
Lake

SPRUCE
SWAMP

BEAR
SWAMP

CAMPGAW
MOUNTAIN

MacMillan Reservoir

Cannonball Trail

The Fyke Creek

MONROE RIDGE

GREEN MOUNTAIN VALLEY

Immaculate
Conception
Seminary

Darlington

GREEN
MOUNTAIN

Stag Brook

Darlington Road

SILVER
LAKE

Ramapo
State
College

Ramapo River

Stag Hill   Road

STAG HILL

Ramapo Valley Road

Ridge Road

Geiger Road

HOLLOW

THE
HOEVENKOPF

FORD
PLANT

Hillburn

Route 17

WEST
MAHWAH

Ramapo R.

Island Road

GROVE ST.

N. J.
N. Y.

N.Y. State Thruway

Erie R.R.

FOUNDRY

SUFFERN

Franklin Tpk.

Mahwah R.

MASONICUS   CRAGMERE

MAHWAH TOWNSHIP

Grove Street with Stag Hill in background

Neighborhood of Grove Street and Island Road

Fire station and former school on Stag Hill

Houses on Stag Hill

Settlement near Silver Lake on Stag Hill

shortly after 1800. They purchased land in the mountains from the Dutch and German farmers in the Ramapo Valley. In 1805 James De Groot bought fifteen acres of mountain land from Richard Wanmaker (Wanamaker).¹² He bought an additional ten acres in 1825 from Garret W. Hopper.¹³ By 1830 there were nine families of Mountain People in this part of the Ramapos. The family heads were Richard Degroot, Joseph Degroot, William Degroot, Ellen Degroot, James Degroot, Elias Mann, Peter Mann, Juliana Mann, and Peter De Friese.¹⁴ According to descriptions in the land deeds, they lived next to each other. This was the nucleus that became the Green Mountain Valley settlement (later renamed Havemeyer Hollow). On Monroe Ridge, overlooking the hollow, was Richard De Groat's farm known as Halifax. Later another settlement of Mountain People was located along The Fyke Creek at Campgaw Mountain southeast across the Ramapo Valley. Neither of these settlements exists today.

Some of the Mountain People evidently attended the Ramapo Dutch Reformed Church in the valley, although there is some evidence that the white Dutchmen hardly considered the colored Mountain People their equals. If one goes into the cemetery to the rear of the church today, he will find the remains of a stone wall that marked the boundary of the graveyard. In the overgrown section beyond this stone wall are the graves of the Mountain People and the former slaves of the Suffern family. In 1857 a Methodist chapel was built by the Mountain People across the Ramapo River at the foot of the Ramapo Mountains near Green Mountain Valley. In 1876 the Methodist chapel was moved farther back into the mountains to the settlement at Green Mountain Valley.

The coming of the railroad brought about a change in the region from subsistence agriculture to large farms owned by wealthy individuals and finally to industrial and suburban development. In 1841 the New York and Erie Railroad completed a line between Piermont, New York, on the Hudson River and Suffern, New York, at the entrance to the Ramapo Pass. This encouraged the Ramapo and Paterson Railroad to build in 1848 a line between Jersey City and Suffern to connect with the Erie. This second railroad line ran through present-day Mahwah. The effect of the railroad on the development of the region is seen in the fact that in 1849 the northern part of Franklin Township was formed into a separate township named Hohokus Township.* In 1860 a railroad station was built, and Andrew J. Winter established a general store nearby.[15] This was the beginning of what was to become the business district of Mahwah.

By the 1870s the large, prosperous-looking farms along Ramapo Valley Road could have been described as country estates. Theodore A. Havemeyer bought the farms of the Hagerman and Bookee families, descendants through marriage of Andrew Hopper. Havemeyer named his estate the Mountain Side Farm. It consisted of 3,200 acres extending into the Ramapo Mountains as far as Bear Swamp. On this farm he raised cattle, chickens, horses, and pigs. Behind the farm was located the Green Mountain Valley settlement of the Mountain People, some of whom found employment on the Mountain Side Farm. After the death of Mrs. Havemeyer in 1914, the farm was sold to Stephen Birch, president of Kennecott Copper, who renamed it the Birch Farm and raised Black Angus cattle.[16] Today part of the former Mountain Side Farm is the campus of Ramapo State College.

Also in the 1870s, A. B. Darling, one of the owners of the Fifth Avenue Hotel in New York City, bought a farm in the Ramapo Valley south of the Mountain Side Farm. There he built stables and a half-mile track and raised trotting horses. Some of the Mountain People also worked for him. The neighborhood of his farm was later named Darlington in his honor. After Darling's death in 1896, the land changed hands several times until it was bought by the Roman Catholic Diocese of Newark as the site for the Immaculate Conception Seminary.[17]

Another large estate was built by Colonel Ezra Miller, son of the inventor of the Miller Railway Safety Coupling, on the west side of the ridge separating the Ramapo Valley from the Saddle River Valley. His mansion, known as Owena, faced west on Owena Lake but was destroyed by fire in 1899. In 1910 George M. Dunlap, owner of silk mills in Spring Valley and Paterson, purchased Owena and built a housing development of single-family, stone dwellings which represent the coming of the suburbs to Mahwah. The development had its own private water system, which was later taken over by the township.[18]

* The name was changed to Mahwah Township in 1944.

In 1902 the Ramapo Wheel and Foundry Company was reorganized into the American Brakeshoe Company, and its foundry in Hillburn was moved to Mahwah. This new industry brought into Mahwah an influx of Polish Catholics to work in the new foundry. In 1915 a Catholic church was organized by the Salesian Fathers. At first, services and a parochial school were conducted in a clubhouse owned by the American Brakeshoe Company. In 1916 the Immaculate Heart of Mary Church was completed on Island Road.[19]

Meanwhile the settlements of the Mountain People were shifting from Green Mountain Valley to Stag Hill and the hollow behind the Hoevenkopf Mountain, nearer the Ramapo Pass. In 1902 Mr. and Mrs. Francis Wheaton, missionaries from Park Ridge, New Jersey, moved to the hollow behind the Hoevenkopf. The Wheatons lived in a crude, three-room cabin, the front room of which was used as a school with Mrs. Wheaton as the teacher—the first school attended by the Mountain children. About the same time Miss Nora Snow, the daughter of one of the managers of the foundry in Hillburn, supplied the funds to build a one-room schoolhouse and a log chapel and to hire Margaret Mack as a school teacher and visiting nurse for the Mountain People on Stag Hill. Miss Snow brought to the attention of the New Jersey educational authorities the conditions on Stag Hill, and as a result the Hohokus Township board of education in 1909 bought land on the mountain and took over the school there.[20] The mountain school was named Lincoln School No. 5.

In the 1920s a number of the Mountain People moved from the mountains to the valley section of Mahwah. Many of them came from Green Mountain Valley back in the mountains, and they resettled near the American Brakeshoe foundry on Sherwood Heights along Grove Street between Island Road and Valley Road. The deeds on file in the Bergen County courthouse indicate that the Moutain People bought the land from the Sherwood family for one dollar per lot. Among the purchasers were Arthur Van Dunk, who bought land in 1923, Asa and Ruth De Groat in 1924, Mildred and Arthur De Groat in 1925, Frederick B. and Rosetta De Groat in 1927, and Sidney De Groat in 1929.[21]

The decade of the Great Depression brought about a slowdown in the migration to Grove Street. During the thirties, only one mountain person, Anna L. Van Dunk, bought a lot there (in 1932).[22] But during World War II the Mountain People again began to purchase lots on Grove Street: Frederick and Florence De Freese buying in 1943, Molly George in 1943, Mildred Castelonia De Groat in 1943, Hartford and Florence De Freese in 1944, and William and Mary Mann in 1945.[23] By the 1950s a second church was founded by the Mountain People on Grove Street—the Pentecostal Full Gospel Church. By this time the earlier settlements at Green Mountain Valley and The Fyke were abandoned. This left the two present settlements of Mountain People in Mahwah: one on Stag Hill and in the hollow behind the Hoevenkopf Mountain and the other on Grove Street in the valley.

During this period Mahwah continued to undergo suburban and industrial growth. In 1932 State Highway Route 17, running through Mahwah into the Ramapo Pass to upstate New York, was completed. A small airfield was built in Mahwah in 1934. In 1955 the Ford Motor Company completed an automobile assembly plant in Mahwah just across Route 17 from the Hoevenkopf Mountain which is now the largest industry in the township; but few if any of the Mountain People work there. Most of the Ford workers commute to Mahwah from the Newark area. This led to a dispute initiated by the United Auto Workers in the 1970s against Mahwah's restrictive zoning law, which excluded multiple-unit dwellings. The Mountain People did not become involved in this zoning dispute. Recently the national headquarters of Western Union located in Mahwah.

Modern Mahwah has several sections. Cragmere, located on the west slope of the ridge separating Ramapo Valley from Saddle River Valley, is an upper-middle-class residential neighborhood. The roads there follow the contour of the ridge and are lined with trees and the stone houses of Mahwah's first housing development. Masonicus, located farther south along the same ridge, contains some undeveloped woodland, some farmland, and a new housing development.

Below in the valley between this ridge and the smaller ridge known as The Island is Mahwah's old business district. A railroad station, several stores and businesses, a bank, the library, the fire and police station, and the municipal building are arranged around a small rectangular park. There is a picturesque little pond on the side of the railroad trestle opposite the business district. North of the business district along the railroad tracks is the old American Brakeshoe foundry, now owned by Abex Corporation.

The neighborhood between the foundry and the Ford plant is known as West Mahwah, which includes the west side of The Island ridge, Grove Street, and a section of Valley Road. This section is both combined industrial and working-class residential. The western border of West Mahwah is Route 17, along which there is a new shopping center that competes with the old business district.

As you continue down the Ramapo Valley on the other side of Route 17 along the Ramapo River and the eastern side of the Ramapo Mountains, you pass one farm and then the new campus of Ramapo State College, opened in 1971. To the southeast is the Fardale section of the township, formerly an area of lakes, woods, and scattered farms, but now being transformed by housing developments.

To the south is Campgaw Mountain, the location of the Immaculate Conception Seminary and a county park, including what was once the settlement of Mountain People along The Fyke Creek.

The Ramapo Mountains northwest of the Ramapo Valley contain several summer camps and middle-class summer homes around Bear Swamp Lake and the settlement of Mountain People around Silver Lake on Stag Hill and in the hollow behind the Hoevenkopf Mountain.

Although the Mountain People in Mahwah have a long history as property owners, they have been largely apolitical, with one exception —a dispute that arose in the 1950s over the need for a new road up to Stag Hill so that buses could safely take the mountain children to and from school in the Ramapo Valley. In 1945 the grammar school on Stag Hill, Lincoln School No. 5, operated by the township's board of education since 1909, was closed, and the mountain children began attending school in the valley. There were several unimproved roads up to Stag Hill on the Mahwah side of the mountain. But because these roads were unsafe and at times impassable, the children were transported on a connecting road down the New York side of the mountain, through Hillburn, and then back into New Jersey. This arrangement worked for nine years, but then the village of Hillburn took action that precipitated a dispute involving the Mountain People, the Hillburn and Mahwah authorities, the Bergen County superintendent of schools, the Bergen County prosecutor, a grand jury investigation, and several court injunctions.

In September 1956 the Hillburn village board threatened to impose a five-ton weight limit and to barricade the road to Stag Hill through Hillburn unless the Township of Mahwah provided a liability bond to cover any accidents that might involve the mountain children being bused through the village. Since the Hillburn road was the only improved access to Stag Hill, the effect of Hillburn's action would be, not only to prevent the public transportation of the mountain children to school, but also to cut off fuel deliveries to Stag Hill.

In 1910 and 1940 the Mountain People had petitioned the township authorities to take over a possible alternate route to Stag Hill that was on the New Jersey side of the mountain. This alternate route was Old Stag Hill Road, which dated back to the time of the Revolutionary War. But no action was taken on these petitions, nor on repeated appeals in 1955, when Old Stag Hill Road was blocked off as a result of Hurricane Hazel. Now threatened with being completely cut off, the Stag Hill residents organized the Stag Hill Civic League. The organization included both Ramapo Mountain People and a few white outsiders who had recently moved to Stag Hill. They retained the Newark law firm of Rothbard, Harris, and Oxfeld.

The Stag Hill Civic League took the position that the Township of Mahwah should reopen Old Stag Hill Road. But township engineer Frank E. Harley estimated that it would cost $300,000 to rebuild the road. And township clerk Raymond F. Dator noted that Old Stag Hill Road ran through private property which would either have to be given as a gift to the township or condemned.[24] Consequently, the township officials decided to improve instead another road on the Jersey side of Stag Hill—Geiger Road, which was steeper than Old Stag Hill Road. Mayor Charles N. Feldman stated the reasons for this decision: Geiger Road would cost only a few thousand dollars to improve and would take only four or five days to complete. The leaders of the Stag Hill Civic League vigorously objected, maintaining that Geiger Road would be too dangerous.

In November 1956 the five-ton weight limit on the Hillburn road went into effect, preventing school buses from using the road. Bergen County Superintendent of Schools Archie Hay decreed that an alternate means of transportation must be supplied by the Mahwah authorities. This forced the Mahwah board of education to transport the mountain children to school down the Hillburn road in taxis at a cost of sixty-six dollars per day. In December the Hillburn village board passed an ordinance closing the Hillburn road, but it granted a limited delay on the enforcement of this ordinance until Geiger Road in Mahwah was completed. Work was begun on Geiger Road in late December, but it was discontinued because of cold weather and snow. Mahwah authorities posted a special liability policy covering the Hillburn road, and the Hillburn authorities repeatedly extended the delay on enforcement of the closing of the road.

By the spring of 1957, Geiger Road was still not completed. In May, Otto Mann, one of the Mountain People and vice-president of the Stag Hill Civic League, warned that even if it were completed, Geiger Road would be "an absolute menace" and "unsuitable for anything but mountain climbers and goats." [25] A Bergen County grand jury threatened to investigate the handling of the affair by the Mahwah authorities, but it delayed taking action on the promise that a road would be provided.

In June, Superintendent Hay inspected the still uncompleted Geiger Road and found it too hazardous for school bus travel.[26] But in July Hay stated that he would approve Geiger Road for school buses if the final road matched the plans shown him by township engineer Harley.[27] Members of the Stag Hill Civic League doubted whether Geiger Road would be finished by the new deadline of September 1, 1957, or whether County School Superintendent Hay would approve it when it was finished. Roy S. Austin, the Mahwah Township superintendent of schools, stated that if Geiger Road was not approved, the mountain children could walk down the road to meet the bus on Route 17. This suggestion was unacceptable to Otto Mann, who responded that Geiger Road was very long and very steep.

"If a car can't get down it without its brakes burning out," he said, "how can you expect children to walk down it—especially in slippery weather?" [28]

One resident of Mahwah, critical of Mayor Feldman's support for the cheaper but unsafe road, said, "In years to come Geiger Road will be known as Feldman's Folly." [29]

Finally, the Hillburn village board decided to enforce their ordinance closing the Hillburn road as of August 1. When informed of this decision, Bergen County Prosecutor Guy Calissi announced that a grand jury would investigate why no alternate road was available to the Stag Hill residents. The Mahwah Township committee initiated proceedings to obtain an injunction against Hillburn to prevent the closing of the Hillburn road.[30]

On August 1, 1957, the Hillburn road was closed as planned. When somebody knocked down the barricade, the village appointed a special policeman to guard it. Otto Mann announced that, on the advice of their attorney, the Mountain People would use the unimproved Stag Hill Road, despite the legal problem that it allegedly transversed private property.[31] Arthur L. Sachs, who claimed a part of Stag Hill Road was on his property, placed his car across the road to prevent its use. Members of the Stag Hill Civic League allegedly pushed the auto to the side. Then Sachs placed a chain across the road, but the chain was cut. Sachs threatened to take legal action to protect his right-of-way.[32]

On August 9 Justice Richard H. Levet of the New York district court issued a temporary restraining order preventing Hillburn from keeping the Hillburn road closed.[33] In August the Bergen County grand jury began its investigation of possible malfeasance or misfeasance on the part of Mahwah officials, but it did not find sufficient evidence for indictments. In September Mr. and Mrs. Arthur Sachs obtained an injunction from a superior court judge preventing Stag Hill residents from using Old Stag Hill Road until the question of title was settled.[34]

Geiger Road was not completed as scheduled on September 1, and a new date for completion was set—November 7. When school opened for the fall term, the Stag Hill children were taxied to school as in the previous year. In October, Federal Judge Sylvester J. Ryan ruled that Hillburn could close its portion of the road up to Stag Hill, but Mayor Harold Williams of Hillburn stated that the road wouldn't be barricaded again before November 7.[35]

Finally, on October 21, 1957, County School Superintendent Archie Hay gave his opinion on the safety of the nearly completed Geiger Road. In a letter to the Mahwah board of education, he ruled that school buses could not use the new road but he would allow either taxis or station wagons to use it providing guard rails were placed at hazardous locations. He concluded,

I am well aware that your municipal officials may object to my refusal to allow school buses to use Geiger Road. I am further aware that other individuals and groups may object to my permitting small vehicles to use the road for personal or political reasons. I can understand the viewpoints of the aforementioned groups or individuals, but I have no concern for them. I am only concerned that the children affected get to and from school safely and I believe this can best be done by using smaller vehicles to traverse Geiger Road.[36]

Otto Mann of the Stag Hill Civic League declared that he would not permit his children to use Geiger Road under any circumstance. "If it's too dangerous for buses," he said, "it's too dangerous for any type of vehicle." [37]

At its October meeting, the Mahwah Township committee defended itself against criticism resulting from the grand jury investigation. In a prepared statement addressed to their constituents, the committeemen stated,

You have been told that the Township has been under investigation by the Grand Jury. That is true. The Prosecutor of Bergen County had a complaint that the mountain folks were being discriminated against. The complaint was referred to the Grand Jury. The Grand Jury heard witnesses of both sides on an impartial presentation. The result! The Grand Jury came to the end of its term, was discharged, and found no cause for action.[38]

What happened next at the meeting was best described in a local newspaper account.

[Otto] Mann jumped to his feet and said, "The statement is a good political coverup and that's all." Mann said discrimination was shown and that Geiger Road was not the shortest route between two points, as was said in the beginning of the [press] release.

[Howard] Pitts [a local resident] said the statement is an innuendo that the Grand Jury has cleared the Committee. However, Pitts said [County Prosecutor] Calissi told him that the case would be presented to the new Grand Jury.

"It's a coverup of facts and it's in there to fool people, but they won't be fooled long," Pitts said.

"They have been fooled for along time," the Mayor replied. Members of the League applauded.

Mayor Acherson then hastened to say he meant they were fooled by misconstrued newspaper accounts of the Geiger Road controversy.[39]

On November 1, Superior Court Judge John Grimshaw, ruling on an application by the Stag Hill Civic League, rescinded the temporary restraining order preventing the use of Old Stag Hill Road granted the previous September. Justice Grimshaw stated that Stag Hill Road should remain open while Arthur Sachs's claim to private ownership of part of the road was being settled.[40] In late November, a federal judge finally ruled that Old Stag Hill Road was not privately owned.[41]

Meanwhile, Geiger Road again was not ready as scheduled. The completion date was moved from November 7 to November 25, and the Hillburn authorities agreed that they would not close the Hillburn road until then. The Mountain People on Stag Hill were prepared to boycott the schools rather than allow their children to be transported over unsafe Geiger Road.

As the day of reckoning drew near, a Mahwah resident named H. E. Serner charged that the Hillburn officials had given Raymond Dator, Mahwah township clerk, for his personal use a key to open the chain that was to blockade the Hillburn road. Dator responded to these charges by saying that the key was presented to him because he paid taxes to Hillburn and that the Hillburn road was the only access to his home. Serner retorted that giving the key to one resident and not to the Mountain People was discriminatory.[42]

On the morning of November 25, the Stag Hill children were taken to school as usual in taxis down the Hillburn road, because the chain was not to be put up until 10 A.M. When they returned from school in the afternoon, they walked up the Hillburn road rather than being shuttled up Geiger Road. The Hillburn officials warned that the children were allowed to walk up the Hillburn road this time but next time they would be stopped because all forms of transportation on the road had been banned.[43]

The next day the school boycott began, with forty-three of the forty-five Stag Hill school children remaining home. Emil J. Oxfeld, attorney for the Stag Hill Civic League, charged that the township had

constructed Geiger Road as part of a deliberate conspiracy to evict the
Mountain People in order to make way for a vacation resort on Stag
Hill.[44]

An editorial in the *Ramsey Journal* expressed a sympathetic opinion
of the cause of the Mountain People.

> With the closing of the Hillburn section of Stag Hill Road Monday,
> the triangular dispute between the Stag Hill residents, the Mahwah Town-
> ship authorities and the educational authorities of the township and county
> entered a new phase, as the parties of the first part respectfully, but firmly
> declined to use the school transportation offered by way of Geiger Road.
> This defiance of constituted authority could be considered regrettable,
> and dealt with harshly, as it probably would in a totalitarian country. One
> can picture the skirmish line of truant officers, armed to the teeth and
> backed up by contingents of state police, national guardsmen and maybe a
> few regulars drawn hastily from the Nike base—just to provide a Little
> Rock flavor to the battle—climbing Mount Houvenkop to demand the white
> flag of school attendance from the entrenched inhabitants.
> On the other hand, one can consider that the Stag Hill residents, in
> refusing to make the best of the bad bargain thrust upon them by Town-
> ship Engineer Frank Harley at the behest of the Township Committee, are
> more concerned with the safety of their children than anyone else could
> be. Despite the fact that Geiger Rd., after being rebuilt, was approved by
> the county school superintendent for taxis and station wagons, the ultimate
> decision as to entrusting a child's life to its curves and grades must be the
> parents'—until the American system yields to one making the family sub-
> servient to the state.
> Whether the parents are right or wrong in their belief that Geiger Rd.
> is too treacherous for them to allow their children on it can be argued ad
> infinitum, but as long as they believe it they are right in refusing to permit
> its use. The Township Committee, Mr. Harley, the school board and
> County Superintendent Hay may be quite correct in their position, but one
> accident would prove them too terribly wrong to be worth taking the
> chance.[45]

County School Superintendent Archie Hay warned that if the Stag
Hill parents continued to boycott the schools, the authorities might be
forced to take action under the provisions of the compulsory attendance laws.[46] But Mahwah Township Superintendent of Schools Roy S.
Austin announced that the local board of education would take no
disciplinary action until after the completion of an independent engi-

neering survey of Geiger Road and Old Stag Hill Road ordered by Bergen County Prosecutor Guy Calissi.[47]

The independent survey by the engineering firm of Savage and Nunno was completed the first week of December. It estimated that Old Stag Hill Road could have been made into a one-way, 10-foot-wide, paved road for only $25,000.[48] The Township of Mahwah had already spent $60,000 on the construction of Geiger Road.[49] According to the survey, Geiger Road had grades of 20 percent for 100 feet and 18 percent for 1,500 feet of its length, but the grades on Old Stag Hill Road did not exceed 16 percent at any place.[50] The survey was submitted to the grand jury that was reconvened to investigate the handling of the matter by the Mahwah Township committee. Again no indictments were forthcoming. But the Stag Hill parents, convinced that the township officials would now agree to rebuild Old Stag Hill Road, ended their school boycott and allowed their children to be transported over Geiger Road in the meantime.

Township Engineer Frank Harley submitted his resignation in a bitter statement, which read in part:

> Never until this year have I been expected to explain my every move and uphold my reputation to people who neither by education or experience are qualified to judge them. They have constantly twisted the facts in order to use them as an instrument to befuddle the people and cause dangerous unrest.[51]

He maintained to the end that the type of road on which Savage and Nunno based their estimate for rebuilding Old Stag Hill Road was ridiculous. He defended his original estimate that it would cost $300,000 to rebuild Old Stag Hill Road into a 30-foot-wide paved and curbed road plus the legal entanglements over the road's ownership.[52]

Construction on Old Stag Hill Road was not begun until seven years later, after two persons were killed in separate automobile accidents on Geiger Road. In the meantime, the Stag Hill Civic League organized in 1961 its own volunteer fire department because of the difficulty in getting the township's fire equipment up to Stag Hill. The old mountain school was transferred to the League for use as a combination firehouse and recreation center. The new Stag Hill Road, finally completed in December 1964, enabled more outsiders, many of whom

were blacks from nearby urban areas, to move to Stag Hill. One result
was racial antagonisms between these blacks and the colored Mountain
People.

The victory of the Mahwah Mountain People in their battle to
have a safe access road up to Stag Hill resulted in the end of whatever
isolation had previously existed.

5 RINGWOOD

In the upper Wanaque River Valley with mountains on the east and west, Ringwood has limited access from the New York City metropolitan area. One can either drive north on Route 17 through the Ramapo Pass into New York State and then turn south at Sloatsburg down Eagle Valley back into New Jersey, or drive southwest on Route 202 to Pompton Lakes, where the Wanaque River joins the Pompton River, and drive up the Wanaque Valley from its entrance on Route 511. The only short-cut is Skyline Drive, which crosses the Ramapo Mountains midway down range at Oakland.

Driving through the Wanaque Valley, one is impressed by its natural beauty. Just beyond the outer fringe of the suburbs of New York City, the valley's natural state is preserved by Ringwood Manor State Park and the Wanaque Reservoir. From the road one sees little evidence of the once-thriving Ramapo iron industry. The manor house and estate of managers of the mines are now a state park, the tracks of the Montclair Railway Company's spur to the mines are no longer in use, and some foundations of buildings that once occupied the site of the reservoir are not visible except when the water level is low.

Turning on Margaret King Avenue in Ringwood, the road goes up a hill and around a curve, and suddenly one gets a glimpse through the foliage of the brown, shingled company houses of the Mine Area, a stark contrast to the beautiful scenery passed on the way. A pot-holed dirt road becomes visible. It extends back about a half mile to the site of old Peters mine, where there are some burnt-out buildings. The mine hole itself is used as a dump for the borough of Ringwood and the Ford assembly plant in Mahwah. The opening to the mine shaft is now a pit of cardboard refuse. One would not guess that a deep shaft with many levels lies below. Between the mine and the main road is a network of dirt roads with names like Riverside Drive, Pipeline Road, and Horseshoe Bend, along which are located the old company houses now inhabited by the Ramapo Mountain People.

The houses are two stories high and contain two family units, one on either side. They are frame dwellings with cement foundations, brown shingled walls, and multicolored (green, brown, and orange) shingled, pitched roofs. A television antenna is often visible. Sometimes there are porches at the entrances. In winter the windows are covered with cellophane in lieu of storm windows. About fifty feet behind each house is a privy. Wash hung out to dry is seen either in the yard or on the porch. Usually an old car or pick-up truck is parked in the yard, and a dog is tied to a tree nearby.

The iron industry of the Ramapo Mountains dates from colonial days.[1] The Ringwood Company, the first large producer of iron in America, was founded in 1740 by the Ogden family of Newark. Later Nicholas Gouvernour became a partner. In 1742 the first blast furnace was built in Ringwood. A London commercial firm known as the American Company, or sometimes as the London Company, bought the Ringwood ironworks in 1764. "Baron" Peter Hasenclever, a naturalized British citizen of German birth and partner in the firm, came to America to manage the company's interests. He brought Germans, Englishmen, and Scotch-Irish workers for the mines and forges. Hasenclever built ironworks at Charlotteburg and Long Pond in New Jersey and at Cortlandt and Cedar ponds in New York. In building the Long Pond furnace (1766–68), he dammed the Long Pond (Wanaque) River, thereby creating the Long Pond (Greenwood Lake). He established Ringwood Manor, an iron plantation combining the medieval institution of a manor with the modern iron industry. The miners and workers in the forges and furnaces lived on the manor, and the surrounding lands were rented to individual farmers and woodsmen.

In 1767 Hasenclever was relieved of his duties by the London Company under charges of extravagant spending. A Scotsman named Robert Erskine was sent in 1771 to become the new manager of the ironworks. When the Revolutionary War broke out, Erskine sided with the colonists. He was commissioned surveyor-general of the Continental Army, in which capacity he made about two hundred maps of the New York-New Jersey area. General Washington was a visitor at Ringwood Manor. In 1782 the New Jersey legislature expropriated the mines and furnaces at Ringwood from the English-owned London Company, but they lay idle after the war. In 1807, Martin J. Ryerson of Pompton, New Jersey, bought the Ringwood mines, but after his death in 1839, his sons, who inherited the ironworks, went into bankruptcy.

In 1853 the Ringwood iron mines and furnaces were purchased by Peter Cooper, the New York industrialist who founded Cooper Union in New York City. Cooper's Trenton Iron Company was managed by Abram S. Hewitt, later a reform mayor of New York City. Near the Ringwood mines they erected a company town consisting of a general store, a tavern, a church, and multifamily, clapboard dwellings for the employees. It was this reactivation of the Ringwood iron industry that drew the Ramapo Mountain People out of the mountains and into the Wanaque River Valley to find employment.

During the Civil War Cooper, Hewitt and Company supplied gun carriages for the Union army's mortars. However, there always had been difficulty shipping the ore out of the Ramapos. In 1875 the Montclair Railway Company built a line from Pompton to Greenwood Lake with a spur to Ringwood, but it was too late. By 1880 iron ore from the Ramapos was being replaced by ores from the Mesabi range in Minnesota. The Peters mine was worked on and off until 1931 and again during World War II and the Korean conflict, but the great days of the Ramapo iron industry were gone forever. The isolation of the Ramapos had taken its toll.

When the iron mines were working in the nineteenth century, several wealthy families owned large estates in Ringwood.[2] Abram S. Hewitt, who was the secretary and business manager for Peter Cooper and who in 1855 married Cooper's daughter Amelia, moved with his bride to Ringwood in 1856. Hewitt built the present Ringwood Manor house near the site of the first manor house built by Peter Hasenclever. It was completed in 1878. As a wedding gift to his daughter Amy, who married Dr. James Green, Hewitt built another mansion on adjoining property. In 1930 this second mansion was sold to the Franciscan

Capuchin Sisters for a convent. In 1936 Ringwood Manor was acquired by New Jersey for use as a state park, except for one parcel of land given to the Cooper Union Schools of Engineering and Science in 1941 for use as the Green Engineering Camp.

Around the turn of the century Francis Lynn Stetson, a wealthy corporation lawyer for J. P. Morgan and the former law partner of President Grover Cleveland, bought 1,075 acres on the slopes of the Ramapo Mountains in Ringwood. He built a large farm, estate, and a mansion he named Skylands Manor. The mansion was rebuilt in 1924 by the Clarence Lewis family, who acquired it after Stetson's death. Conservative Protestant minister Reverend Carl MacIntyre bought the estate in 1953 for his religious school Shelton College. The college remained on this location until 1964, when it was moved to southern New Jersey. In 1966 Skylands Manor was purchased by the State of New Jersey in connection with its Green Acres program.

In addition to these wealthy families, Ringwood's population also included employees in the mines and furnaces and on the farms. Some of these employees were white, others were colored Mountain People. All lived in housing supplied by the Ringwood Company in the mine area. There were also several small farms on the slopes of the Ramapos and in the Wanaque Valley at Stonetown, Monksville, and Boardsville, towns which became part of Ringwood when it was incorporated as a borough in 1918.

With its incorporation, the new Borough of Ringwood signed a water agreement with the North Jersey District Water Supply Commission, consisting of Newark, Paterson, and other north Jersey cities, for building a reservoir by damming the Wanaque River. Construction was begun in 1920. In 1928 the reservoir, 6 miles long and 1½ miles at its widest point, was finished, permanently changing the physical setting of Ringwood. Boardsville disappeared under water. The roads and railroad had to be rerouted and several cemeteries moved.

The mountain lakes in the Ramapos—Cupsaw Lake, Erskine Lakes, and Skyline Lakes—brought about the transformation of the old Ringwood of the iron mines to modern Ringwood. In the late 1920s and early 1930s, the Ringwood Company advertised lakefront lots for vacation cabins. After World War II, Skyline Lakes Corporation, owned by Winston-Holzer Associates, began the development of the

Skyline Lakes region as a summer and year-round community. These development schemes brought about a population boom in Ringwood, the population doubling in each decade after World War II. In 1930, the population was 1,038; in 1940 it was 977; in 1950 it was 1,752; in 1960 it was 4,182; and by 1970 it reached 10,393.[3]

Today Ringwood is divided into three sections. Most of the population resides on the slopes of the Ramapo Mountains near Cupsaw, Erskine, and Skyline lakes. Permanent year-round houses have replaced the original seasonal cabins. Private swim clubs restrict the use of the lakes to members only. This section also contains two small shopping centers, two elementary schools, Skylands Manor, Shepherd Pond State Park at Thunder Mountain, a Catholic church, a Presbyterian church, a Lutheran church, and a Baptist church.

The valley is divided into two sections by the Wanaque Reservoir. West of the reservoir is the Stonetown section, which with a few remaining farms is still rural although it is beginning to be developed as a residential area.

North and east of the reservoir are the Eleanor C. Hewitt Elementary School, the municipal building (a large Victorian house formerly the home of one of the managers of the mines), Mount Saint Francis Convent, the Green Engineering Camp of Cooper Union, Ringwood Manor State Park, the Episcopal Church of the Good Shepherd (attended by the Mountain People), and the Mine Area.

Despite the transformation of Ringwood from colonial iron plantation to nineteenth-century millionaires' estates to twentieth-century lake resort and suburban development, the end of mining in Ringwood left the Mountain People in the Mine Area in a pocket of poverty. After the mines closed in the early 1950s, the Mine Area was purchased by the Ringwood Realty Company, a corporation consisting of Ford Motor Company executives. The land was managed by J. I. Kislak Realty Corporation of Newark and was used as a dump for the Mahwah Ford assembly plant. Rents for the company houses in which the Mountain People live ranged from $25 to $60 per household per month. Kislak collected total rents averaging $14,000 per year on these rundown houses. Efforts to improve the housing conditions in the Mine Area led to a dispute involving a private, federally funded housing

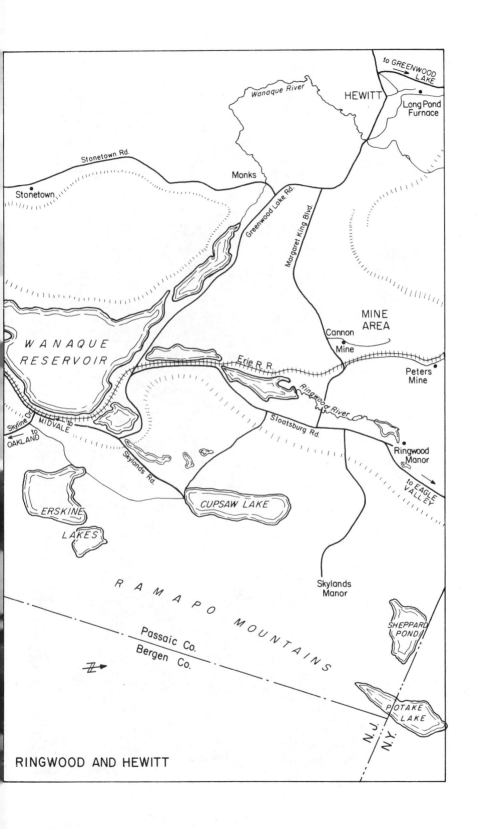

to GREENWOOD LAKE

Wanaque River

HEWITT

Long Pond Furnace

Stonetown Rd.

Monks

Stonetown

Greenwood Lake Rd.

Margaret King Blvd.

MINE AREA

Cannon Mine

Peters Mine

W A N A Q U E RESERVOIR

Erie R.R.

Ringwood River

Skyline Dr.   to MIDVALE

to OAKLAND

Sloatsburg Rd.

Ringwood Manor

to EAGLE VALLEY

Skylands Rd.

CUPSAW LAKE

ERSKINE LAKES

R A M A P O   M O U N T A I N S

Skylands Manor

SHEPPARD POND

Passaic Co.
Bergen Co.

N.J.
N.Y.

P O T A K E LAKE

RINGWOOD AND HEWITT

New houses built by HOW-TO, Inc.

Company houses in the Mine Area

Anna De Freese

Melvin "Mousy" Morgan

Leroy Van Dunk, Hewitt, N.J.

Eveline Morgan

Folk artist Ed Morgan, Haskell, N.J.

"Uncle" Charlie De Freese

Cannon Mine by Ed Morgan   *Photograph courtesy of Newark Public Library*

Long Pond Furnace by Ed Morgan

The Ringwood Mine Area with the Wanaque Reservoir in the background

corporation, the Ford Motor Company, a local public Solid Waste Disposal Authority, and the borough of Ringwood.

In 1965 the President Lyndon Johnson Administration's War on Poverty came to the Ringwood Mine Area in the form of the Community Action Council of Passaic County (CACPC). One of their first programs was Operation Headstart, a preschool nursery project. Other programs initiated by CACPC were a Neighborhood Youth Corps and Legal Aid.

In the winter of 1966–67 the Community Action Council made a survey of the Mine Area to determine the degree of poverty there. There were 92 families, 417 individuals. The average family income was $2,609 per year. The unemployment rate was 52 percent. Out of a labor force of 139, only 55 had full-time jobs, 11 had part-time jobs, and 73 were without work. Thirty families were on either municipal or county welfare, 9 were on social security, and 16 were on unemployment compensation.[4]

In 1966 plans were made for a self-help housing project to be financed by Farmers' Home Administration mortgages. But the inability to acquire suitable land led to the tabling of this proposal. In 1969 Ken Ryan, the new executive director of the CACPC, revived the idea of self-help housing through a separate housing corporation. HOW-TO, Inc. (Housing Operation With Training Opportunity, Incorporated), a private federally funded, nonprofit housing development corporation under the auspices of the Community Action Coun-

TABLE 7   YEARLY INCOME OF RINGWOOD MINE AREA FAMILIES, 1966–1967

Income	Number of Families
Less than $1,000	13
$1,000–$2,000	11
$2,000–$3,000	18
$3,000–$4,000	22
$4,000–$5,000	10
More than $5,000	8
Unknown	10
Total	92

Source: Community Action Council of Passaic County survey, 1966–67.

49490

cil of Passaic County, was incorporated in May 1970. Initially funded with a $105,000 grant from the Office of Economic Opportunity, the grant was renewed in March 1972 with $60,000 from OEO supplemented by $63,700 from the New Jersey Department of Community Affairs.

The purpose of the corporation is to initiate self-help housing for the people living in the Ringwood Mine Area. The male participants are trained in construction skills, including carpentry, electrical work, masonry, and plumbing, and then provided with tools and materials to build their own houses. The women are trained in sewing and reupholstering furniture. While the Mountain People themselves provide the labor, the cost of the materials for the houses and the land is paid by 100 percent Farmers' Home Administration no-down-payment mortgages with interest credit for low-income rural residents, decreasing the interest from 7½ percent to 1 percent according to need and family size

HOW-TO, Inc., is run by a board of directors, a majority of whom are residents in the Mine Area. The chairman of the board, William ("Pooch") Van Dunk, is one of the Mountain People. A full-time paid director and his staff administer the program. Andrew Marshall, a former Peace Corps volunteer in Guinea, West Africa, was hired as the director in December 1970. The headquarters of HOW-TO, Inc., is a former bowling alley in Hewitt, New Jersey.

HOW-TO began an evening meal program for the Mine Area people three times a week in the spring of 1971 with a grant from the New Jersey State Department of Education. This program was continued by two local churches and the Community Action Council until a new grant from OEO in February 1972 included the meal program. An adult education program for remedial reading and mathematics established in January 1972 was funded by the New Jersey Department of Education and run by the West Milford board of education. Also a Consumer Education Program sponsored by the New Jersey Division of Vocational Education was started in the HOW-TO headquarters. In March 1972 a Manpower Development Training Program was opened to unemployed or underemployed individuals to provide training in building maintenance. And the Fairleigh Dickinson Dental School, Division of Community Dentistry, started in the summer of 1972 a free dental clinic for children in the Mine Area.

In September 1970 Ringwood's Mayor John Kulik (Democrat) proposed a plan for the borough to build a solid-waste disposal plant in the Mine Area. The plan was to purchase the Mine Area, sell part of the land to the residents in the Mine Area, purchase a solid-waste disposal plant, and open the rest of the land for industrial use. On October 9, 1970, the Democratic majority on the borough council established the Ringwood Solid Waste Management Authority (SWMA) over the objection of the two Republican councilmen. Republican councilman Dale Peters opposed the creation of the Authority on the ground that the main beneficiary of the solid-waste plant would be the Ford Motor Company, not the borough of Ringwood, since Ford dumps more waste in the Mine Area than does the borough.

In late October 1970 the Ford Motor Company undermined the opposition to the Authority by making a free gift of 290 acres of land to the Authority. Ford executive T. R. Reid, in a letter to Andy Marshall dated March 29, 1971, stated that part of the reason for conveying the property to the Authority was the Authority's concern to secure land for a housing project, and that it was Ford's understanding that part of the land donated would be used for that purpose.[5] Reflecting on this one year later, Councilman Dale Peters was quoted as saying,

Now let's set the record straight as to how the borough came into ownership of the 290 acres of land in the Mine Area. It was quite simple—the land was simply given to the town because of the most difficult set of social problems existing on this piece for so many years. The Ringwood Realty Company and their representatives, the Kislak Realty Co., felt that Ringwood could and should assume responsibility for solving housing problems for nearly 400 people—a task they felt was outside of their corporate purposes.[6]

Andy Marshall offered the opinion that "Ford, rather than suffer adverse publicity from its slumlord capacity, decided to wash its hands of the entire matter and instead of giving the town the 50 acres they had initially requested for their solid waste disposal project, donated 290 acres to the town." Marshall noted that Ford still retained 180 acres with no housing on it adjacent to the tract given to Ringwood. He concluded that the grant was "very definitely gerrymandered."

Dale Peters ran against Mayor Kulik in November 1970. He won the election but did not take office until after the lame-duck, Democratic-controlled council appointed Kulik and four other Democrats to the Solid Waste Management Authority. One appointee, Henri Dimidjian, was the head of the local Democratic club and Kulik's campaign manager.

Considerable emotion was generated by the solid-waste disposal controversy. One irate Ringwood resident, former Councilman Wendell J. Reed, wrote to the local newspaper,

Who paid for Mr. Kulik's trip to England? Ford Motor Company, who owns the Ringwood land? O'Connor trucking who hauls Ford's trash? Who put Mr. Kulik up to this scheme? Who would benefit most? Obviously, not the people of Ringwood. Ford needs a dumping facility badly. Why not make a deal with Ringwood in the guise of good citizenship, and let the Ringwood taxpayer bear the burden of payment? Sell the land to the Borough for low cost housing—who pays? The Ringwood taxpayer. Don't be misled—Federal funds are tax dollars, too. Who benefits? Not the Ringwood taxpayer, not the citizens of Ringwood who really deserve to be helped, not the hard-working citizen who may be currently struggling to own his own home. His only benefit will be to help a minority group, steeped in the history of the area, but not steeped in ever doing much to help itself.

We all respect the right of minority groups, but the time has come when we must respect the rights of the majority. Many of us have long realized the need to do something for the Mine Area. Many of us have spent long hours working with these residents, actually picking up the trash in their own yards, while these same people stood idly by. The housing proposal is not new. Do we change our zoning for these low cost units and still oppose zoning changes for low cost senior citizen housing? This is housing for the people who really built Ringwood, housing for those who have earned it . . .

Wendell J. Reed
Ringwood [7]

When he took office, Mayor Peters set up a Mine Area Housing Planning Committee made up of representatives from the borough's planning board, zoning board, board of health, council, SWMA, and HOW-TO to coordinate the transfer of part of the Authority's property to HOW-TO for self-help housing. Andy Marshall maintains that the SWMA boycotted all the meetings of the Housing Planning Committee except one. He argues that the committee responded with "evasive rhetoric" to all queries by HOW-TO about transferring the land. Henri Dimidjian, then chairman of the SWMA, responded by accusing HOW-TO director Marshall of being too impatient and "wanting all the problems of the last hundred years solved in the next 24 hours." Dimidjian gave as his reason for not attending the meetings: "There is no need for HOW-TO to take part in planning for the whole 290 acres." [8]

A few days later Dimidjian issued a statement to the local newspaper criticizing HOW-TO and accusing Marshall of being an "outsider" whose "only concern is to keep his job and get another federal grant from taxpayers' money." He added that "the only people who should worry about community affairs were people who live in the community."

I will say now as I have said in the past that the Ringwood Solid Waste Management Authority has pledged its full support in any project designed to help alleviate the Mine Area's problems. This support will continue in the future.

I also have to say that the self-help plan as proposed by Mr. Marshall is not the best means of helping all the people . . . Unfortunately, a program such as this can, by its very nature, only help a small number of the Mine Area residents; the rest of the residents would not qualify financially for the program.

At present, the rents we receive for the homes in the Mine Area are very minimal, averaging $25 per month and we have had difficulty in collecting these rents. Even a mortgage at the lowest percentage available, one percent, would increase the monthly outlay for these residents.

The body that can most help the majority of the Mine Area residents will eventually be the Authority.[9]

Andy Marshall responded to these charges in the same edition of the paper.

Mr. Dimidjian's reaction ignores the crucial issue, that is—when does the Authority intend to keep its promises to make home sites available to residents of the Mine Area? In lieu of a direct answer the self-help participants in HOW-TO are told that they must wait indefinitely while the 15 month grant period that would pay for construction skills training lapses—taking with it all aspirations to become taxpaying property owners in Ringwood.

The Authority's inaction is rationalized with claims that since ALL of the Mine Area residents aren't eligible for self-help housing mortgages, therefore NONE should be allowed to become home owners and share the municipal tax burden. . . .

Pledges of support are significant only when they are endorsed by actions. Homes are not built upon foundations of rhetoric. HOW-TO Corporation offers an immediately available solution to alleviate the Mine Area housing crisis . . .

The participants in the self-help HOW-TO program do not want to plan the industrial development of the Authority's 290 acre gift. The people are merely requesting that a small home site be decided upon before their construction skills training grant expires. These descendants of North Jersey's original pioneers are understandably miffed to learn that industry has priority over human needs.[10]

HOW-TO attempted to mobilize community support by sponsoring, along with the local Community Church of Ringwood and civic groups, an "Awareness Day" to publicize their plight. The Sunday preceding Awareness Day, Reverend Alva G. Decker, pastor of the Vicar Church of the Incarnation in West Milford and the Church of the Good Shepherd in Ringwood, delivered a sermon addressed to the SWMA, the mayor and council, and concerned members of the church.

I call upon Mr. Dimidjian and the other members of the Ringwood Solid Waste Management Authority. I call upon the members of the Ringwood Borough Council. I call upon these persons who can make possible the fulfillment of the dream of the Mine Area people for better housing. I call upon you to continue the step taken yesterday and to take the next necessary step Now—make land immediately available not in some dark, dim future after construction of your disposal unit as is mentioned by you, Mr. Dimidjian, but Now. Share your power and authority with these people so they too can begin to taste the reality of the American dream. Never let yourself get into a position where these words of Isaiah can ever be said of you: "Woe to those who decree iniquitous decrees and the writers who keep writing oppression, to turn aside the needy from justice and to rob the poor of my people of their right, that widows may be their spoil, and they make the fatherless their prey." [11]

The next meeting of the SWMA on Thursday, April 1, was attended by about sixty Ringwood residents who wanted to know about the land promised to HOW-TO. After the public session, the

SWMA reconvened in executive session in which the authority agreed that a parcel of ten acres be turned over to HOW-TO. But rather than give HOW-TO an option on the land then, the SWMA insisted that the transfer not take place until HOW-TO plans gained the approval of the county and municipal planning board, the municipal board of zoning adjustment, and the mayor and council.

Wendell J. Reed again wrote to one of the local newspapers.

You are to be commended for your editorial this date. The stand you and the other "Nellie-Do-Gooders" take on How-Too [sic] is excellent. After all; where else can a person learn "how-too" get his hand in the taxpayers pocketbook.

If you would spend half of your effort encouraging these people to achieve something really constructive, we in the Borough of Ringwood would all be the better for it.

I am curious about one thing. In all the years the mine people have been in this community what have they really achieved. I would submit, over a hundred years to accomplish it and they blew it. This is except ride the Welfare roles.

I too would like to buy one of those building lots when they are offered. I do, however, realize I'm not eligible. I work for a living and pay my taxes. That's an automatic disqualification.

In the meantime keep up the editorials. If you write enough of them, perhaps the silent majority—the overburdened taxpayer—will rise up and demand the end to this and many other of the welfare boondoggles.

Wendell J. Reed
Ringwood [12]

HOW-TO then began preparing plans to submit to the local and county boards. They hired an engineer to survey the land for subdivision. This work took several months through the summer of 1971.

Meanwhile, a new complication arose jeopardizing the Farmers' Home Administration mortgages. These mortgages were earmarked for rural areas, defined as towns with a population less than 10,000 persons. But the 1970 federal census listed Ringwood's population as 10,393. Senator Harrison Williams's office set up an appointment for HOW-TO representatives with the assistant administrator of the Farmers' Home Administration in Washington. The matter was referred to FmHA lawyers, and the response was negative. HOW-TO then began lobbying through the regional director of OEO, the office of Senator Clifford Case, the governor's office in Washington, and the Rural Housing Alliance, a lobbying group. HOW-TO was refused the rural housing mortgages three times. On the fourth try, in August 1971, it succeeded in having the state director of the FmHA granted discretionary power to wave the arbitrary 10,000 population cut-off figure for a program that had begun before the population exceeded that number.

By the fall of 1971 the preliminary sketch plat was ready to be submitted to the borough's planning board for subdivision approval. The newly hired, full-time municipal engineer recommended that the town's road standards be changed to allow for different grades of roads, thus making the HOW-TO plan to build on the side of a hill viable. The plan was approved, and the board recommended that the planning board's application fee of $825 be refunded. Then the plan was sent to the mayor and council for approval. An application for a variance for the 8.2 acre residential area within the 290-acre tract zoned for industry was submitted to the board of zoning adjustment. After its approval the plan went to the county planning board. Finally, in the spring of 1972, the plan came back to the mayor and council for final ratification of the preliminary plans. The agenda consisted of two items: the ratification of the application refund, and ratification of the plan. The refund vote was split 2-2. Mayor Peters cast the deciding vote in HOW-TO's favor. The two dissenting votes were Democrats, one of whom, Robert Hadley, was also a commissioner on the SWMA. The vote on the ratification of the preliminary plan was unanimously in favor of it.

Meanwhile, the make-up of the SWMA was slowly changing. The five original commissioners had been appointed for five, four, three, two, and one years. For one vacancy, Mayor Peters appointed a civil engineer named Burton Bassett, who agreed with Peters that Ford would be the main beneficiary of the disposal plant. The other vacancy, which opened in February 1972, was filled by Ken Ryan, former executive director of the Community Action Council of Passaic County and a firm supporter of HOW-TO. But a Democratic majority remained on the Authority.

During this delay, tragedy struck in the Mine Area. On March 25, 1972, three children—twins age six and their two-year-old sister—

perished in a fire in one of the company houses in the Mine Area. Firemen had to dam a nearby stream to get sufficient water to put out the fire. Mayor Peters, who was on the scene, praised the local volunteer firemen and reflected,

Everyone quite naturally asks, "Who is responsible?" Certainly no one person or group can be or should be singled out for blame in a situation that developed over so many years. But certainly, this latest in a long series of tragedies in this area should serve to drive home a point some of us have tried to make for many months—the responsibility for rectifying the housing situation in the Mine Area is Ringwood's. There is no out-of-town realty company to point to. We accepted a responsibility for the population on the land when we accepted the gift of the land in October, 1970. Clearly, the time has come to put aside the petty suburban fears—totally without foundation as they are—and eliminate the unbelievably substandard housing conditions in the Mine Area. The help in the form of federal programs is there—all we have to do is ask for it.[13]

In the spring of 1972, HOW-TO, having completed the lengthy approval procedure for its preliminary plans, approached the SWMA for their land. The Authority's attorney informed them that legally the land could not be simply given away. There were three alternatives: First, they could secure a change in the state statute governing municipal solid waste disposal authorities. Second, the Authority could grant the land to the town, which in turn could grant it to HOW-TO. Third, the land could be declared excess property and put up for public auction. The first alternative might delay the project for years, given the innumerable bills before the state legislature. The second alternative was supported by the mayor and council, who sent a letter to the Authority expressing their willingness to accept the land. The Authority considered this letter unwarranted meddling on the part of the mayor and council, and at their next meeting on May 4, the SWMA declared the land excess property but did not put it up for auction right away. Ken Ryan made two motions to put the land up for auction, but they did not receive seconds. During the following week, concerned citizens telephoned the members of the Authority to pressure them into taking action. Finally, a meeting was called for May 12, at which the land was put up for bid with the restriction that the land had to be used for low-income, single-family residences.

The bidding was scheduled for June 8, 1972. A legal notice appeared in the local newspapers for two consecutive weeks. At the meeting, the Authority's attorney read aloud the HOW-TO bid of $912 for the 8.2 acres. This bid was based on the median family mortgage approved by the FmHA. Then came a surprise. Michael Newman, a Ringwood salesman of automobile tune-up equipment, entered a bid for three dollars higher than the HOW-TO bid. Newman maintained he wanted to build low-cost housing as an investment but had no contractor in mind. HOW-TO's attorney protested, but the Authority's attorney, John Running, offered the opinion that the second bid was valid. The meeting was recessed while the Authority tried to decide what to do. The Authority was split. Ryan and Kulik voted that the bid was improper. Bassett and Hadley voted that the bid was proper. Dimidjian was "out of town." In the absence of a majority vote, all bids were rejected. The meeting was recessed until a future time, when new bids would be received.

At a special meeting of the Authority on June 12, it was decided that a new requirement be added: that the bidder submit a written statement establishing his eligibility to apply for a site development loan from the Farmers' Home Administration. The bidding had to be advertised again for two more consecutive weeks. The meeting was scheduled for June 30, but it was further delayed by the failure of the advertisement to appear during the second consecutive week as required by law. Meanwhile the residents of the Mine Area were without water for two weeks because of a faulty pump and a leak in a water pipe. They had to carry water in bottles from nearby streams and springs until the pump was repaired.[14]

Finally, on August 3, 1972, the Ringwood Solid Waste Management Authority convened. HOW-TO was the only bidder with its bid of $1,100 for the 8.2 acres. After several hours' deliberation, the Authority voted 3 to 2 in favor of the bid—Ryan, Kulik, and Bassett voting in favor, Dimidjian and Hadley dissenting. Hadley explained his vote by saying, "I doubt the integrity of the HOW-TO organization in what they are trying to do. The houses they are going to build are going to depreciate rapidly." Dimidjian let loose one parting blow at Andy Marshall:

My vote has been changed because I have no faith in Andy Marshall, the program director of HOW-TO. Since the beginning of this project, we have been subject to pressure . . . I am asking the authority's secretary to send a letter to the HOW-TO corporation asking that Marshall be removed.[15]

Former mayor John Kulik, who originated the idea of the Authority, said, "I have never seen a program with such emotion. HOW-TO has the majority of the town behind it." [16] Kulik then summed up the whole controversy by saying, "I wish the best of luck to the HOW-TO participants. The town, county, state, and perhaps the country will be watching your progress. You must become a symbol throughout the country." [17]

Like the white mountain people in Appalachia, the Ramapo Mountain People in Ringwood are the victims of the closing of the mines. The economic prosperity experienced by the Hillburn Mountain People, and to a lesser degree by the Mahwah Mountain People, by-passed the Ringwood Mountain People. This was partly because of the geographic isolation of Ringwood and partly because of the fact that, while the Hillburn and Mahwah Mountain People have a history of being property owners, the Ringwood Mountain People have always been tenants. The self-help housing program in the Mine Area is designed to make the Ringwood Mountain People home-owners and to give them a stake in society.

6   HILLBURN

Hillburn, New York, is a small village nestled in the entrance to the Ramapo Pass on the banks of the Ramapo River. It's tree-lined, residential streets give the impression of a small, quiet, typical American town. The streets were laid out in 1873 in a grid pattern—on one axis the numbered streets (First, Second, Third, Fourth, Fifth, and Sixth), and on the other axis the named streets (Terrace Avenue, Lake Avenue, Rockland Avenue, Fox Hollow Drive, and Boulder Avenue).

The neat grid lay-out of the village was disrupted by the construction of Route 17 in 1932 and the New York Thruway in the 1950s. Both these highways pass through the village on their way through the Ramapo Pass to upstate New York. As a result the village is divided into three sections: East Hillburn (east of the Thruway), the main section (between the Thruway and Route 17), and the Hollow (west of Route 17). East Hillburn contains a power station for the Rockland Power Company, a warehouse for the Avon cosmetics factory in Suffern, and several private dwellings. The main section contains private dwellings, two grocery stores, a grade school, a post office, the white Presbyterian church, the colored Pentecostal church, the abandoned Methodist church, a two-story frame apartment building called the Beehive, and a building that serves as a combination village hall, fire station, assembly hall, and gymnasium. The Hollow contains private dwellings and the colored Presbyterian church.

The Hollow used to be the colored section of town, and Route 17 was the dividing line segregating the races. But now the Mountain People are moving into the main section along Sixth Street and Chestnut Avenue and up several other avenues. The Beehive is mostly colored. But most of the Mountain People still reside on the west side of town and the whites on the east. Most of the streets on the colored side of town do not have sidewalks, whereas there are sidewalks in the white section. The village board hires a snow plow for the sidewalks in the winter. Some of the Mountain People feel that this is an unfair luxury for the benefit of the Hillburn whites. But one of the Mountain People told me that some of the Mountain People are unwilling to give up part of their property frontage to have sidewalks.

Even before Hillburn was founded in the late nineteenth century and the Mountain People moved there, the Ramapo Pass attracted industry because of its location near the colonial iron mines of the Ramapo Mountains and because it was the main land route through the mountains to upstate New York.[1] In 1773 John Suffern settled near the mouth of the Pass at a place he named New Antrim after his home town in Northern Ireland. The name was later changed to Suffern in his honor. He kept a tavern that served as Washington's headquarters for a time during the Revolutionary War. In 1792 Suffern built a saw-mill in the Pass at what is now Hillburn. In 1808 he and his son Andrew established in New Antrim an ironworks which was to include a forge, a rolling and slitting mill, and works for cutting and heading nails. His grandson James later established a charcoal forge on the site of the sawmill, added a rolling mill, and specialized in making railroad car axles.

In 1795 Josiah G. Pierson, the owner of a nail factory in New York City, purchased 119 acres of land in the Ramapo Pass from John Suffern. Pierson owned a patent on machinery to cut nails, and in 1797 he and his brother Jeremiah began manufacturing nails and hoops for sugar barrels at what they called the Ramapo Works. They built a company town just north of the site of Hillburn. In 1803 a company store was built, in 1807 a post office was established, and in 1810 the Presbyterian Church of Ramapo Works was founded by Jeremiah Pierson. At that time the village had a population of 700, with 150 people directly employed in the works and at least 400 peo-ple employed part-time as woodcutters and charcoal burners. In 1814 a cotton mill was erected to manufacture spun yarn to trade for high-quality Russian iron. Jeremiah Pierson leased the ironworks to another company in 1851, but by 1855 it was closed.

In the early 1870s a company to manufacture railroad car wheels and brakeshoes was incorported—known originally as the Ramapo Car Works, and later as the Ramapo Wheel and Foundry Company, the Ramapo Car Wheel Company, the Ramapo Iron Works, the Ramapo Foundry Company, and the American Brakeshoe Company. Later it expanded to produce railroad track equipment, automatic switch stands, split switches, and frogs. The founding officers of the company were Henry L. Pierson and Charles T. Pierson (descendants of Josiah and Jeremiah Pierson), George Church, and William W. Snow.

In 1873 the Ramapo Wheel and Foundry Company purchased from James Suffern fifteen acres in the Ramapo Pass where a company town consisting of a foundry, dwelling houses, and a store was established. The town was originally named Woodburn, but the name was changed to Hillburn when it was discovered there was already another Woodburn in the state. The town was incorporated in 1893.

Hillburn's population was predominantly made up of workers in the foundry. The occupational distribution in 1875 included 1 superintendent in the foundry, 1 pattern maker, 1 foreman in the foundry, 7 moulders, 1 iron melter, 2 carpenters, 15 laborers, 1 watchman in the foundry, 1 machinist, 1 core-maker in the foundry, 1 machinist/moulder, 1 blacksmith, 1 butcher, 1 locomotive engineer, 2 farmers, 2 servants, 1 farm laborer, and 1 landscape painter. Among these first residents were three of the Mountain People—John Mann, Elliot Mann, and Samuel De Freese, all laborers. Elliot Mann, however, was also a landowner.[2] In the following years they were joined by other Mountain People attracted to Hillburn by employment in the foundry. Many of them bought land in Hillburn during the 1880s and 1890s. John and Thomas Van Dunk purchased land in 1883,[3] Sarah De Groat in 1884,[4] John D. De Groat in 1887,[5] Samuel De Freese in 1891,[6] and John Van Dunk, Jr., in 1892.[7]

A few leading white families possessed a large amount of political and economic power in the town—the Snows, the Davidsons, the Piersons, the Churches, and the Sufferns. With the exception of the Sufferns, who were large landowners, all these families were associated with the Ramapo Wheel and Foundry Company. Members of these families were also active in the local Ramapo Presbyterian Church, the Mountain Spring Water Company (supplying water for the village), the Hillburn Power and Building Company (supplying electricity), the school board, and the local government.[8]

Today the foundry is gone from Hillburn. The tight social control of the company town structure no longer exists. Most of the powerful families of the managers have since moved elsewhere. But the residents of Hillburn, both white and colored, are today still predominantly blue-collar workers. Of the total number of Hillburn's white males in the labor force in 1960, close to half were craftsmen, foremen, operatives, or laborers; approximately one-quarter were in professional, technical, managerial, and proprietor occupations; and only about one-eighth were service, sales, or clerical workers. Of the total number of Hillburn's nonwhite (colored) males in the labor force in 1960, close to 90 percent were craftsmen, foremen, operatives, and laborers. In 1959, two-thirds of the white families had an annual income below $8,000, 30 percent between $8,000 and $15,000, and only 3 percent between $15,000 and $25,000. In the same year 88 percent of the nonwhite families had an annual income below $8,000, and 12 percent earned between $8,000 and $15,000.[9]

Although the Hillburn Mountain People are not as affluent as the Hillburn whites, they are more affluent than the Mountain People in Ringwood and Mahwah. Possibly this is related to the fact that Hill-

TABLE 8   NONWHITE OCCUPATIONAL DISTRIBUTION FOR
HILLBURN, N.Y., 1960

	Male	Female
profess'l, techn'l & kindred workers	8	5
mgrs., off's & propr's, incl. farm	—	—
clerical & kindred workers	—	5
sales workers	—	4
craftsmen, foremen & kindred workers	24	—
operative and kindred workers	33	17
private household workers	—	24
service wkrs., exc. priv. household	—	7
laborers, except mine	25	—
occupation not reported	4	5
women in labor force, hus. present	—	41
Total	94	67

Source: U.S. Census, 1960.

TABLE 9   WHITE AND NONWHITE ANNUAL FAMILY
INCOME FOR HILLBURN, N.Y., 1959

Income	White	Nonwhite*	Number of Families
Under $1,000	...	8	8
$1,000 to $1,999	...	8	8
$2,000 to $2,999	11	9	20
$3,000 to $3,999	11	16	27
$4,000 to $4,999	14	28	42
$5,000 to $5,999	18	32	50
$6,000 to $6,999	18	11	29
$7,000 to $7,999	27	9	36
$8,000 to $8,999	...	4	4
$9,000 to $9,999	9	4	15
$10,000 to $14,999	36	8	44
$15,000 to $24,999	3	...	3
Total	149	137	286

Source: United States Census, 1960.
* Although census takers do not have a separate category for colored, in Hillburn the nonwhite category consists almost totally of Ramapo Mountain People.

burn is the least isolated settlement. The median annual family income of the Hillburn Mountain People in 1959 was approximately $5,000.[10]

None of the Mountain People in Ringwood own their homes. In Mahwah 39 mountain families own property, 17 in the vicinity of Grove Street and 22 on Stag Hill. In 1972 the average property valuation was $16,800 for those on Grove Street and $7,600 for those on the mountain.[11] But in Hillburn 64 families owned property, and their average property valuation in 1972 was $11,300.* [12] Perhaps because the Hillburn Mountain People have a greater financial stake in society, they have been more successful than those in Mahwah and Ringwood in organizing to achieve political and social reform.

Race relations in Hillburn are outwardly cordial. Some of the whites are life-long friends of some of the Mountain People. They

* The property in Mahwah is assessed at 74 percent of full value, and the property in Hilburn is assessed at 30 percent of full value. The above figures are a computation of full value based on these fractional assessments.

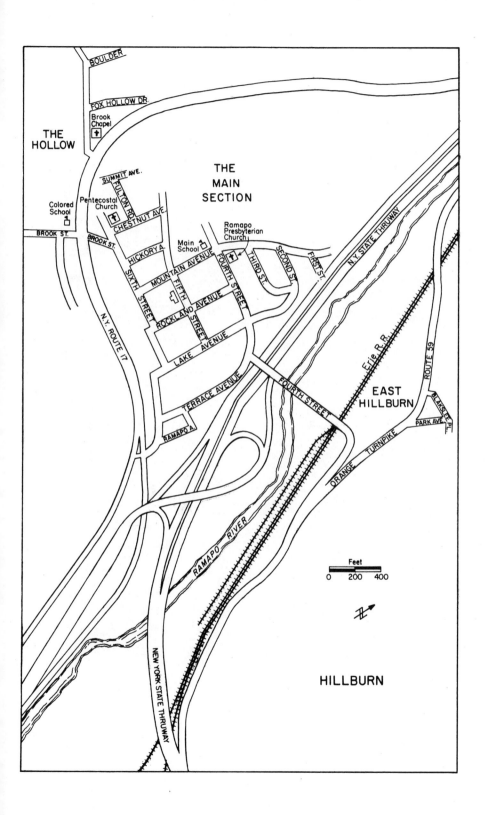

WOODBURN TOWNSHIP RAMAPO, N.Y.

From *Combination Atlas of Rockland County, New York*
(Philadelphia: F. A. Davis and Co., 1876)

The Ramapo Pass with Hillburn in foreground, the Hoevenkopf Mountain on the right, and Mahwah beyond

Homes of the Hillburn Mountain People

Howard Morgan

Brook Chapel

Hillburn Village Board: left to right, Harvey Coleman, trustee; Mayor Lester Lepori; "Tracey" Powell, trustee; Patti Lyn Van Dunk, village clerk

The Galindez home

The Galindez children

Vic De Freese

grew up together and remained in the village. But these friendships tend to follow a pattern of deference on the part of the Mountain People and paternalism on the part of the whites. Most of the whites and some of the Mountain People maintain that there is "no race problem in Hillburn." However, close beneath the surface of this outward cordiality there are suspicion and distrust between the races which tend to surface during times of controversy.

One such development involved the Hillburn school district, which was established in 1880. It was segregated from the outset. A separate school for the colored children, named Brook School, was organized at about the same time and maintained by private subscription. In 1888 Brook School became part of the Hillburn school district. Colored children living in Ramapo or nearby in New Jersey were allowed to attend Brook School. The first session of the school was held in a log chapel. In 1889 it was decided to build a new school building. The school accommodated grades one through six.[13] Both races attended the same high school in Suffern.

Brook School was located in the Hollow on the colored side of town, and the white Main School was located on Mountain Avenue on the white side of town. The facilities were blatantly unequal. As late as the 1940s, Brook School had outdoor privies for the children. In 1943 there were approximately one hundred children crowded into the three-room Brook School, while only approximately fifty white children had the use of the eight-room, modern Main School building.[14]

In the fall of 1943 the Mountain People in Hillburn decided to try to improve the educational situation. A chapter of the National Association for the Advancement of Colored People (NAACP) was formed, and Thurgood Marshall, then the special counsel for the NAACP in New York City, came to Hillburn to help organize a protest. Marshall pointed out that the segregated school district in Hillburn was in violation of a New York law of 1938 that repealed an earlier law permitting segregated schools. Marshall notified the New York state commissioner of education of the situation in Hillburn.

On the first day of school, September 8, 1943, the mother of five-year-old Allan Morgan, Jr., accompanied by Thurgood Marshall, attempted to register her son at the white Main School. Young Allan was not allowed to register. Meanwhile, across town a boycott of

Brook School was begun. A telegram from the counsel of the state education department was sent to the Rockland County superintendent of schools: "Necessary for your board to arrange school facilities for both white and colored children without segregation." [15]

That evening a special meeting of the district school board was held, and the following statement was issued:

We take the position that *there is no segregation in the district* since a number of the schools are being attended by both Negro [sic] and white children, including the new central high school. In order to clarify the issue that has been raised the board has established the following *geographical* lines for attendance of pupils in the Main and Brook Schools in Hillburn. [Italics added] [16]

This "geographical" boundary roughly followed the line of segregated housing in the village. The president of the board of education was J. Edgar Davidson, who was also an official of the American Brakeshoe Company. Davidson said that the students who failed to attend their assigned school would be considered truant.[17]

The Mountain People filed a petition with Davidson charging that the Brook School facilities were inferior and that the territorial division was deliberately designed to continue de facto segregation. The petition demanded that the school board grant a public hearing on the question, that it abolish the policy in which the colored children were required to attend Brook School, that it abolish the policy of refusing to admit colored students to the Main School, and that it abolish the present geographical boundary lines.[18]

On the day scheduled for the reopening of the Hillburn schools, the colored parents again refused to register their children at Brook School and instead went en masse to the Main School to attempt to register there. They were met at the schoolhouse door by Davidson and Miss Stickle, the principal. Thirty-two colored children who resided within the white geographical zone were allowed to register, but the rest were told by Davidson:

There is no use of *you people* coming up here one by one. The same information is for all. We expect children to enter school as laid out in geographical line; and those children on the west side of the tract will go to the other school. [Italics added] [19]

"You people" had become an offensive phrase to the Mountain People. Like the name Jackson Whites, it was not so much the meaning of the phrase as the tone in which it was said that was offensive.

The next day, the parents of the "truant" children received the following notice from the school board: "Unless you comply with the law, it will be necessary for the Board of Education to take such steps as are provided by law to compel your compliance." [20] The boycott continued, and the parents were served with summons for violation of the state truancy law. A hearing was held on September 29 at New City, the county seat. Justice John A. McKenna presided. He fined the colored parents $10 each but suspended sentence providing they send their children to an accredited school within a reasonable period of time.[21] A school for the boycotting children had been established, and a licensed teacher was hired, but it was not accredited.

Thurgood Marshall appealed to the state authorities to override this decision. Representatives from both sides met in Albany with Dr. George Stoddard, the state commissioner of education. Stoddard promised to send two representatives to investigate the situation. Until the matter was settled, the children would be allowed to boycott the Brook School. On October 12, Stoddard handed down his ruling— the effect of the "geographic" division was "to maintain the Brook school entirely for Negro [sic] children." He ruled that Brook School be closed and "that the Board of Education provide educational facilities for all the children in this area at the Main School." [22]

The reaction of the whites to the integration order was the same as that in the South in the following decade. On October 18, when the Main School was to be integrated, only one white child attended. The rest of the white children were transferred to private schools. Some attended the parochial school in Suffern, several enrolled in the public school in nearby Tuxedo, and many enrolled in the Suffern School for Boys, a private school headed by Reverend Robert Jones, the minister of the Ramapo Presbyterian Church.[23] In the years following the dispute, the white children gradually returned to the Hillburn public school, mainly because their parents could not afford continued private schooling.

During this dispute, the local county newspaper sided with the whites of Hillburn. When the Stoddard decision integrating the school was delivered, the *Nyack Journal News* ran an editorial entitled "Hardly a Local Victory." It read in part:

Technically, of course, and on the basis of cold fact, with complete disregard for the human element involved, it [Stoddard's decision] is a step forward and an action in which as a matter of general principle Rockland County people unanimously concur.

Fortunately for Dr. Stoddard, however, he does not have to live in the county along with the way in which he rendered his decision . . .[24]

The editorial admitted that "there has existed a problem at the Brook School requiring a solution," but it continued:

This has not been a problem for solution by the state—Dr. Stoddard included in spite of his decision—but for solution by the local district and by the local people. Futhermore, by local is meant the people of the Hillburn district in particular and the Ramapo central district in general.[25]

In a later editorial the paper approved the white boycott as "a silent slap . . . not to the Negro [sic] children and their parents, but to the method by which the change was effected." [26] The *Journal News* also condemned "reporters from the New York tabloids [who] attempted to make a field day of the event for themselves." [27] Undoubtedly this was a reference to the newspaper *P.M. Daily*, edited by Socialist Ralph Ingersoll, which crusaded for the Hillburn Mountain People by giving the controversy extensive coverage including pictures.

The two major political parties in Rockland County remained aloof from the dispute, but a third party, the American Labor Party, championed the cause of the Mountain People. The American Labor Party invited both the Republicans and the Democrats to take a stand.[28] The Republican Party answered that it would not intervene, because "being a political party, it would establish a bad precedent to inject politics into any school matter." [29] The chairman of the Democratic county committee issued a statement saying that "there is no place for politics in the management of our public school system."[30]

The Hillburn school dispute was one of the few times that the Mountain People were willing to accept the support of a black civil rights organization like the NAACP. A rally was held in the Golden

Gate Ballroom in Harlem in New York City to gain support and raise money for the Mountain People.

In contrast to the successful desegregation of the Hillburn school was the failure to integrate the colored and white Presbyterian churches. Brook Chapel, the colored church, and the white Ramapo Presbyterian Church are loosely affiliated. The old stone Presbyterian Church of Ramapo Works founded by Jeremiah Pierson was the parent church of both. When Hillburn was founded, it was decided to build a branch of the Presbyterian church there. The land was donated by James B. Suffern, and the white-frame Ramapo Presbyterian Church was finished in 1873. The old stone church was attended by the upper class—Piersons, Snows, Sufferns, and Davidsons. The new frame church was attended by the white employees in the foundry.

Samuel De Freese, Jr., conducted prayer meetings for the colored workers in the home of William De Groat. In 1876 Reverend George A. Ford, minister of the Ramapo Presbyterian Church, expanded the congregation to include the Mountain People. In 1877 Brook Chapel was established, and a log chapel was constructed. The present small white frame church was constructed in 1893. Samuel De Freese is considered one of the founders of Brook Chapel, and a picture of him with his white beard, dark clothing, and stern expression hangs in the church.[31]

There exists a nominal cooperation between the two Presbyterian churches in Hillburn. When the minister of one church goes on vacation during the summer months, the other minister conducts joint services alternately in each church. But these joint services are not as well attended by the visiting members as their own services. Each year Brook Chapel sponsors a pre-Thanksgiving church supper that is attended by both white and colored Hillburn residents. But there is an underlying tension in these joint church activities. After plans were announced at a Brook Chapel religious service for a joint breakfast at the white church to follow Easter sunrise services, one of the Mountain People joked, "You go first, and then I'll follow."

About ten years ago an attempt was made to merge the two Presbyterian churches in Hillburn with the larger Presbyterian church in Suffern. The merger was urged by the local presbytery because, it was argued, Hillburn was too small to support two Presbyterian churches. The minister of the Suffern Presbyterian church, Reverend Wissler, who was then the moderator for the two Hillburn churches, told me that most of the whites were in favor of the merger "with a few reservations." He said that these reservations were "subtle," based on the "age-long racial prejudice situation there." He admitted that there was "some foundation" to the contention that some whites in Hillburn didn't want to unite with the colored church. There were also reservations on the part of the Mountain People. Some felt a sense of tradition for their own church and didn't want to give up their own building. Others thought they weren't wanted in the white church, and they didn't want to go where they weren't wanted. Still others didn't want their children to cross Route 17 to attend Sunday school. But some Mountain People favored the merger. The issue never came to a vote in the white church. The merger plan was voted down by the session of Brook Chapel, so there was no need for a vote in the Ramapo Presbyterian Church. The desire of the older Mountain People to preserve tradition won out over the desire for integration. There was no outside civil rights organization to keep up the momentum.

TABLE 10   WHITE AND NONWHITE POPULATION
OF HILLBURN, NEW YORK, 1875–1969

	White	%	Nonwhite	%	Total Population
1875	148	(88.6%)	19	(11.4%)	167
1900	. . .	. . .	. . .	. . .	824
1905	755	(86.0%)	123	(14.0%)	878
1910	. . .	. . .	. . .	. . .	1,090
1915	699	(68.9%)	317	(31.1%)	1,016
1920	. . .	. . .	. . .	. . .	1,112
1925	695	(61.5%)	437	(39.5%)	1,132
1930	819	(63.0%)	481	(37.0%)	1,303
1940	678	(58.5%)	483	(41.5%)	1,161
1950	676	(55.8%)	536	(44.2%)	1,212
1960	562	(50.4%)	552	(49.6%)	1,114
1963	546	(51.1%)	522	(48.9%)	1,068
1966	503	(49.8%)	508	(50.2%)	1,011
1969	460	(43.9%)	587	(56.1%)	1,047

Source: United States and New York State Censuses.

TABLE 11 POLITICAL PARTY ENROLLMENT FOR RAMAPO DISTRICT NO. 5
(HILLBURN, N.Y.)

	Repub-lican	Demo-cratic	Prohi-bition	Progres-sive	Amer-ican Labor	Liberal	Conser-vative
1914–15	168	48	7	6	...	...	...
1930–31	346	97	...	...	...	...	...
1940	481	169	...	...	4	...	...
1950	295	83	...	...	7	2	...
1951	271	58	...	...	1	1	...
1952	382	150	...	...	3	2	...
1955	224	123	...	...	...	1	...
1960	291	158	...	...	...	5	...
1965–66	130	154	...	...	...	4	1
1968–69	197	172	...	...	...	6	43

Source: Rockland County Courthouse, Bureau of Election, New City, N.Y.

An event of historical importance for the Hillburn Mountain People occurred in March 1969 during my stay in Hillburn—the election of the first colored trustee to the village board in its seventy-six-year history. In 1875 the Mountain People had constituted only 11.4 percent of the population of the village.[32] Their number increased to 31.1 percent in 1915 [33] and 37.0 percent in 1930.[34] After reaching a peak in 1930, the total population of Hillburn began to decline as the result of a white exodus from the village. As the percentage of whites declined, the percentage of Mountain People increased, until in 1966 the Mountain People outnumbered the whites for the first time.[35] Some of the Mountain People held minor political offices such as commissioner of recreation or county committeeman in the Democratic Party. A Republican official in the county government told me that the only reason one of the Mountain People was elected a Democratic committeeman was that the party members didn't know he was colored until after he was elected. But Hillburn still had no colored representative on the village board, which consists of a mayor and two trustees.

Traditionally, Hillburn was staunchly Republican. Until the 1950s both colored and white tended to vote the same way. One informant said that many of the older Mountain People voted Republican because of the economic pressure exerted by the leading families in the company town. In the early 1950s the Democratic Party began to gain support as a rival party.[36] But even then both major parties tended to be controlled by whites, and the race issue was kept out of politics, because it was too sensitive. Party affiliation was a matter of convenience, rather than of ideology. It was common for a candidate to switch parties if he lost the nomination on one ticket. In many elections, candidates ran unopposed or on both tickets.

There had been several previous attempts by the Hillburn Mountain People to gain political power by electing a colored trustee to the village board. In two of the three attempts, the colored candidate had to run as an independent or on a third-party ticket. In 1947 a colored candidate ran for trustee on the American Labor Party ticket. He was defeated by the white Republican candidate by a vote of 243 to 77.[37] Another attempt was made in 1960 by another colored candidate running as an independent. He was defeated by a vote of 208 to 134.[38] In 1968 a colored candidate for trustee gained the Democratic nomination. But he too was defeated—by a vote of 209 to 136.[39]

There were several reasons for the failure of the Mountain People of Hillburn to gain political office. In the 1950s and 60s political support of the Mountain People was divided between the Republican and Democratic parties. It is estimated that in 1968 approximately 100 colored voters were registered Democrats and 55 were Republicans. Many of the older Mountain People with a strong sense of tradition have remained Republicans. The political efforts of the Mountain People also have been frustrated by personal antagonisms and family jealousies. The involvement in politics of the Powell family, who have been Mountain People for only three generations, has resulted in antagonism among the older mountain families. The strong antipathy for blacks felt by the Mountain People has prevented an alliance with the few blacks in the village. One of the Mountain People told me that he thought the whites took advantage of this feeling by running a black against a mountain person for committeeman. A black woman in Hillburn who had political ambitions told me that she couldn't hope to gain the support of the Mountain People if she were to run for political office.

The turning point in the political situation in Hillburn came with the formation in the late 1960s of the Citizens for Better Representation. In theory this organization was nonpartisan and "for all the people of

Hillburn," but in practice only the colored Mountain People participated in the meetings in Brook Chapel, and its business dealt mainly
with the problems of the Mountain People. There was a strong self-
help attitude among the members of this organization coupled with a
refusal to accept help from outside civil rights groups. There was also
a commitment to work within the political process and to accept gradual reform. "You have to crawl before you walk" was a saying heard
at several meetings. One of the Mountain People noted with pride that,
unlike the blacks in Nyack, they were working within the political
process. The stated purposes of the Citizens for Better Representation
were to acquaint the colored population of Hillburn with the political
process, to inform them of their rights and the procedures of redress,
and to serve as an intermediary between the Mountain People and the
village board. But the main accomplishments of this organization were
a successful voter registration drive and efforts to get out the vote on
election day.

In the March 1969 election the mayor and one of the trustees were
up for reelection. Nominations were made at party caucuses in which
all registered members of the party were eligible to vote. The incumbent, Mayor Lester Lepori, received both the Democratic and Republican nominations and ran unopposed. The incumbent trustee, Walter
Stead, received the Republican nomination, but he was challenged by
colored candidate Benjamin T. ("Tracey") Powell, who won the
nominations of both the Democratic and Liberal parties. The main issue
was a referendum on whether or not the village-owned water system
should be sold to the Spring Valley Water Company. The colored
candidate opposed the sale, and both the incumbent mayor and trustee
supported the sale.

The chairman of the Liberal Party sent the residents of Hillburn
a mimeographed letter stating that race was the main issue in the election. His letter read in part:

I know that you believe in the democratic principle of fair representation!
To date, the colored people of Hillburn have been taxed and exploited for
the common welfare without having had the fair representation to which
they are entitled. . . .

If elected, Mr. Powell will be the first colored person to hold public
office in Hillburn since it was incorporated. Isn't it about time?

In rebuttal Walter Stead sent out his own letter.

I am pleased that others are also, interest [sic] in our village and desire to run for office. Namely, Mr. Tracy [sic] Powell, perhaps you to [sic] were shocked by the letter sent out by the, so called, Liberal Party of Sloatsburg, with the old familiar lies of explotation [sic] of the colored people of Hillburn.
If Mr. Powell, accepts support from fringe charactors [sic] such as this he is welcome to it, I don't believe the colored people or white people want any part of Mr. Koch [head of the Liberal Party] or his philosophy.
I sincerely, believe the colored people of our village are outstanding. They are respectable, hard working and proud. They are proud of their homes and property, their children and everything they posses [sic]. The white people of our village respect them for these traits. This is the reason *we have no racial problems in Hillburn. If outsider rable* [sic] *rousers would stay out of our village we will have no problems.* [Italics added]

On the evening of March 18, 1969, when the polls closed and the results were announced, Tracey Powell had been elected trustee by a vote of 251 to 171. Powell polled 115 votes on the Democratic line and 136 votes on the Liberal Party line. Never before had the Liberal Party polled so many votes in Hillburn.

Mayor Lepori was reelected with 161 Republican votes and 75 Democratic votes. It was evident that a large number of people abstained from voting for the mayor because only 226 votes were cast for mayor as opposed to 424 votes for trustee. The sale of the village water system was voted down 197 to 48.

After the election the Citizens for Better Representation issued a victory statement assessing the election from the point of view of the colored population of Hillburn.

The election of Mr. Tracey Powell as Trustee of Hillburn marks a new era in the village.
After more than 75 years of taxation without representation in the village government, the colored people of Hillburn now have an elected official to speak for them and to keep them informed about current events in the village.
After more than 75 years of pretence by the village government that Hillburn has no racial problems, the village may now face these problems publicly and work to resolve them fairly.

. . . Walter Stead was way out of line when he blamed the controversy of the election on outside agitators. If raising such serious issues during an election campaign is "rabble rousing," then the Citizens for Better Representation are rabble rousers and proud of it.

The Liberal Party of Rockland County, through its chairman, was invited to participate in the election by the village of Hillburn. This village is in Rockland County, all part of New York. The Liberal Party of Rockland County is no more an outsider than the Republican, Democratic, or Conservative Party.

Now that the election is over, we hope that all the citizens of Hillburn will join together in trying to improve the village for everyone.

Strong feelings were aroused by the election. Soon there was a rumor that the brother of the losing candidate for trustee had said that their side was going to contest the election because "they [the opposition] brought in outside niggers from Mahwah [to vote]." However, the election was not formally contested. I was present in the municipal building to hear the results when the polls closed. After the results were announced, a white Hillburn resident came up to me and accused me of being an "outsider." When I informed him that I had been living in Hillburn since the preceding August, the man changed his tone and welcomed me to Hillburn.

The day after the election I was on the street talking to Harvey Coleman, one of the Mountain People who had been active in the Citizens for Better Representation. A young mountain woman passed us and joked, "Now that 'you people' have power, what are you going to do with it?" This woman passed us again on her return, when she said, "What are you going to do now, Harvey, sit back while the whites move out of town?"

At the next meeting of the Citizens for Better Representation, it was suggested that, now that the Mountain People had gained representation of the village board, the name of the organization ought to be changed. Possible names were discussed. Someone suggested the name the Hillburn Civic Club, but it was noted that the whites in the village might object, because the group didn't represent everyone in Hillburn. Another person suggested the name Brook be used, because Brook Community referred to the Mountain People in Hillburn, as in Brook Chapel and Brook Grammar School. At this point someone facetiously offered the name Brook Civic Club of Hillburn *and Poor Whites.*

Concurrent with the village election campaign, there arose another political issue, although it did not become an issue in the election itself. This concerned the leasing of a community swimming pool from the Town of Ramapo Recreation Department. According to the arrangements, the village would lease the pool for one dollar, but it had to pay the maintenance, including electrical power, personnel, and insurance. The pool had been leased for part of the preceding summer, but the village board was considering refusing the offer for the following summer.

The issue was raised early in 1969 at a meeting of the Citizens for Better Representation. Many of the Mountain People considered this a racial issue. During the preceding summer only the colored children had used the pool. The Mountain People believed that the white parents had refused to allow their children to use the pool, but they couldn't prove that there was an organized boycott by the whites. Now that there was a chance of losing the pool altogether, the Mountain People were irate. It was decided to send a delegation to the next village board meeting to petition the board to reconsider its decision.

There was an overflow crowd of over fifty Mountain People in the small second-floor meeting room in the village hall at the village board meeting on March 12, just one week before the election. Mayor Lepori was conciliatory. He said that his opposition to the pool was based on the expense to the village of maintaining the pool. He wanted the Town of Ramapo to take over this expense. He also noted that there had been some vandalism at the pool. One of the Mountain People said he believed the pool was voted down because it was used only by the Mountain People. The mayor answered that he represented *all* the people of Hillburn, and he denied that *he* dealt with people on the basis of race.

At one point in the meeting, the village attorney used the term "you people," which was taken as an offense by the Mountain People present. At the close of the meeting, the mayor complimented the Mountain People on their conduct during the meeting. One man took offense at this statement and said that this wasn't Nyack (a reference to the black population there) and that the Mountain People never caused trouble.

The mayor and council said that they would take under advisement the opinions expressed at this meeting. Soon after the election, the village board decided to lease the pool for the summer.

7 RACE

The Ramapo Mountain People have no strong sense of racial identity except in negative terms. They feel they are not black, not mulatto, not white, and not full-blooded Indian.

"So what are we?" one man asked.

"I'm one of those *different* ones," said a teen-age girl from Ringwood. "Just put 'other,'" she says when asked to identify her race on forms.

Scholars have used the terms *WINS* (white-Indian-Negro), *quasi-Indians, pseudo-Indians, mestizos*, and *triracial isolates* to refer to similar racial groups in the United States.[1] But the exact racial makeup of the Ramapo Mountain People has not been scientifically determined. Some of the Mountain People will say they are "mixed" or "mixed up like a dog's breakfast." Others use the term *colored* to describe their race. To them *colored* is not a synonym for black; they use it to mean nonwhite. They tend to think of themselves as biracial, not triracial, asserting Indian and white ancestry, denying any black ancestry. Yet there is definite genealogical evidence of black ancestry.

In recent generations there have been some marriages to Indians from North Carolina and Oklahoma, but not enough to affect substantially the racial makeup of the entire population. There is no genealogical proof of early Indian ancestry. Some Indian mixture is possible, however, because Indian and colored interracial matings probably were not recorded in the Dutch Reformed churches.

The term *racially mixed* has been used in this book, but even this term is not completely accurate. There are no pure races; all races are racially mixed. According to recent definitions by biologists, a race is a breeding population.[2] Since the Mountain People have tended to marry among themselves for many generations, they certainly fit the criterion of being a breeding population. Nevertheless, there is a difference between the biological and the sociological definitions of race.[3] Most people think of race in terms of the major categories—black, white, Indian, and so forth. In terms of these sociological categories, the Mountain People are racially mixed. It has been suggested that such groups as the Ramapo Mountain People constitute "little races." [4]

Despite this lack of a clear sense of racial identity, some of the Mountain People do identify with American Indians. These people believe the part of the folk legend that asserts Tuscarora Indian ancestry. In fact, some of the men from Hillburn enlisted in World War I as Tuscarora.[5] One man from Hillburn told me that his father was a full-blooded Cherokee Indian and his mother Irish, even though my genealogical charts showed this was not true. He spoke about his difficulty having the racial classification on his driver's license changed from "Bl" (black) or "M" (mulatto) to "R" (red). He was finally successful in getting the change.

One of the Mountain People in Mahwah said that a minister had visited the Tuscarora reservation in upstate New York and told the Indians there about the "Indians" in Mahwah. The minister brought one of the doubting Tuscarora chiefs to Mahwah for a visit. After seeing the Mountain People, the chief said, according to the informant, that "these were his people," and he welcomed the Mountain People to visit the Tuscarora reservation anytime. Some of the Mountain People make periodic trips to upstate New York Indian reservations. Sometimes a bus is chartered for these trips.

With the possible exception of the herb cures, there are no authentic survivals of Indian culture in the culture of the Ramapo Mountain People. Consequently there is a certain poignancy to some of their expressions of identification with Indians. It can be seen in the folk etymology of proper names. One woman said her mother told her that the name Conklin was an Indian word for "little shell." Another person told me that Dennison was an Indian name.

The identification with Indians also comes out in the humor. Some of the Mountain People semifacetiously refer to themselves as "the mountain tribe" or "the tribe of the Ramapos." Sister Anna Solomon, who married a mixed-blood Cherokee from North Carolina, repeatedly jokes that she makes good fires in her fireplace because she is an Indian.

Dress and hair styles reflect this identification. Sister Anna has on her mantel a picture of herself as a young woman with her hair in braids and wearing an Indian blanket. Another woman agreed that her mother wore braided hair in a conscious attempt to appear Indian. About ten years ago in Hillburn there was a fad among the boys for Don Eagle haircuts, in which the head was shaved except for a shock of hair on top. The girls used to wear headbands and moccasins.

According to one woman, when the children used to go berry-picking in the mountains, motorists would stop and ask if they were real Indians. One family in Hillburn have on their lawn a name sign in the shape of an Indian head. Jimmy De Freese in Ringwood has prominently displayed on his living room wall a picture of an Indian in a canoe. And Sister Anna Solomon has one corner of her home devoted to Indian artifacts. They consist of tourist souvenirs such as pennants, postcards, Indian dolls, and toy canoes.

Some of the Ramapo Mountain People also identify with southern Appalachian and Ozark Mountain whites. Once in a while one of the Mountain People might facetiously refer to himself as a hillbilly. This identification tends to be stronger in Mahwah than in Hillburn or Ringwood. Perhaps this is because the Hillburn and Ringwood people live in valleys rather than in the mountains. In fact, some of the Hillburn people dislike being called Mountain People. Like the identification with Indians, this identification with hillbillies is both cultural and racial. But here there is a better case for cultural similarity. The settlement patterns in hollows and along ridges, the mountain agriculture of earlier times, the mining industry, the family and kinship system, and the folklore and musical tastes indicate that the Ramapo Mountain People are part of an overall Appalachian Mountain culture area.

A premium is placed on physical traits associated with the white race. Reference often is made to "good" hair, meaning straight or curly hair as opposed to kinky or woolly hair. One young mother in Ringwood told me with pride that her son has red hair and that she was going to buy a tinted wig for herself because of her dark, kinky hair. Several Hillburn and Ringwood people told me that the Mahwah people tend to have lighter skin, which enables some of them to pass as white. This was said with a certain resentment against the Mahwah people.

Racial jealousies sometimes divide families. A man in Ringwood confessed to me that he dislikes his sister-in-law because she is too dark. A young man in Hillburn spoke of a family in which an uncle disliked his nephew solely because the nephew was too dark. Even within the nuclear family, race is sometimes a divisive factor. It is not uncommon for there to be racial differences between siblings in the same family. One teen-age girl from Ringwood with light skin said that she has a sister with "brown" (dark) skin, a brother with "brown" skin, a brother with "light" skin, and a brother who is an albino. Her dark-skinned brother thinks she ignores him in public because she is light-skinned. She denies this, saying "brothers and sisters don't turn their backs on each other." Nevertheless, when they eat together in a restaurant, the dark-skinned brother sits at another table.

"Are you prejudiced?" she said to him once.

"Let you light-skinned people sit alone," he answered.

Some of the light-skinned Mountain People try to pass as white. To pass, the person often has to change his name because the surnames are usually recognized by local whites. A De Groat might change his name to De Graw, or a Suffern to Smith. Sometimes the person wishing to pass will move to another place where he won't be recognized. But not everyone with light skin attempts to pass.

The Black Pride movement has modified somewhat this negative attitude among the younger people. A few of the younger Mountain People are willing to be classified with blacks, but they remain a minority. One teen-age girl in Ringwood said she was going to get a "natural" wig, even though her own hair is naturally straight. She said she wanted the wig because it is now the fashion, but she insisted that this didn't mean she considered herself black.

Relationships between the colored Mountain People and blacks are often strained. Several Mountain People said they have more trouble in their relationships with blacks than with whites. Blacks resent that the colored Mountain People consider themselves different. Blacks use the epithets "high yellow" or "high yellow nigger" to refer to the Mountain People.[6] One man said that he was called a "pale face" by blacks. Another man stated that, when he was in the army, blacks called him "Charlie's man." A black woman from Mahwah called the Mountain People "rock jumpers." [7] Another black woman explained this term by saying the Mountain People were too lazy to move rocks so they jump over them. The epithets are returned by the Mountain People. One black woman mentioned the following saying she has often heard used by the Mountain People: "You tell a white man once, a Chinaman twice, and a nigger until he understands."

There is informal opposition among the Mountain People to their children dating and marrying blacks. A teen-age girl told me that she generally didn't date boys with dark skin—not because she was prejudiced, she insisted, but because no dark-skinned boys ever asked her out. Another girl confided that her mother had told her not to date anyone darker than she. In 1939 an informant who was seventy-five years old said that when he was a young man, there was strong opposition to marriage with blacks. He often heard girls say they wanted "only men with white skins and blue veins." [8] A Hillburn woman admitted that there is opposition in some families to marriages with blacks. When such a marriage does occur, the black spouse is regarded as an outsider, but the children of these mixed marriages are accepted. Despite this opposition, there have been numerous marriages to blacks. In one marriage in which the husband is one of the Mountain People and the wife a black from South Carolina, antagonisms exist among the relatives. The woman is made to feel like an outsider, and she associates with nearby blacks more than with the Mountain People. This woman likes to prepare what she calls soul food, including pigs' feet, brains, chitterlings, and sweet potato pie. But her husband dislikes these foods. At one family gathering, she was ridiculed by her in-laws for liking chitterlings and brains. They said they would never eat that kind of food.

In Mahwah the history of the local African Methodist Episcopal (A.M.E.) church reveals the strained relationships between the Mountain People and blacks. The church was founded in 1857 and was named The John Wesley Chapel of Darlington, New Jersey. It was originally located back of the Havemeyer estate at the foot of the mountains. Later it was moved farther into the mountains to Green Mountain Valley, where there was a settlement of Mountain People. In 1876

Elliot Mann was the local preacher and William Mann the licensed exhorter. In 1904 this Green Mountain Valley church withdrew from the Union Conference and joined the A.M.E. Zion Conference. In 1915 the church was moved to its present location on Grove Street in West Mahwah.[9]

The small congregation of about twenty-five today consists of both blacks and a few Mountain People. The singing style is distinctly black gospel. The pastor is a black who comes from out-of-town every week to conduct services. He gave me a different version of the history of this church. He said that the Mountain People applied for but were refused membership in the white Methodist church. So they reluctantly became affiliated with the A.M.E. Zion church, a black denomination. When the church began to attract neighboring blacks, he said, a group of the Mountain People withdrew from the A.M.E. church and began attending the Pentecostal church down the road. When I spoke to the minister of the Pentecostal church, he accused the blacks of stealing the title to the A.M.E. church. But another member of the Pentecostal congregation denied that race was behind the affair. She said that evangelical movements like the Pentecostal church often get converts from other churches.

In Ringwood antiblack feelings are focused against the blacks in Paterson, New Jersey, the nearest city with a large black population. There is some contact with Paterson blacks through Mountain People from Ringwood who have migrated to that city. Occasionally Paterson blacks come up to Ringwood to see colored mountain girls. The Mountain People call blacks "southerners," assuming that most blacks come from the South. Unaware of the strong antiblack attitudes in Ringwood, the federal government's Office of Economic Opportunity (OEO) hired a black executive director of the Passaic County Community Action Council, the antipoverty agency whose jurisdiction included the Ringwood Mine Area. This resulted in distrust and ill will among some of the Ringwood Mountain People. Racial problems impeded the effectiveness of other federal antipoverty programs. A teen-age girl from Ringwood spoke about her experience at a Job Corps training camp in Maine in 1968. She said she felt like an outcast. Although she "fit in alright" with the whites and Puerto Ricans, she said, she "had no chance" with the blacks. She left without finishing the program.

In Hillburn the white owner of a grocery store said that he once was given some advertising materials aimed at the black consumer. When he started to distribute these advertisements, he was told by one of the Mountain People that they were not black and would not favorably receive this kind of promotion. The grocer sent back the advertisements.

Most whites who live in the vicinity are unaware that the colored Mountain People make a distinction between themselves and blacks. Even the United States Census has always listed the Mountain People as either black or mulatto. Many neighboring whites do not know that the terms *Negro*, *black*, and even *Jackson White* are considered derogatory, and many well-meaning whites have offended the Mountain People without intending to do so. Other whites intending offense use the term *nigger*, which is doubly offensive, first, because it implies they are black, and, second, because it is offensive even to blacks. Another offensive term used by whites is *half-breed*. In his novel about the Mountain People, Albert Payson Terhune refers to the "blue-eyed niggers." I have been unable to verify whether this term was ever in common use.

One factor underlying the white attitude toward the colored Mountain People is a disapproval of miscegenation. The bartender in a white bar in Suffern told a customer that there was a "mixed couple" (colored and white) in the bar the other night. The bartender said that he doesn't "go for that stuff" and added that if his daughter ever dated a colored man, he'd kill them both. A male customer commented that the mountain girl in the bar the other night was pretty. A woman customer disagreed, saying the girl wasn't pretty at all. The man responded that she was colored, but pretty nonetheless.

The fact that some of the Mountain People can easily pass as white creates a problem for some whites. One white informant said that a while ago some white soldiers from the Nike base in nearby Franklin Lakes had been dating some girls from Mahwah. When their commander informed them that these girls were not white, the soldiers, who were from the South, were quite discomfited by the news. This same informant said that there was a lot of interracial dating at Mahwah

High School but that he wouldn't allow *his* daughter to date a colored boy.

One young colored man from Ringwood bragged that, when he is in Paterson, he only patronizes white bars and will only date white girls. A young man from Hillburn said that he sometimes dated white girls, but he didn't think there was any special prestige in this. Another Hillburn man said that when he was younger he wanted to marry a white girl. His mother opposed the marriage, and he ended up marrying "one of [his] own kind." He also felt there was no special prestige attached to dating white girls.

Some of the Mountain People take advantage of this white fear of miscegenation. They hint at past miscegenation in white families as a kind of threat. One Hillburn woman told me that the whites in the village wouldn't be very happy with the results of the genealogies I was compiling. Another colored woman in Hillburn stated that her mother used to say that certain white families in the village were "all [her] people." Another informant said his grandmother used to say that many of the so-called white people in the village were actually mixed-bloods who had changed their names and were passing as white. Some of the Mountain People cite as evidence of miscegenation the fact that several white families have the same surnames as colored families. The whites argue that this occurs as a result of freed slaves taking the surnames of their former masters.

A second element in the white attitude toward the Mountain People is the fear that the Mountain People are dirty. One colored woman from Hillburn said that, when she graduated from high school in 1947, she applied for a job at a local bank in Suffern. She wasn't hired because, as she was later informed by a friend, the employees at the bank wouldn't use the washroom facilities after her. A white woman from Hillburn said that, as a child, she and her friends used to swim in the Ramapo River. Reminiscing about this once with a colored man her own age from Hillburn, she was amused to find out that the colored children were told by their parents to swim farther upstream. Her amusement came from the reversal of the white view of the Mountain People as the dirty ones. When told about this conversation, another white woman remarked that the colored children probably urinated on the white children.

Race is one of the main factors that socially isolate the Ramapo Mountain People. Identifying with American Indians and white hillbillies, they reject any black ancestry. Yet the surrounding society will not let them, as a group, pass as white. In a sense, they constitute a separate little race.

8 FAMILY AND KINSHIP

There has been much confusion concerning the family and kinship structure of the Ramapo Mountain People. Misunderstandings range from the idea that "they have no organization. . . . Two people agree to live together; they may be cousins, or they may be brother and sister . . . and it is probable that their ceremony of marriage is as informal as that of barn-yard fowls" [1] to the equally erroneous idea that they have a clan structure—"the common ancestry and interests of the whole clan, rather than the narrower divisions of the family, have been their spiritual support. . . . For upwards of hundred years, the Jackson Whites . . . were thought of as shiftless, illiterate mountaineers, unbelievers in soap and marriage." [2] Some observers have even suggested that the people have a tribal structure.

The Ramapo Mountain People do not distinguish between the family and the kinship system. They use the term *family* to refer to both. They refer to the Van Dunk family or the De Freese family, by which they mean everyone with that surname. But anthropologists do distinguish between family and kinship. According to anthropologist George Peter Murdock, the family is

a social group characterized by common residence, economic cooperation, and reproduction. It includes adults of both sexes, at least two of whom maintain a socially approved sexual relationship, and one or more children, own or adopted, of the sexually co-habiting adults. [3]

Murdock distinguishes between two types of family structure. The nuclear family consists of one conjugal unit—the cohabiting couple and their offspring. The extended family consists of two or more conjugal

units residing in the same household.[4] It has been widely believed that
the extended family was predominant in American culture until the
Industrial Revolution. Recent genealogical research has challenged this
concept, showing that the nuclear family has been predominant since
the founding of America.*

In addition to the real historical origin of the Ramapo Mountain
People, my genealogical research indicates the past and present family
structure. True, these sources tend to overestimate the stability of the
family. Church records do not include consensual unions. The Mountain People probably told census takers that they were married even
if they weren't. And my informants for genealogical information probably wanted their families to be seen in the best light. Nonetheless, these
sources indicate that the family structure of the Mountain People remained stable, relatively unchanged over almost three centuries. The
families have always been predominantly large, nuclear, and male-
headed.

In the late seventeenth and eighteenth centuries, according to the
genealogies of the Van Dunk, De Freese, Mann, and De Groat ancestors, the average age of first marriage for males was 29.9 and for females
22.2.† The average number of children born into these families was 5.2.

* One study demonstrates that there were no extended families in colonial
Plymouth. (John Demos, "Notes on Life in Plymouth Colony," *William and Mary
Quarterly* 22, no. 2 [April 1965]:264–86.) Another study uses the term *modified
extended family* to describe the economic dependence on their parents of married
children living in separate households in seventeenth-century Andover, Massachusetts. (Philip Greven, Jr., "Family Structure in Seventeenth Century Andover,
Mass.," *William and Mary Quarterly* 23, no. 2 [April 1966]:234–56). Actually
modified nuclear family would be a more appropriate term to describe this structure. Greven makes this change in terminology in his book *Four Generations:
Population, Land, and Family in Colonial Andover, Massachusetts* (Ithaca: Cornell
University Press, 1970), pp. 15–16n.

† These findings are in accord with recent research on the Puritan family.
John Demos shows that the mean age of first marriage in Plymouth for the period
from 1675 to 1700 was 24.6 for men and 22.3 for women. He concludes that this
average was considerably higher than it is today, contrary to the popular view
that people married at an early age in the colonial period. (Demos, *A Little
Commonwealth: Family Life in Plymouth Colony* [New York: Galaxy Books,
Oxford University Press, 1970], p. 274.) Greven shows that the average age of
marriage for the second generation in Andover, Mass., was 22.8 for women and
27.1 for men. (Philip J. Greven, Jr., *Four Generations* . . . [Ithaca, N.Y.: Cornell
University Press, 1970], pp. 241–42.)

Because the Dutch didn't recognize the right of primogeniture, all the offspring, including daughters, inherited property equally.[5] Elizabeth Claessen inherited land along with her brothers Lewis and Manuel after the death, sometime prior to 1704, of their father Claes Manuel.[6] When John De Vries II died, sometime between 1708 and 1715, his property was inherited by his widow and all his children, including his two daughters Maria and Lennah.[7] Augustine Van Dunk II, in his will probated in 1793, left his property to be divided among his widow, his daughters, and his grandchildren.[8] As far as can be determined, married children set up their own households near the parents from whom they inherited property. The families tended to be male-headed.

In the nineteenth century there was a drop in the age at which males and females married. The average age of marriage for males was 22.4, for females 19.4.[9] The size of the families remained large. The average family had 6 persons in 1830, 6.7 in 1840, 6.4 in 1850, 5 in 1865, and 5.1 in 1880. The families continued to be predominantly male-headed. In 1830 there were 15 male-headed families (88 percent) and only 2 female-headed families (12 percent). In 1865 there were 41 male-headed families (93 percent) and only 3 female-headed families (7 percent). And in 1880 there were 69 male-headed families and no female-headed families.[10] The few female family heads were probably either widows or divorcees.

In the 1880 federal census, which lists the relationship of every member of the family, there were 68 mountain families (12 in Ramapo, 29 in Mahwah, and 27 in Ringwood and West Milford). Fifty of these families (75 percent) consisted only of parents and their unmarried children. There was only *one* extended family (1.5 percent), in which a married couple lived in the household of the wife's parents. In three families (4.4 percent) one parent lived with the married couple; in one it was the wife's mother, in another the wife's father, and in the third the husband's mother. There were 12 families (18 percent) in which some relative, other than married children or parents, lived in the household. In 5 families (8 percent) one or more grandchildren lived with their grandparents, rather than their parents. In 2 families (3 percent) a cousin of the head lived in the household, in one family (1.5 percent) a nephew of the head, in 3 families (4.4 percent) a brother or sister of the head, and in one family (1.5 percent) a sister-in-law of the head. In one family (1.5 percent) there was a boarder unrelated to the head living in the household. And there were three cases (4.4 percent) of two unrelated nuclear families living in the same household.[11]

The New York State census for 1915 provides the relationship to the head of every member of the household for Hillburn. There were 57 mountain families in Hillburn, a total of 317 people. The average size of those families was 5.6 people. Of these families 54 (95 percent) had male heads, and only 3 (5 percent) were headed by females. Forty-six families (81 percent) consisted of only parents and their unmarried children. In two families (3.5 percent) one grandparent was living in the household, the wife's mother in both cases. In 3 families (5.4 percent) grandchildren were living with the grandparents, rather than with their parents. In one family (1.8 percent) a daughter and her child were living in the household of her parents. In one family (1.8 percent) a nephew of the head was living in the household, and in another (1.8 percent) a niece of the head was in the household.[12]

According to the 1960 federal census, 121 (96 percent) of the 125 nonwhite married couples in Hillburn had their own households. In Ringwood 61 (92 percent) of the 66 nonwhite married couples had their own households. Other relatives of the head (cousins, nephews, nieces, brothers, and so forth) were sometimes included in this nuclear family structure. In Hillburn in 1960 there were 127 persons listed as "other relative of head" (neither spouse nor children). In Ringwood there were 96 persons in this category. The average number of persons per household was 4.21 in Hillburn and 5.98 in Ringwood.[13]

Further breakdown of the modern Ringwood family structure is provided by the 1966–67 survey conducted by the Community Action Council of Passaic County. Data are available on 51 families. In only one of these families were married children and their spouses living with their parents. This extended family consisted of grandfather, grandmother, son, grandson, daughter, her husband and three children, second daughter, her husband and two children, and a boarder. In three families at least one grandparent lived with married children, in one case both parents of the wife, in another the husband's mother, in the third the relationship was unspecified. One family in the survey consisted of husband, wife, children, brother-in-law, his wife and son, and another unmarried brother-in-law. The average number of persons per family was 6.8. Forty-seven of the 51 families were headed by males, and only 4 families had female heads. In 41 families both parents were living at home.[14]

Anthropologist George Peter Murdock defines kinship as "a structural system of relationships in which individuals are bound to one another by complex interlocking and ramifying ties."[15] The kindred or kinship group includes those relatives who are outside the family or household unit. The Ramapo Mountain People might be considered one large kinship group. Everyone is related in this complex of interlocking relationships.

The Mountain People determine whether an individual is one of them by asking to whom the person is related. An outsider can become one of the mountain people only by marrying into the group, and even then his acceptance will be only partial. The children of intermarriage, however, are given full acceptance. As the only institution that is exclusively their own, the kinship system provides the main structure of the group.

Like kinship in American society at large, the kinship system of the Ramapo Mountain People is characterized by bilateral descent. This means that the individual recognizes relatives on both his father's and his mother's side of the family, even though the surname is taken from the father. But unlike the open-ended kinship system in American society at large, which extends outward like an inverted pyramid, the kinship system of the Mountain People is relatively closed. The Mountain People tend to marry among themselves, a practice anthropolgists call endogamous marriage. This practice among the Mountain People dates back to the eighteenth century, when their free colored ancestors living in the Hackensack River Valley were practically forced to marry among themselves by the racial attitudes of the society in which they lived. After they migrated to the Ramapo Mountains, geographic isolation further encouraged endogamous marriage. One result of endogamous marriage is to multiply the ways the same individuals are related to each other. For example, they may be double cousins, that is, cousins on both the maternal and paternal sides. Rather than interlocking with the surrounding society, the kinship system of the Mountain People is turned in upon itself, making for a tighter, more exclusive group. The Mountain People are very aware of kinship relationships, and they often will interject into their conversation how certain individuals are related to them. Endogamous marriages, multiple kinship ties, and the fact that the kindred and the community coincide make the kinship system of the Ramapo Mountain People similar to that of the southern Appalachian mountain people.[16]

Despite the tendency to marry within the group, there has always been some marriage outside the group. I made a survey of endogamous and exogamous marriages based on the genealogical charts I compiled during the field work. A total of 567 marriages in Ringwood, Hillburn, and Mahwah covering the period from the early nineteenth century to the present were included.[17] Of this total, 385 (68 percent) marriages were within the group, 182 (32 percent) outside the group. One Hillburn woman said the Mountain People in Hillburn used to be much closer years ago but that this is changing as a result of increased marriages to outsiders. Other Mountain People said that they used to be able to tell to which family a person belonged just by his features but that today this is no longer possible because of outside marriages. When the data were broken down into thirty-year generations, they indicated that marriage outside the group was on the increase.

As might be expected in a relatively small endogamous group, cousin marriages are a fairly frequent occurrence among the Ramapo Mountain People. Thirty-eight cousin marriages were identified on the genealogical charts. This figure does not reflect the number of cousin marriages as a percentage of the total number of marriages

TABLE 12 ENDOGAMOUS AND EXOGAMOUS MARRIAGES BY GENERATION

Generation	Endogamy	Exogamy	Total
I (born 1810–39)	11 (85%)	2 (15%)	13
II (born 1840–69)	49 (75%)	16 (25%)	65
III (born 1870–99)	112 (69%)	51 (31%)	163
IV (born 1900–29)	130 (67%)	63 (33%)	193
V (born 1930–60)	83 (62%)	50 (38%)	133
Total	385 (68%)	182 (32%)	567

Source: Compiled from author's genealogical charts.

TABLE 13 Exogamous Marriages to Blacks,
Whites, and Others by Generation

Generation	Marriages to Blacks	Marriages to Whites	Marriages to Others	Total
I (born 1840–69)	3 (33%)	6 (67%)	...	9
II (born 1870–99)	19 (51%)	18 (49%)	...	37
III (born 1900–29)	26 (58%)	16 (35%)	3 (7%)	45
IV (born 1930–60)	20 (50%)	18 (45%)	2 (5%)	40
Total	68 (52%)	58 (44%)	5 (4%)	131

Source: Compiled from author's genealogical charts.

because in many cases the kinship of the marrying couple could not be determined. But of these 38 cousin marriages 7 involved first cousins, 1 first cousins once removed, 19 second cousins, 3 second cousins once removed, 6 third cousins, and 2 fourth cousins. Many of the Mountain People told me that they are now wary of marrying too close in the family, especially first-cousin marriages. But it was admitted that in some cases the partners in marriage didn't know the closeness of their kinship until they were told by one of the older Mountain People.

Another pattern of endogamous marriage is the marriage of two or more siblings from one family to two or more siblings from another family. There were thirteen such occurrences in the genealogical charts. In three cases a brother and sister from one family married a sister and brother from another family. In nine cases two brothers from one family married two sisters from another family. And there was one case in which three brothers from one family married three sisters from another family. This same marriage pattern is found among whites in the southern Appalachian Mountains.[18]

In 131 marriages outside the Ramapo group, the race of the person marrying into the group was known. Sixty-eight (52 percent) of these exogamous marriages were to blacks, 58 (44 percent) were to whites, and 5 (4 percent) were to others. The high percentage of marriages to blacks may seem surprising, considering the strong prejudice of the Mountain People against blacks. But when one remembers the intensity of white attitudes against miscegenation, it's not so surprising that when the Mountain People marry outside the group, they tend to marry blacks.

The pattern of endogamous marriages over many generations has resulted in the occurrence of certain recessive genetic traits within the group.* These include polydactylism (extra fingers or toes), syndactylism (webbing between fingers or toes), and albinism (lack of pigmentation in the hair and skin). In the past these abnormalities have been exaggerated by writers. In 1940 two doctors from Hackensack, New Jersey, presented a paper to the Medical Society of New Jersey on polydactylism and syndactylism in four generations of one family of Ramapo Mountain People. They found that

Polydactylism and syndactylism are dominant characteristics, passed along by both male and female parents. They developed in the second and third generations in about 50 percent of the children; and in the fourth generation, in seven out of nine, although each mating was with a normal individual. Male and female occurrences are about equal. Fecundity and sub-normal intelligence are apparent throughout.[19]

But this study was based on just *one* family, and the doctors made no attempt to determine how frequently these mutations occur in the population at large. I saw no examples of either polydactylism or syndactylism among the Mountain People. However, one of the Mountain People told me that he knew some Mountain People who had had the beginning of an extra finger surgically removed.

Albinism is more visible, but it too has been exaggerated. Pulitzer-prize-winning journalist George Weller, in an article for the *New Yorker* in 1938, apparently intended to draw a favorable picture of the Mountain People, but he stressed albinism.[20] I know of no more than 5 albinos out of the population of 1,500 Mountain People in Hillburn, Mahwah, and Ringwood. While geneticists consider this a high incidence of albinism, it is not as high as many laymen believe. Albinos tend to have poor eyesight, and many Mountain People believe that they are especially talented either musically or manually by way of compensation.

* This kind of inbreeding is more common than most people think. European monarchy, eastern European Jews, southern Appalachian Mountain whites—in fact, any group that either restricts or is restricted in its marriage choice—run the risk of recessive genetic traits appearing in their population.

The Ramapo Mountain People use the same kinship terms used by the rest of American society: mother, father, son, daughter, sister, brother, aunt, uncle, nephew, niece, cousin, grandfather, grandmother, grandson, granddaughter. Often more familiar forms are used. Daddy is used instead of Father even by grown men, and a young child may be called Babe.

Many times a kinship term is used as a nickname. One woman in Hillburn is widely known as "Sister" or just "Sis." The terms *aunt* and *uncle* are often used before the names of older people even though they are not the aunt or uncle of the speaker. One woman in Ringwood said, "I call her 'aunt,' but she ain't nothing to me" (not a relative). One elderly woman was called "Aunt Sis."

Since the Mountain People are descended from a few families that began intermarrying in the eighteenth century, nearly everyone is related if you go back far enough. The Mountain People have a special term to refer to distant relatives. They are called "woodpile relations."

Even illegitimate children are taken into account in the kinship terminology. The expression "cousins in the bush" is used to refer to a cousin born out of wedlock.

There are several naming patterns among the Ramapo Mountain People. One son, usually the first, is named after the father. This pattern, which dates from the seventeenth and eighteenth centuries, when there were four generations of Augustine Van Dunks and five generations of John De Freeses, continues. Sometimes the middle name will be different in successive generations, as in the case of John Felix Morgan, his son John W. Morgan, and grandson John Allan Morgan. Sometimes the name will skip a generation and reappear in the third generation. Other times the name will go from grandfather, to father's brother, to father's son.

The same naming patterns apply for women. It is common for daughters to be named after their mothers or grandmothers, although this pattern is not so frequent as among the men. Again the middle name may vary, as in the case of the daughter of Ora Madeline Morgan, who is named Ora Bernice Morgan.

The naming pattern, like the kinship system, is bilateral, except for the surname, which comes from the father's side. A son is more likely to be named after his father's father and a daughter after her mother's mother. In one case a woman named her daughter Alexandria after her maiden name, which was Alexander.

Because of these patterns, there is considerable duplication of names. Nicknames are often used to avoid confusion. In fact, the nicknames are so widely used that many of the Mountain People know other Mountain People *only* by their nicknames, having forgotten or never having known their real names. One woman is called Mary Gil, her first name followed by her husband's first name, Gilbert. Junior is a common nickname for a son whose father has the same given name, but in one case the wife of a man nicknamed Junior also was known by her given name followed by Junior. The nickname may refer to a physical characteristic of the person, as in the case of James ("Red") De Grote, who has red hair. It may be humorous or ironic, as with Leonard ("Big Pee Wee") Van Dunk, who is anything but small. It might refer to a habit for which the person is known. An old-timer was called John J. ("Rock") Van Dunk, because he was known to sit often on a rock in town. The nickname may take the form of an epithet, such as "Pete the Tramp." It may reflect stories and rumors told about a person behind his back. One old woman was called "Black Mag" because she was suspected of being a witch. The mass media may even play a part in nicknames. One young man in Ringwood was called "the Judge," because he used to wear a three-quarter-length coat like Judge Roy Bean on television. Another man is nicknamed "Wimpy," because he has a passion for hamburgers like the comic-strip character of the same name. And, finally, nicknames also may be the shortened or familiar forms of given names, such as Becky for Rebecca, Bert for Roberta, Teddy or Dory for Theodore, Rainey for Lorraine, and Meal for Emilia.

Family feuds are fairly common. Rather than fitting the stereotype of two hillbilly families shooting at each other, these feuds consist of informal antagonisms and jealousies between families. A member of the Morgan family in the Ringwood Mine Area told me about a feud between the De Freeses and the Morgans. When a De Freese family moved out of the Mine Area, a Morgan arranged to rent the house. Since housing in the Mine Area is much in demand, some De Freeses resented that a Morgan got the house. According to my Morgan informant, one elderly De Freese woman turned the whole family, including the children, against the Morgans. The Morgan children were told they couldn't play house anymore with the De Freese children. The informant said that this was alright with him, because now he wouldn't have the De Freese children "wearing down the carpet" in his house. He added that the De Freese family "sticks together like white to rice."

Relations between in-laws may be strained. One man in Ringwood refused to attend his son's wedding because he disliked the relatives of the bride. A fight between one father and his son-in-law developed at one party over the son-in-law's insistence on taking his wife home early. One Ringwood man told me that 90 percent of the family feuds start with a marriage between two families and the subsequent attempt by one spouse to win the other over to his or her family.

Kinship solidarity sometimes is involved in barroom brawls. Ten minutes after a brawl in a bar in Suffern, the son of one of the participants, evidently called from the phone booth, came down from the mountain to help out. The other fighter, an outsider who knew the Mountain People fairly well, realized before the son arrived that he was in trouble, that it would be "open season" on him. When the son arrived, the man was conciliatory, the son was mollified, and the issue was resolved without more fighting.

One often hears the Mountain People state that if you offend one member of a family, you offend the whole family. This maxim is also used in reference to the group as a whole. Throughout my field work, I was warned that if I offended one person, I'd offend all the Mountain People. When the group is threatened by outsiders, such as newspaper reporters, individual differences are forgotten, and the entire group responds as one family.

The following comparison of two families, one in Hillburn and the other in Ringwood, shows how difficult it is to generalize about the Ramapo Mountain People. These two families are not in any sense typical; no family is. In some ways the Hillburn family is no different than other middle-class families. In the same way the Ringwood family resembles other lower-class rural families. Yet there are some important aspects of the family and kinship organization that differ from those of American society in general.

In the Hillburn family the husband, age forty-one, is one of the Mountain People and the wife is a black, born in the South. They met in New York City, married in 1958, and moved back to Hillburn. They have four children, two of their own and two foster children, ages eight, six, three, and one. The husband works at the Chevrolet assembly plant in Tarrytown, New York, to which he commutes fifteen miles in the family car, a late-model Chevrolet.

The family own their house, a recently constructed split-level style which is mortgaged and is assessed at $13,800.[21] It is located on a hill, and a short, steep driveway leads up to it. On the bottom level are a partially finished basement, in which the husband installed wood paneling, and the garage. The roof of the garage is used as a patio and is accessible from the first floor. The front-door entrance is approached by cement steps leading from the driveway to a small front porch. On the first floor are the kitchen, a dining room, a living room, two bedrooms, and a bathroom. The furniture is simple and inexpensive. On the top floor are a bedroom and a storage room. The parents and the youngest child sleep in the downstairs bedrooms, the three older children in the upstairs bedroom. The house has indoor plumbing and central heating. In the back yard there are a small vegetable garden and a house for the family dog.

The family usually eat together in the kitchen, although sometimes the children might eat before the parents. There is a dining set in the dining room, but it is hardly ever used. The living room is another place where the family gather. But often the three older children go upstairs to their bedroom to watch television. Sometimes they are sent to their room as punishment. Central heating makes possible this private use of space. When the weather is warm, the children play together on the patio or in the back yard. The parents entertain guests on the patio, in the back yard, on the frontporch, or in the living room. The family take pleasure rides or sometimes go shopping together in the family automobile.

The husband is away from the house more than any other family member. He gets up early to go to work five days a week. Often he will stop off on his way home from work to talk with his male friends among the Mountain People. During warm weather, they gather on the banks of the Ramapo River on the outskirts of town and talk for hours.

The wife is home most of the time, taking care of the children. In the afternoon, she likes to watch soap operas on the television in the children's bedroom upstairs. The older children help take care of the youngest one, who is just learning to walk. The two oldest children attend school. The wife likes to tell how proud she is of one daughter's good grades. On Sundays the wife takes the children to Sunday school at Brook Chapel.

The husband has three brothers and eight sisters. They are all married and have separate households. Four of them live in Hillburn, one in Haskell, New Jersey, near Ringwood. Four of them married within the Mountain People. Six of the rest married blacks. On the Fourth of July and other occasions, the family gather for outdoor barbecues. But there is tension in the family between the Mountain People and the blacks who married into the family. The wife feels that she has never been fully accepted into the family.

In contrast to this family in Hillburn is a Ringwood family. The grandparents live in the Mine Area in a brown shingled company house which they rent for $25 per month. With them live an unmarried son and a granddaughter born out of wedlock to one of the daughters. Down the road in another company house live a married son, his wife, originally from Hillburn, and their daughter. Another son lives in consensual union with a mountain woman and their son in a company house elsewhere in the Mine Area where they have set up a stable household as if they were married. One married daughter lives elsewhere in Ringwood, not in the Mine Area. The grandparents have two other married daughters who live in separate households. There was one other daughter, who died young.

Unlike most of the company houses in the Mine Area, the house in which the grandparents live is one-family. In the yard are a small garden, an outdoor privy, and a small kennel. Steps lead up to a wooden porch and the front door. A side door opens into the kitchen. On the first floor there are the kitchen, the living room, and a bedroom. Upstairs there are bedrooms. The kitchen contains a table and chairs, a new refrigerator-freezer, an old-fashioned, cast-iron, wood-burning range used for cooking and heating the kitchen, and a sink that is not used because the water pipes in the Mine Area often don't work. A granddaughter is sent down the road to bring back potable water in milk bottles. The living room is cluttered with an old sofa, two sagging easy chairs, an inexpensive Danish-modern coffee table, and a television set. On the walls are photographs of the children in the family, and there are knickknacks on shelves. In one corner of the room is a coal-burning, potbellied stove. A pipe leading from the stove through a hole in the ceiling provides the only heat in the upstairs bedrooms.

In the winter the living room and kitchen are kept uncomfortably hot in order to heat the rest of the house. The lack of central heating and of effective insulation cause the house to be drafty. The lack of central heating also results in a greater amount of family interaction than in the middle-class family. Most of the family life takes place in the living room and kitchen. At any one time, the children might be watching television, while a baby is asleep on the sofa, and the adults are engaged in conversation, eating, or playing pinochle in the same room. The noise level in the house tends to be loud. There is little or no privacy. A person is not going to spend more time than is necessary in an unheated bedroom.

Members of the family who live in the Mine Area gather at the grandparents' house several times a week, usually in the evening, to play cards, watch television, or talk. They use affectionate kinship terminology. Adult sons and daughters still call their parents Daddy and Ma. Yet there is a respect for the parents expressed in deference to them in conversation.

The littlest grandson, age two, is called Babe. The grandmother calls him a bird, meaning he is full of mischief. But she says this in an affectionate tone, indicating that his mischieviousness is cute. In conversation, the women of the family say that babies are not forced to be toilet trained, and they are allowed to keep their bottles until they want to give them up. Generally, the child gives up the bottle of his own accord by age three, but some give up their bottles as young as ten months. In a few cases, children are still using a bottle when they begin school, but this is unusual.

The children in this family are allowed much freedom. They are allowed to eat and sleep when they please. They tend to be familiar, affectionate, and even boisterous. They called me by my first name. Parents do insist on certain forms of etiquette. Children are taught to say "Excuse me" when they interrupt a conversation. All members of the family show open affection for the little children. Discipline, when it is administered, tends to be corporal punishment. Adults will not swear in front of the children. On one occasion a man was swearing when a young girl walked within earshot. When he saw that she had overheard him, the man stopped and said, "Oh, excuse me, dear."

The adults in the family are a bit prudish about sex. Although obscene jokes are told, these sessions are never in mixed company. When a woman or child enters the room, a man will stop telling the joke until the woman or child has left. Adults in the family say they are against sex education in the schools because when children learn about sex too young they get into trouble. One woman said she told her daughter never to let a boy "put his hands on any part of your body he has no business touching." Despite these admonitions, early sexual experience is common among teen-agers. But if an illegitimate child results, little or no stigma is attached and the child is accepted into the family. This is a reflection of the strength of the family tie.

Thus, contrary to the stereotype of them, the Ramapo Mountain People have a very strong family and kinship structure. The families have tended to be large, nuclear, and male-headed. The practice of endogamous marriage has multiplied the kinship bonds within the group, rather than diffusing the kinship and integrating the Mountain People into the outside society. Along with race, kinship is one of the main factors in their social solidarity. In a sense, the Ramapo Mountain People are one kinship group.

9 FOLKLORE AS
AN EXPRESSION OF
THE CULTURE

The folklore of the Ramapo Mountain People is an integral part of their culture. It is their own artistic communication.[1] Folklore is traditional, passed from generation to generation by word of mouth or customary example.[2] Folklore is a group expression. Although it is created and performed by individuals, folklore is shaped by many individuals over the years. Thus folklore is more characteristic of the culture of a group than is the work of the atypical artist or writer. Folklore contains tale types and motifs that are international,[3] but folklore functions within the local culture. Tale types and motifs appear in local versions which are placed in a local setting and told about local people.[4] (See Appendix A.)

When I began my field work among the Ramapo Mountain People, I was told that the Mountain People no longer possess any folklore or folksong tradition. I doubted this for several reasons. Folklore usually can be found among people oriented toward oral communication. In the past, illiteracy among the Mountain People had been a factor in the stress on oral, rather than written, communication. In 1850, 65 percent of the adult Mountain People listed in the federal manuscript census could not read or write. Illiteracy among the Ramapo Mountain People has progressively declined since then. In 1880, illiteracy declined to 39 percent, and by 1915 only 9 percent of the adults could not read or write.* [5] Today, although illiteracy has not been

* The 1850 and 1880 federal manuscript censuses contain literacy information for all the settlements of the Mountain People. The 1915 New Jersey state manu-

completely eliminated, most of the Mountain People have at least a grade school education, many have completed high school, and a few have attended college. Nevertheless, folklore is not necessarily limited to illiterate groups. Oral communication continues in any relatively small group in which there are face-to-face relationships.

Today most of the Mountain People, including the poorest of those in Ringwood, have television sets. Before the invention of television, many had radios. These mass media made it more difficult for the folklore to survive. I suspected that it might be difficult to find a folk tradition not at all influenced by mass culture. But did this mean that the folklore had died out completely? I suspected that folklore and mass culture fulfill different needs and that they could exist side by side.

I thought I would most likely encounter their folklore in the most isolated settlement of the Mountain People. So one Sunday afternoon in July 1968 I went to Ringwood for the first time. I drove around on the dirt roads in the Mine Area, past the brown-shingled company houses and the abandoned automobiles. Then I came upon the site of the old mine hole of Peter's mine, which was being used as a dump for the Ford plant in Mahwah. One would never guess that the soggy, sponge-like pit of cardboard trash was actually the entrance to a deep mine shaft with a network of underground levels. A bulldozer was leveling the trash, and a number of Mountain People were standing around, waiting for the trucks to come and dump refuse that the Mountain People would scavenge for copper wiring that could be sold in Paterson. (I later learned that some of the Mountain People in the Mine Area disapprove of those who scavenge rather than work.)

I began to talk with one old man, who was so bent over with arthritis that he appeared to be partially sitting as he leaned on his walking cane. His name was Charles De Freese, but he was generally

script census lists literacy for only Mahwah, Ringwood, and West Milford. The New York State manuscript census for the same year does not contain information on literacy, thus the literacy rate in Hillburn cannot be determined. Since the Hillburn Mountain People had a higher standard of living than the other settlements, the literacy rate in Hillburn was probably even higher than in the other settlements. Thus if the 1915 illiteracy figure of 9 percent were to include Hillburn, it would be even lower. Unfortunately, neither the state nor federal manuscript censuses more recent than 1915 are available, making it impossible to determine present illiteracy among the Mountain People without a door-to-door survey.

known as Uncle Charlie. He said he was in his eighties, but he still retained a trace of the jaunty manner of his youth. In his pocket, he carried a tin can that he used as a spittoon. I asked if there were any people around who told old-time stories. He answered that there used to be. One old man, he said, used to talk for half a day.

While we were talking, a car drove up, and a man and his sons got out. He said his name was Bob Milligan and that he used to work in the mines when they were open. In the course of our conversation, Bob mentioned that his daughter was "born with a veil." I asked him what he meant. He answered that his daughter had a caul or membrane around her when she was born and that this meant she could predict the future. He cited several times when she had indeed predicted the deaths of individuals.

Over the following months, I visited the Mine Area and talked with the people there. One day an old man told several stories for our amusement. One was about the time he had confronted the Devil on the stairs when he came home drunk. On another occasion Bob Milligan and John Morgan, the operator of the bulldozer, mentioned some old-time remedies. We got into a conversation about folk remedies, herb cures, healing, magic, and prediction, which I recorded on a portable cassette tape recorder.

By early winter I was being invited into people's homes. One evening in December 1968 I was introduced to the family of John and Madge Morgan (not the John Morgan who operated the bulldozer). I was taken to their house by their granddaughter, who told me they knew many old-time herb cures. That night the whole family were present: John and Madge, their unmarried son "Mousy," their married sons John Allen and Wally with their wives Barbara and Lois and children. I was offered a cup of coffee, and while I was sipping it, I told them that I was collecting old-time cures. With the tape recorder on, the Morgans began talking about different herb cures. John and Madge did most of the talking, their sons reminding them of others. I didn't have to ask a single question. They proceeded from folk cures to magic to ghost stories to tall tales. This story-telling session went on for two hours.

As my field work progressed, I began collecting folklore from other informants. Wally Morgan introduced me to Frank Milligan, who proved to be one of the best tall-tale tellers I ever encountered. I also collected folklore in Hillburn and Mahwah, but I found that the oral tradition was best preserved in more isolated Ringwood. Whereas the people in Hillburn and Mahwah remember their parents and grandparents using herb cures, for example, the Ringwood people still use them themselves.

There is evidence that years ago there was a large repertory of traditional folk music among the Mountain People. In 1967 Charles Kaufman, a graduate student of ethnomusicology at Columbia University, collected in Hillburn a fragment of the Anglo-American ballad "Bar'bry Allen."

Oh Mamma, Mamma, go make my bed, go make it long and narrow.
Little Jimmy Groves has died for love, and I will die of sorrow.
Oh, Mamma, Mamma, go make my bed, go make it long and narrow.
Little Jimmy Groves has died today, and I will die tomorrow.
Little Jimmy was buried in the old churchyard, and Barb'ry close beside
    him.
And out of his grave grew a red rose, and out of hers a briar.[6]

Fragments from another Anglo-American ballad, locally called "The Butcher Boy from Jersey City," were collected in Hillburn by Anne Lutz, an amateur folklorist from Ramsey, New Jersey.

He courted me through rain and snow,
'Twas when my apron string hung low;
But now my apron's to my chin,
He passes by, but he never looks in.
. . . .
He has another; you know why—
Because she has more gold than I;
Her gold will melt and her silver will fly;
And then she'll be as poor as I.[7]

Kaufman collected several traditional fiddle tunes in Ringwood from Jimmy De Freese, who played a violin—he called a Stradivarius—in the traditional folk manner, holding it against his side, rather than under his chin: "Fisher's Hornpipe" (an Irish reel), "Nigger Wench,"

"Sailor's Hornpipe," "Irish Washerwoman," "Jordan Is a Hard Road to Travel," "Poppa Kicked Me Out of Bed Before I Got My Britches On" (a Scottish reel known as the "Devil's Dream" in the rest of the United States), and "Buck and Wing" (better known as "Turkey in the Straw").[8]

Vince Morgan of Mahwah and Wally De Groat of Hillburn said that years ago some of the old-timers used to have jug bands.

Vince Morgan: Well, my grandfather and them they used to have a little sort of a band. Guitar and—what did they used to?—banjo, and they used to have what they called a "sweet potato whistle"—I don't know what—they have a name for it.
Wally De Groat: Hoccarina.
Vince: Hoccarina. And jugs and they had washboards, you know. They'd put thimbles on their fingers and—talk about rhythm. That's an awful rhythm, ain't it?

Other instruments used in these bands were the Jew's harp, the fiddle, the accordian, and drums made out of hollowed logs. Additional rhythm was supplied by slapping hands against the body.

The folk music of the Mountain People has been less durable than their verbal folklore. Today this traditional folk music has almost disappeared because of a ready substitute in the country and western music performed on the radio and records. Years ago people in Ringwood used to listen to a radio program named "Hometown Frolics." Radio station WJRZ in nearby Hackensack programmed country and western music exclusively.

In the barrooms in Suffern and Mahwah patronized by Mountain People the songs most frequently played on the jukeboxes are country and western. When I lived in Hillburn during 1968–69, Jeannie C. Riley's "Harper Valley PTA" and Johnny Cash's "Folsom Prison Blues" were the two most popular songs. Many of the men play electric guitars, and their repertories consist of country and western songs and hymns learned from records and the radio. Even the gospel music and hymns in the Pentecostal churches in Hillburn and Mahwah are sung in the nasal style of country and western music.

This preference of the Mountain People for country and western music reinforces their racial and cultural self-image. They call this hill-

billy music, and it reflects their identification with southern Appalachian mountain whites. Actually, hillbilly music is only one of many
sources of country and western music. The commercial production
center of this style is in Nashville, Tennessee, but it can be heard
throughout the United States. Country and western music is normally
associated with whites, unlike the blues and soul music associated with
blacks. Thus their musical tastes are related to the fact that the Mountain People do not consider themselves black.

In recent years a new musical preference has been developing
among the younger generation of Mountain People. Teen-agers are
now listening to black soul music. This trend might be attributed to
the Black Pride movement. It appears to herald a developing generation
gap between the adults and their teen-agers, and it might indicate a
future willingness of some of the Mountain People to accept a black
identity.

The appeal of country and western music and the folk songs that
preceded it is more than simple racial and cultural identification. The
sentimental themes in the lyrics strike a deep sympathetic cord with
the Mountain People. Take, for example, the following folk song sung
by Sealey Morgan of Ringwood.

Dad was a dutiful father,
He always thought of home.
While we'd eat meat with each other,
Wrastle with an old ham-bone.

Now, people would ask where Daddy
Got crippled on the way.
Then I'd just say, "If you want your back bent,
Just try and carry Daddy's load."

Oh, the load that Daddy carried
Made him bend so low.
Since the night that Daddy got married
He's been always on the go.

We watch him in the evening
Come scrubbling [?] down the street.
When all of us kids would shout, "Hey, Ma!

Here's Dad with his motor car."
Yodel-layee, Odel-layee, Odel-layee.

This song about a hard-working, dutiful father can be viewed in terms of the respectful yet affectionate attitude toward their fathers by mountain children. The attitude toward mothers is similarly expressed in song. The country and western song "God Walks These Hills With Me," sung for me by Wally De Groat, reflects strong feeling for the Ramapo Mountains.

We all have treasures we call our own.
Mine are these hills, I call my home.
Just let me live till eternity,
In these hills God walks with me.

Yes, he walks these hills,
These beautiful hills,
Where my soul is always free.
What a comfort to know
I'm never alone.
'Cause God walks these hills with me.
Yes, God walks these hills with me.*

If you were to go to one of the colored bars in Suffern or Mahwah, not only would you hear country and western music, but you might also see one of the Mountain People dancing a type of shuffling tap dance in which the upper part of the body is kept loose and the arms are left to swing freely. This is what the Mountain People call buck-and-wing dancing or simply buck dancing. Vince Morgan and Wally De Groat maintain that this style of dancing comes from the American Indians.

Cohen: Why do they call that buck-and-wing dancing?
Vince Morgan: I think it comes back to the Indian days, like bucks with the Indians. You know. Bucks. And it's more or less like a tribal dance.
Wally De Groat: They used to fashion wings out of feathers and strap them to their arms, and, ah, that's where I got it from. And that's where it got the name buck-and-wing dance, because the old miners used to do that.

They got it from the Indians. From the Indian tribes they got that dance.
Cohen: So it's not a hillbilly dance?
Wally: Anything I ever heard about it was derived from the Indians. And
there was buck-and-rain dances and all that stuff. And they used to fashion
wings from feathers and strap them to their arms and they would flap these
wings while they were dancing. They'd call it buck-and-wing dancing.
Vince: They'd slap their legs—slap their legs, you know. They'd go all
around the circle first just shuffling their feet. Then the first thing you
know, they'd stop. When they stopped, boy, then they'd start real dancing.
Them old-timers they all slapped their legs.

This folk etymology demonstrates the identification of the Mountain
People with American Indians. However, this derivation of the dance
is unlikely. The movements in buck-and-wing dancing are not at all
similar to the dances of the North American Indians.

The terms *buck-and-wing* and *buck dancing* can be traced back
to Lancashire, England, where they are used to refer to step dancing
in clogs, a kind of shoe with a thick sole worn by miners and weavers
in the cotton mills.* This style of dancing is similar to Scottish step
dancing and Irish jigs. The Scotch-Irish (Presbyterian Scots who resettled in northern Ireland in the early seventeenth century) brought
this dancing tradition to the southern Appalachian Mountains, where
it became the basis for American square dancing. Irish immigration in
the nineteenth century reinforced the tradition. Buck-and-wing dancing
was performed in minstrel shows and vaudeville, where the English,
Irish, and Scottish traditions merged with the buck-and-shuffle style
of American blacks with the addition of a more syncopated rhythm.[9]
The buck-and-wing dancing of the Ramapo Mountain People is one
evidence of their similarity to southern Appalachian Mountain whites.

* "The etymology of 'Buck' and 'Wing' is not clear. Maybe they are descrip-
tive by comparison with the movements of a horse, 'wing' meaning to kick out
sideways, also 'buck' knees are inclined inward. Note also 'winge' (with a soft 'g')
meaning to shrink or draw in, applied to a 'horse . . . when about to strike.'
'Wang' on the other hand, according to *Tum O' Dick O' Bob's Lankisher Dick-
shonary* (n.d., but after 1873), is equivalent to 'bang,' which brings us to 'buck-
thwang, buckwang, buckfang,' given in Taylor's *Folkspeech of South Lancashire*
(1901), 'a form of punishment inflicted by schoolboys who hold their victim by
the hands and feet and swing him against a wall.' 'Whang' can also mean a shoe-
lace, being derived from the Anglo-Saxon 'pwang = a thong.'" (Julian Pilling,
"Buck and Wing; Notes on Lancashire Clog Dancing," *English Dance and Song*
23, no. 1 [January 1959]:25.)

Previous observers of the Mountain People have noted a peculiar, unknown folk speech. The reporter for *Appleton's Journal* who visited the Ramapo Mountains in 1872 described it as follows:

There has developed among them a *patois* of singular character, and the ear is so outraged by uncouth utterances, that one readily believes himself fallen among madmen. There is little gesticulation. When a man speaks, he lowers his head, and drawls his words with a guttural sound, and delivers his sentences in so strange an idiom that one must guess his meaning and be content. A distinct syllable is not to be heard. Their speech is a succession of make-shifts. Their scant ideas are expressed by methods still more scant, and so awkwardly do they mouth their words that the ear grows weary and impatient.[10]

This *patois* that so "outraged" the *Appleton* reporter was shown in 1910 by Professor John Dyneley Prince to be a variant of Jersey Dutch.[11] One of Professor Prince's main informants was William De Freece (age seventy-five in 1910), a laborer on the Abram Hewitt estate in Ringwood. Prince described Mr. De Freece as "an excellent authority on the negro variant of the dialect"; and those whites in Bergen County who still spoke Jersey Dutch

characterized many of his [Mr. De Freece's] words as distinctly "nigger," an interesting circumstance showing that the negro slaves of the old settlers used an idiom tinged with their own peculiarities. There is a small colony of old negroes living on the mountain back of Suffern, N.Y., who still use their own dialect of Jersey Dutch, but they are very difficult of access, owing to their shyness of strangers.[12]

Although Prince was wrong about the ancestry of the Mountain People, he did prove that they had their own variant of Jersey Dutch, known as *nêxer däuts* (Negro Dutch) by his white informants. Prince's description of Jersey Dutch as characterized by "curious jerky intonation, unclear diction, and [a] marked singsong tone of voice"[13] helps explain the misconceptions of the *Appleton* reporter.*

* Jersey Dutch should not be confused with Pennsylvania Dutch, which is not Dutch, but a dialect of German. According to Professor Prince, "Jersey Dutch was originally the South Holland or Flemish language, which, in the course of centuries (ca. 1630–1880), became mixed with and partially influenced by English,

Professor Prince collected from William De Freece the following charm in the form of a riddle:

Negro Charm

Altāit än zômer	Always in summer
Stât de zûve bôme	stand the seven trees;
äske'n äike än al de	ash and oak and all along
lāng vôrbāi	past they cannot proceed.
Kän nît rolle;	What are they standing on?
wāt er opstât	

William De Freece, who gave me this rather incomprehensible charm says that the seven trees symbolize the seven stars (qv. the planets?), and that they seem to be standing on nothing. They, therefore, cannot go along. Then follows the query, as to what they are standing on. I am inclined to doubt the accuracy of De Freece's text, and prefer to read *kän nît rāde wāt er opstât,* "I cannot guess what they are standing on," which makes sense of the text at least. De Freece regards this as an excellent cure for rheumatism.[14]

Appendix C contains a list of Jersey Dutch words and phrases collected from William De Freece and a pronunciation guide.

Today the Jersey Dutch dialect is no longer spoken as such by the Ramapo Mountain People. Survivals of this dialect, however, still exist in their speech. In many cases those who use these words and expressions are unaware that they are Jersey Dutch and not English. One Jersey Dutch expression still common is "I'm *feest* of it," which means "I'm disgusted by it" or "I find it obnoxious or dirty." * Several Mountain People remember their grandparents using foreign expressions.

having borrowed also from Minsi (Lenape-Delaware) Indian language a few animal and plant names." (*Dialect Notes* 3, pt. 6 [1910]: 459.)

Jersey Dutch differed significantly from Holland Dutch. Prince noted that those who spoke Jersey Dutch said that "our language is low Dutch and theirs is Holland Dutch; quite different." (Ibid.) He added that an intelligent Fleming or South Hollander with a knowledge of English could understand Jersey Dutch but that those who spoke Jersey Dutch couldn't understand Holland Dutch. According to L. G. Van Loon, another variant known as Mohawk-Hudson Dutch developed farther north in upstate New York. (*Crumbs from an Old Dutch Closet* [The Hague: Marinus Nijhoff, 1938], pp. 46–47.)

* This appears in a word list of Jersey Dutch, listed as *feest,* meaning "stomach disgust." (James B. H. Storms, *A Jersey Dutch Vocabulary* [Park Ridge, N.J.: Pascack Historical Society, 1964], n.p.)

One woman in Hillburn remembers her grandfather saying, "*dause* the *glim*," meaning "dim the light," which is not Jersey Dutch, but Gaelic.* Another woman in Hillburn remembers the use of the words *häuze* and its plural *häuzen* to mean house.† A man who lives behind the Hoevenkopf remembers his grandfather James De Groat using the expression "*Gehst du hein*," meaning "Go home," ‡ *hunt* meaning "dog," § and *heit* meaning "hot." ||

One reason for the survival of the Jersey Dutch dialect among the Mountain People is the isolation of the Ramapo Mountains. The survival of older forms of language in isolated regions is a well-documented phenomenon. For example, the syntax and some expressions of old, early, and Elizabethan English have been found in the southern Appalachian Mountains.[15] The main significance of the Jersey Dutch dialect for the Ramapo Mountain People, however, is that it corroborates linguistically what we have already seen genealogically—that the Mountain People are the descendants of the Dutch rather than of Hessians.

For an analysis of the overall speech pattern of the Mountain People, a sample tape was sent to Professor Raven I. McDavid of the University of Chicago and some of his colleagues who responded:

> As far as we can determine, there is no evidence of any Southern influence in grammar, phonology, supra-segmentals, or paralanguage. Al Davis said that it seemed "old fashioned Inland Northern." My own feelings are that it is very much like the older generation rural speech of Upstate New York and Southern Michigan. These conclusions, of course, are more or less what we would expect, in Rockland and Bergen counties. But it is interesting that even the isolation of the group isn't enough to set off their speech patterns.[16]

* "*Glim*, sb. [substantive] and v. [verb]. In gen. [general] dialect in Sc. [Scotland] and Eng. [England]. 1. sb. [substantive] A candle, lantern; a fire or light of any kind; the eye. Sc. [Scotland] Ware Hawk! Douse the glim! Scott, *Guy M.* (1815) iii," (Joseph Wright, ed., *The English Dialect Dictionary* [London: Henry Frowde, 1900], p. 643.)

† The Holland Dutch is *huis*, pl. *huizen*. (Prince, p. 475.)

‡ This expression appears to be closer to German than Dutch. The Jersey Dutch imperative for "go" is *xân*, and for "home" is *täus*. (Prince, *Dialect Notes* 3, pt. 6 [1910]:474, 475.)

§ The Jersey Dutch pronunciation was *hont*, and the Holland Dutch pronunciation was *hond*. (Ibid.)

|| Prince lists this word as Jersey Dutch. The Holland Dutch word is *heet*. (Ibid.)

The Mountain People have a strong affection for the Ramapo Mountains. This emotional tie to the mountains as their home has helped to preserve their group identity and to help prevent their dispersal. It is not surprising that this strong sense of place should be expressed in their folklore.

Place-names reflect the various cultural overlays in the region. The Indian occupation is reflected in such names as *Ramapo* (slanting rock), *Hackensack* (hook mouth of a river), *Mahwah* (meeting place or assembly), and *Wanaque* (place where the sassafras grows).[17] The Dutch also left an influence on the place-names. The peak at the entrance to the Ramapo Pass is known as the *Hoevenkopf* (high head) Mountain. The Tappan *Zee* (sea) refers to the widening of the Hudson River near Nyack. High Torne Mountain in the Ramapo Pass (not to be confused with High Tor near the Hudson River) takes its name from the Jersey Dutch word *torn*, meaning steeple or peak. Smith's Clove is derived from the Dutch word *kloof*, meaning gap.[18] And the residence of the colored Mountain People in the Ramapos since the early nineteenth century is reflected in the fact that old maps show one of the mountain lakes named Nigger Pond.

A myth or legend sometimes explains a place-name. In the mountains there is a rocky place known as "where the devil broke his apron strings." Vince Morgan told me the following myth associated with that place:

Cohen: We were talking the other day about a place back in the mountains called "where the devil broke his apron string."
Vince Morgan: Oh, that's up near the Cranberry [pond].
Cohen: Ever heard the story that goes along with that [name]?
Vince: The story was—like the Devil had a lot of rocks—oh, 'bout this big around, some smaller and bigger. But it was just one big rocky mess. And they claim the Devil was going through there with these rocks in his apron. Then something happened, and the string broke, and he spilled all those rocks there. And they claim that's where the Devil broke his apron string.

There is also a place-name legend from the Revolutionary War period about a military road through the mountains named the Cannon Ball Road. Otto Mann gave the following account of the legend.

Otto Mann: Well, the Cannon Ball Road, which used to go up over the top of the High Mountain, was put—as I've been told—there by the American troops to stop the British from going up these valleys, and they used to transport those cannons by horses or mules or whatever, and those roads went over these Jersey Mountains, and so into New York State up around —near Sloatsburg, and that's—. In fact, in Hillburn, they tell us—that was— they had one of the battle grounds. In fact, there is some old graves— cemetery—there's an old cemetery up there yet that has some of these grave markers.

In his book *Vanishing Ironworks of the Ramapos,* James Ransom reconstructed the route of the Cannon Ball Road.[19]

When Fred ("Snoozy") Powell from Hillburn talks about the Ramapo Mountains, he gets so enthusiastic that he slips into tall-tale exaggerations.

Snoozy Powell: But anybody that would ever want to see the beautiful terrain that the Lord has put here on earth, they got to come to Hillburn. Everybody calls it a little piece of town. But you come to Hillburn, and I'll be your guide. I'll show you everything that Hillburn offers. And that's the prettiest thing you ever seen in your life.
Cohen: There's a real feeling for the hills here, isn't there?
Snoozy: Definitely. We was born here . . . Well, you walk these hills, and I'll guarantee you, when you come down, regardless where you come out—you come out in Suffern, Sloatsburg, Ramapo, Tuxedo, or even Harriman—you've walked a good distance, 'cause everything you've seen was experienced. Everything. You'll see turtles walking around that you wouldn't believe. You'll see mosquitoes with buck teeth. You got owls that look at you and smile at you right away. They're right here 'cause the Lord put 'em here. But everything you see from the time you leave Hillburn 'til the time you get to Tuxedo Park, you'll see every kind of animal—other than what I'm talking about, like piranha fish and things of that nature— alligators and things like that—that's down the road. That's down South. You'll see all that here, and this 'll be the prettiest country you ever walked through.

Snoozy demonstrates how pride in the Ramapos can take the form of exaggerated stories about the animal life found there. The same is true about this tall tale about a squirrel that used lightning to open nuts.

Frank Milligan: They used to tell years ago, you know, when we were kids, they tell that this red squirrel—and none of us kids could figure how a red squirrel, you know, that old—'cause generally they're long and slim—he was so old his teeth were all broken off, so naturally, he couldn't crack a nut, but how he could stay so fat. We were asking, and we said, "Now how can that red squirrel eat with no teeth?"

"Well, he eats nuts."

We said, "Well, how's he gonna crack it?"

[He] Said, "Well, anybody knows that."

We said, "How?"

"Well," he said, "he gathers all them nuts up, you know, in the fall, and then he hibernates, and he don't eat. Then just as soon as summertime comes—the lightning—he'll take them bunch of nuts, and he climb up. He picks a nice dry tree. And every time the lightning crack and split the tree, he shove a nut in, and crack it, and take it back out." And he said, "Yup, and that's how he was—get—you know, stay fat."

When the lightning would crack that would split it. He would shove the nut in, crack it, and take it right out, 'cause they're awful fast, you know.

Some of the Mountain People consider these tall tales outright lies because they are told with a straight face and the teller will swear that they're true. But they express a playful exuberance about the mountains in the spirit of the hoax.

The Ramapo Mountains are the natural habitat of many kinds of snakes, including the rattlesnake and copperhead. Snakes are an everyday fact of life for the Mountain People. Some of the people used to catch rattlesnakes and sell them to zoos and pharmaceutical companies. Snakes are a frequent topic of conversation, and some of this talk contains the traditional motifs of the tall tale.

Vince Morgan says that his mother told him that as a baby he shared his food with a copperhead.

Cohen: Someone was saying that a snake would never bite a baby.

Vince Morgan: That's true. When I was a baby—just crawling—creeping around, and our neighbor she used to—our neighbor used to live up on a hill above us at the foot of the mountain, so I used—my mother used to tell me—every day I'd crawl up to our neighbor's house, you know, and I'd be sitting out there talking to something. And, ah, they always used to give me a biscuit or something to eat, and I'd be up there talking to something.

So this lady up there by the name of Mrs. Caldwell, she stood on the porch and happened to see this big copperhead in my—you see, in them days we used to wear dresses, you know, babies—big dresses, you know—and that snake lay right in my lap. And I was feeding it copper crumbs—uh, you know, biscuit crumbs.

So she hollered for my mother. And my mother come up there and she was afraid to touch me—afraid the snake would bite me. So they had to stand right there, 'til that snake—I filled it up and he went on back into his hole. And she grabbed me by the end of my shirt tail, she said, and drug me back to the house. Didn't let me go up there again.

Mrs. Morgan (Vince's wife): She told me then she knew why he went to that spot. He must have been feeding that day after day.

Cohen: Why is it that a snake won't hurt a baby?

Wally De Groat: You can't answer that. I can't answer that. Like they say, God takes care of fools and babies.

Madge Morgan (not related to Vince) in Ringwood tells a similar story about a black snake that lapped up a baby's milk. "Snake eats milk and bread with child" is an international folktale motif collected in Germany and Denmark.[20]

Many of the snakelore tall tales are about imaginary snakes.

Snoozy Powell: A hoop snake will put his tail in his mouth and he'll roll down the road behind you. And you stop short, he'll drop his tail and go the opposite direction. As soon as you go the opposite, like you're running again, he'll chase you again. And he'll pass you and he won't bite you, and he won't hurt you.

Cohen: Have you ever seen one?

Snoozy: Yes, I've seen one.

Another imaginary snake is the crown snake.

John Morgan: Yeah, they throw their crown. But you can't get it. Once they throwed their crown that's the end of them. They die. They die. They go off and die. Yeah, that happened right down here by the old school teacher's.

Cohen: What kind of crown is that?

John: It's a—like an ordinary crown. You've seen the crown from these—high people in foreign country, you know what kind I'm—

Cohen: With jewels on it or something like that?

John: Yeah. Yeah. . . . That's worth money. They're worth millions of dollars . . . That's the king of snakes.

The joint snake was explained by Vince Morgan.

Vince Morgan: They used to talk about a snake—a joint snake, too. You'd see a head over here, a part of a body here, part of a body there. They said then when you come up by him, they'd jump right together and come after you. A joint snake.

Snoozy Powell told the following story about a joint snake.

Snoozy Powell: I know this old man that lives down in Mahwah and he's told me a lot of stories. His name is "Rabbit Nose" Bill. He told me about this big snake that he'd seen going to the Nigger Pond. This snake was so long—it was across the road—he took his hatchet out, and he cut the snake's head off. He cut it down the center. When he got finished cutting that snake, both ends crawled away and both ends had heads on 'em. And that's the truth. I don't know who's gonna hear this, but that's the blessed truth.

The joint-snake motif was being told in America as early as 1737.[21]

Finally, there is the racing snake or the blue racer, as it is known elsewhere.

Snoozy Powell: Now this is the God's honest truth. I seen this. I seen this with my own blessed eyes. I was standing with Pop Peterson—I was standing with my grandfather, Bill Peterson's father—Pop Peterson—and I was standing with my Uncle Eddie, before he died—as a matter of fact he died while I was in the army. He told me to go out and burn the papers, and I went out to the dump there. You burn the papers and beyond that was the well—spring. So I went out to get the water for grandma, too, at the same time. And I stepped on this snake. He was about six foot long. I stepped on his tail. That snake raised up on its tail and then started running. And I seen that myself. No old man told me. This snake started running back towards the house. This snake raised up on its tail, it's whole body extended into the air, and that snake chased me all the way from the spring back to the house. When I got to the house, my Uncle Eddie come out of the door, seen the snake behind me, and what he doed was stamp his foot and the snake laid right down and curled up, and he started chasing the snake, and the snake got in the same position and run in the opposite direction. Now what kind of snake that was I don't know. But it was a black snake—long, skinny—and it had a ring around its neck. But it chased me good. I'll say about three hundred yards. Had a yellow ring around its neck and it chased me on its tail.
Bill Peterson: A racing snake.

Despite the avowals that these snakes actually exist, these stories contain international folktale motifs adapted by the Mountain People and localized to the Ramapo Mountains.

Hunting, trapping, and fishing were at one time essential food-providing activities in the economy of the Mountain People; today they are primarily sports. Although trapping is not as common as it used to be, most of the men own a fishing rod, a shotgun, and a hunting dog. The opening of the fishing and hunting seasons are important dates on their calendars. The seasonal change is anticipated by such activities as "running the dogs."

Wally Morgan: Like say, you have a hunting dog, and even though you buy a dog that you know he hunts, well, you don't even have to take him out, you know. Well, every year we get together. This time of year [August] we get—our lives change, you know. And you want to run your dog. You get him used to running. His feet harden up. His body—his muscles start tightening up. He's working. And this is what we call running the dog. You taking him out and letting him run rabbits, and getting him warmed up for when the season starts. See? This is what we do . . . You take your dogs out. Like if you got a rabbit dog, you see your dog bring 'em to. "Well, he's working good. He's gonna be ready for the coming season, you know." And if you got a squirrel dog or a coon dog—It's like buying a dog, you get a free trial. Only thing, we've got the dog, and we just take as long as we want. And this is what we—testing the dog, breaking him, working with him.

Frank Milligan: See, now, I like that, and I like to trap too. See, now, just as soon as the weather changes—like last night—right away I get my traps out. I'll boil them and wax them. You gotta hang them in the tree so no human odor is on them, you know. And I'll start to get my tip-ups out to get ready for the ice fishing season. 'Cause I'm not a summertime fisher. I like it when the ice—when that ice gets on that pond, that's when if you want me you gotta make an appointment. And it gotta be before six in the morning and after nine at night, because other than that, that appointment will have to be kept on the ice.

With such intense enthusiasm for hunting and fishing, it is not surprising that they are common subjects in the folklore.

Frank Milligan is one of the best hunting and fishing tall-tale tellers. He says he learned these tales from the old-timers. Many of these tales follow common folklore motifs, such as this one about an extremely dedicated hunting dog.

Wally Morgan: Frank, who was the one that had the dog there that was running a rabbit?

Frank Milligan: Oh, that. That was old Zike De Groat. See, he said his dog he was a real good dog. I mean, it was a fox dog. It would run a fox, but it would run anything, see. And he hadn't been running the rabbit lately, you know, so he took him out rabbit hunting, 'cause, you know, when a fox he gets going straight off. A rabbit gets dodging in and out, so it kind of fooled him. And he got behind that rabbit and he was just about ready to snap him, and the rabbit dove behind a tree. Well, he made the turn so fast, he hit the tree, and it split him right in half. Of course, Zike, he said he was right behind him, and he picked up the two halves and slapped them together. But he slapped two legs up and two legs down, and, he said, "Do you know, that dog run until he got tired on two legs, flip over, and run on the other two, 'til he run that rabbit right down."

This is one of the most common tall-tale motifs. It has been collected in England, Canada, and throughout the United States. It has been told about both Paul Bunyan and Baron Munchausen.[22] It has been traced back as early as 1808 in an American jestbook.[23] Yet in this version, the tale is localized and told about one of the Mountain People.

Frank Milligan told another tall tale about an extraordinarily smart hunting dog.

Frank Milligan: He [Zike De Groat] said—you know, this dog was really a smart dog, too. He said, "He was so smart, you couldn't fool him." So one night, he said to his wife—it was snowing out, about two feet of snow out. The dog wanted to go hunting. He said, "I'm going to fool him," he said, "Watch."
The old dog lay in front of the fire place.
"Well," he said, "I think I'm going up to Greenwood Lake and do a little fishing."
He said the old dog got up and disappeared. So he grabbed the shot gun. Figured he'd put his hunting coat on. That way he'd fool the dog.
He said, "Do you know when I went out that door, you know what that dog was doing?"
I said, "No, I have no idea."
"Out there by the toilet he was digging worms!"

Huckleberry picking in the Ramapos is a common activity for the Mountain People, especially the youngsters. In the following tall tale it is assumed you know that huckleberry picking is a summertime activity.

Frank Milligan: You know, the guys tell us, one time, years ago, one of the boys went out. He wanted to pick some huckleberries, you know. His mother was gonna make some huckleberry pie. Well, they says, he goes out with a water pail. Get up right here in the mountains, and starts picking. He had his pail just about full, and this bear looks up over the huckleberry bush right in his face.

Well, he took off. Started to run. He run over these mountains, up over the Ramapos, cross the Ramapo River on out, you know, went on up over the other range out here towards the Delaware, and finally he come to this big lake. Well, when he got there, he put his ice skates on, and he skated right across.

That boy said, "Now wait a minute. He was picking huckleberries. How could you be skating?"

"Oh," he said, "I forgot to tell you. That bear run me from July to January!"

The motif of a bear chasing a man from summer to winter has been collected elsewhere,[24] but this tale is localized with references to local place-names and the activity of huckleberry picking.

Vince Morgan tells a tall tale he heard from his grandfather about a man who mistook a turtle for a rock.

Vince Morgan: One of these old fellas down here—my grandfather used to tell me—ah, they called him George Diamond. Like up at Greenwood Lake, he used to tell some awful tall tales. He told me he was up there fishing, you know. And the fish wasn't biting very good. So he saw this big rock, oh, about three foot out in the lake. So he jumped on the rock and started to fish. He said the first thing he know he was out in the middle of the lake. He happened to look down. He was on a big turtle's back.

In the *Walam Olum*, the creation myth of the Delaware Indians, there is mention of a great flood from which the Indians escape by seeking refuge on the back of a turtle.[25] But the motif "Man thinks big turtle in river is an island, goes to sleep on its back, wakes up miles from starting point" has also been collected from the mountaineers in the Ozarks and lumberjacks in Michigan.[26]

Bragging plays an important part in the tall tales. In a sense, these tales are bragging carried to an extreme. Sometimes the story-telling sessions become a kind of semihumorous competition. It is significant that this competition is expressed in terms of physical skill, strength, or agility. The men pride themselves on both their real and imaginary accomplishments in hunting and fishing.

In the following tall tale, two men brag about the ranges of their hunting guns.

Frank Milligan: Today they have shot guns, you know, and they, you know —the guys get out and talking about them.

Well, some guy said, "Well, I shot—I shot a squirrel out of a tree a hundred yards away."

And another guy said, "Well, the other day I was out a hunting with my muzzle-loader, and I seen a rabbit, and he went back across the Beech place field," he said, "and so the further he run, you know, I figure, the sooner"— you know a rabbit always turns—"so I kept loading the powder and loading the powder and loading the powder, so finally when he turned, I figured I had enough. I'd load that—put the shot in. I shot him about half a mile away."

The other guy said, "Well, that gun you got don't shoot at all. Well," he said, "my gun—I—when I load it," he said, "there when I go rabbit hunting like that, I load that gun," he said, "always when I put the powder and then the shot, I always put salt."

I said, "What the heck is the salt for?"

He said, "I can shoot it so far away, I put the salt in so when I—er— when I kill him, it'll give me time to walk up to him so it won't spoil!"

The bragging in the next tale concerns a very lucky shot.

Frank Milligan: But now, you take Uncle Roy had the gun—remember?— when he was a boy. Now grandpop told him, you know, 'cause he wanted a box of thirty-two, twenties. He told Roy, "If you go out and you get me some pigeons, I'll buy you a box."

So he figures, "Shucks! Now how you going to get any pigeons"—you know, wild pigeons—"with one bullet?"

That's all he had. One bullet. So, he said, he go out there and he sat there, sat there, and sat there, and figuring over there by Mine Pond, he said, it was. Figuring, "Now how am I going to get a mess of pigeons with one bullet?"

He can't—he can't figure it out. After a while, he said, he looked down in the water and the old dog was pointing, and there was a big pickerel.

"Boy, oh boy!" he said now.

He wanted to shoot the pickerel with that one bullet, and then he looked up and there was a mess of pigeons setting on a dead limb. Now he figured, boy, he didn't know what to do.

Finally, he said, "Well." He'd take a chance. So he turned his back to the water, aimed at the limb, shot, split the limb, caught all the pigeons by the toes, they fell in the water, and he come up with that doggone pickerel!

That tall tale fits the international tale type, "shot splits tree limb, bird's feet caught in the crack, and other lucky accidents bring much game." [27]

In the fish stories the bragging reaches its apex.

Frank Milligan: We were all together, talking about fishing. And the guys up there were saying the size of the fish they got.

And one guy said, "Oh, I got one the other day six pounds."

Another got one bigger.

I said, "Let me tell you a story about the one I got." I said, "We were on Greenwood Lake the other day, fishing. Up went the flag on the pickup. I run over, pulled it up, and couldn't get him through the ice. So we got a couple of axes and saws and we got quite a hole there. Finally, we got the fish through the ice. And that fish was so big we couldn't get a scale big enough to weigh it. So we took a picture of him, and the picture was nine doggone pounds! And that's the truth," he said, " 'cause if you don't believe it, my boys are right over right now shingling the house with the scales!"

This tale contains two motifs, "Fish is photographed because it is too big to weigh" and "Scales of big fish are used for shingles, provide new roof for every house in the valley," both previously collected in the Ozarks.[28]

John Morgan remembers one tale that Frank Milligan's father used to tell about how far he could cast a fishing line.

John Morgan: Yes, Frank's father told us that he had a fish line one time. He was gonna broadcast to show the kids how to cast out down from Riverdale. He cast it out. His line went down to the Great Notch [approximately 20 miles away]. It hooked fast, and he sent one of the boys down on the train to unhook it for him.

Closely related to the tall tales are hero legends, celebrating great feats of strength or agility performed by individual men. These legends have become exaggerated over the years and contain international folk-tale motifs, but the tale teller will swear that these feats were actually performed by the individual. These men have become culture heroes, and the legends express the ideal-type male personality traits valued by the Mountain People.*

Snoozy Powell told me three stories about the remarkable speed of Ted Dunk.

Snoozy Powell: Old Ted Dunk was the faster man ever come around here, other than my grandfather, Pop Peterson. Ted Dunk seen a rattlesnake going cross the road. He got out of the car, and he took his foot and laid it on the ground. And that snake crawled across his foot. A rattlesnake. He kicked that snake straight up in the air, and before the snake hit the ground, he had his knife out and he cut the snake's head off. And that is the truth.

Now another one. Same man. Ted Dunk. The rattlesnake was crawled up, ready to strike. And Ted got on his hands and knees, and faced that snake, nose to nose. The snake was ready to strike. He slapped that snake with his left hand, which he was a right-handed man. He slapped that snake twice along side his head with his hand, and got away before that snake had a chance to strike. That was the fastest man that ever came into Hillburn. And he died at the age of a hundred and six years old. He was in the Spanish-American War, and he was a good man right up until the day he died.

And he could get in the barrel, and jump out of that—stand in the barrel up to his waist, and jump out of that barrel and back in that barrel with never touching the sides.

While Old Ted Dunk was known for his speed, most of the hero legends deal with extraordinary strength. John and Madge Morgan and their family sat at home one evening and talked about the strength of Old Raymond ("Bub") De Freese.

John Morgan: I seen him—I seen him buried under thirty-eight hundred pounds of cement, and when they dug into him, he stood. He held it on his back. When he stood, they got to him, he stood just the way he was holding that cement all along on his knees.
Madge Morgan (his wife): Raymond De Freese.
John: Old "Bub" De Freese. Right up here. Thirty-eight hundred tumbled down [garbled]

* Social psychologists distinguish between ideal-type personality, which embodies all the socially approved character traits, and modal personality, which embodies the most frequently occurring personality traits in the society. (Alex Inkeles and Daniel L. Levinson, "National Character: The Study of Modal Personality and Socio-cultural Systems," in *Handbook of Social Psychology*, ed. Gardner Lindzey [Reading, Mass.: Addison-Wesley, 1954], pp. 977–1020.)

Madge: It didn't hurt him.

John: When they got into him, they said, "Bub, you hurt?"

"No, no. No," he said, "I ain't hurt a bit."

Wally Morgan (their son): He was powerful.

John: Ho. Ho. Good job that he, you know, didn't want to fight or nothing . . . But would take a—he'd take one of these two by sixes [garbled] He wouldn't draw back. He just took—just like that—and snap that, boy, and it'd plunk right into a can.

The most legendary strong man of all was Uncle Rob Milligan, who used to work in the Ringwood mines. There is a whole cycle of tales about Uncle Rob's feats of strength. The Morgan family spoke about him. They said that Uncle Rob never swore. Instead he would say, "Thunder and lightning."

John Morgan: Well, one time. Tell you what happened to my brother and him. One time they rode over to Sterling. And, ah, he had the car. And they got to this curve, and this car keep—was coming right in the face. Well, Uncle was nervous. So it—he turned off the road. His car jumped out on this big flat rock, right off the road. Well, he was—he was stuck. That's all.

So he said to my brother. My brother says, "How'd we going to get out?"

Uncle Rob always sniffed like that. He says, "Never mind. We'll get out."

He walked around. He grabbed the front of that car—he grabbed the front of that car and he throwed that off the rock. He went around to the rear, and he tossed that around. He went around to the front, and he tossed that car back and forth 'til it got out on the road. That shows how strong that man was.

And right down here—this mine hole—I heard my father and them say —they was there—that they snugged him [Uncle Rob] fast with a rope around his body to a tree until he reached down and pulled a mule up out of that mine hole down here, right by the halter. Yes.

Cohen: How big was he?

John: Oh, he was—he was a regular giant. I don't know. He must of been pretty near eight feet tall. Yeah. He was three feet or more across the shoulder. He was! He couldn't get in the door without—when he coming through an ordinary door, he had to—he had to bend down to walk through the door.

Madge: He must have been seven feet tall.

John: He was that big. He could take—I've seen him working in the mines. I know this is true. I've seen him from the mines, when the boys would be

tightening up pipes—I've seen him take one hand on the pipe and tighten it. Two men would get on one of them long wrenches and couldn't move it, and they had to put a pipe on the end of the wrench to break it loose. See. That's how powerful he was. A car was nothing. He lifted his own car up with one hand, and set a jack under it with the other. Just like he set that [garbled] and lay it on that little table. Yeap. He was a regular giant.
Cohen: How did he finally die?
Madge: His car run off the road up there. He—he was going up to Hewitt. His car run off in the snow bank. He was all alone, and he went to lift the car out of the ditch, and they think that he musta—put—taking all that weight to just lift the car up on the road—that it musta put him in cerebral hemorrhage to him.
John: Yeah.
Madge: He—he went right in the coma, like, and he never came out of it. He musta bursted a vein of some kind.

This conversation contains several motifs common in strong man and hero legends, such as "Strong hero lifts cart" and "Strong man lifts horse (ox, ass)." [29] In the heroic legend formula, the death of the strong man is usually in connection with some extraordinary circumstance. For example, the Maine coast fisherman-strong man Barney Beal supposedly died from straining the muscles around his heart when he hauled a dory from Pond Island. [30]

The Morgans mentioned two other incidents about Uncle Rob: the time he killed a horse with a blow from his fist and the time he pulled a horse back on its rear by the reins.

Wally Morgan: Dad, wasn't Uncle Rob that—er, killed that horse by dragging him or something? Or a mule or something with his fist?
Madge: Yeah. He dragged it off the ice.
Mousy (another son): He killed that one horse with his fist.
Barbara (daughter-in-law) (doubting): Oh.
Madeline (granddaughter): (laughs)
John: Yeah. But it was his neck. He broke his neck. Hit him and broke his neck. Yeah.
Wally: That was the same one. Tell him, daddy.
John: The horse got balky. He pet him down. I seen him that night. I know. That's—you're taking it down [on the tape recorder]. I'll tell you what I seen him do. He had a black mare off the racing track. I seen him with the reins [garbled] and set her right back on her honkey. Set her right back on her honkey. That's how powerful he was.

Mousy: What did he break her neck with—his fist, **right?**
John: Oh, yes. Hit him with his fist.

Jimmy De Freese, John's brother-in-law, tells the story differently. According to him, Uncle Rob broke the reins.

Cohen: I think you told me another story about Uncle Rob? Remember that?
Jimmy De Freese: Oh, ah—pulled the lines in two on his mules. Yes. Started to run away with him. He was that strong. He just got his hand like that and braced his feet and away went the lines. Busted them right in two. And they was made strong. Them mules too. He was a powerful man.

But Vince Morgan claims it was his Uncle Dode, not Uncle Rob, who knocked down the horse.

Vince Morgan: They claim my Uncle Dode—they used to have them horses, you know—drive them. He used to drive them out at Hewitt. He used to drive for Miss Sally Hewitt and them rich people. And the horse messed up with him—didn't do what he wanted to do. He got off the wagon—a lot of people told me this—them Ringwood people, too—he got up there and hit that horse right between the eyes with his fist and knocked him down. A horse! My Uncle Dode.
Cohen: I heard that same story about Uncle Rob.
Vince: You take the whole family up there, they'll tell you it was Uncle Dode that did it. He had a fist about like that. He had an awful hand. My father did too.

Obviously there is a bit of family rivalry about who did this amazing feat, suggesting that these strong men are not only culture heroes, but family heroes as well.

Another story about Uncle Rob was told by Jimmy De Freese.

Jimmy De Freese: I heard say—remember the wheels under a box car? He'd just straddle them wheels. He'd raise them wheels up to his [garbled]. Awful powerful man. [garbled] They was all on his—standing there. To all the men to stand on there. Lift that right up and down. He was an awful powerful man. I think he was the powerfullest colored man that was around here. He was a colored man. A big colored fellow. He was six foot—six foot-one, six foot-two. I think he was. He was a powerful man. Awful nice man, too, Rob was.

This is a more realistic estimate of Uncle Rob's height than the eight feet mentioned by John Morgan.

Those who knew Uncle Rob claim that these stories are not exaggerations. Lewis West, who knew Uncle Rob, said, "Yes, I seen him lift up an automobile. I seen him lift up the front end of a Ford automobile while the other fellows put tires on it. This is no exaggeration." Mr. West explained that the Model T Ford was not as heavy as modern automobiles, and a strong man could indeed lift it. The point is not whether these tales have become exaggerated with repeated tellings but that these tales express the ideal-type male. Masculinity among the Mountain People is defined in terms of physical strength and prowess.

A peculiar part of the folklore about the Ramapo Mountain People is what might be called chicken-stealing lore. A common stereotype, applied to rural blacks dating back to the days of slavery, was that they liked to steal chickens. This stereotype was also applied to the Mountain People.

An elderly white man living in Hillburn told me the following joke that used to be told about fifty years ago by the old-timers around Airmont, New York.

Informant A: There used to be a story going around about a man by the name of C—— De Groat. He lived up north of Tallman. He used to be pretty handy around people's hen houses, and one night he was overheard saying to his partner, "Don't be choicey; they all have to come!"

Before recording this joke, the informant made clear that being "pretty handy around people's hen houses" meant that he was a chicken thief. He said that when people saw this individual coming with his horse and wagon, they knew he was out stealing chickens.

The Vineland Training School study of the Mountain People provides another example of this negative stereotype.

Being familiar with the J-W [Jackson White] character and kindly disposed besides, Mr. and Mrs. C. knew both how to make these people happy and how to get the best possible service from them. Under these conditions the young couple lived and flourished. "They're exactly like children," Mrs. C. said more than once when telling about the J-W who had worked for them. "They occasionally took things, but nothing that was of any value. They would steal chickens whenever they got the chance, but they were so funny." She continued laughing. "On one occasion, Mr. C. missed several chickens and without knowing exactly who to blame, said to York J., 'York, there are some chickens missing and I want them put back tonight.' 'All right, Boss,' said York, and by night the chickens were all there." [31]

In response to these stories, some of the Mountain People have adopted the negative stereotype and turned it to their advantage.

Informant B: People used to steal chickens out of people's houses, and they say if you can walk up to a chicken and you tickle the bottom of the feet when they're sleeping, you can put all them chickens in the house—all the chickens in the place—you can put them on a stick and walk right away with them. They say if you tickle the bottom of their feet.
Informant C: Now, I don't know—I never heard about tickling their feet, but if you warm—especially if you take cold weather—warm a stick and you get it good and warm, you walk in a hen house or a duck coop, either one, and you put that warm stick there, they'll step off the roost and step right in. And you put a lantern in the bag. And you just bring them over and put them in the bag by that lantern, and you can clean out a hen house or a duck coop.

These admissions might seem to be the proof of the kernel of truth said to be behind all stereotypes. Be that as it may, in this case the negative stereotype has been transformed into a positive body of lore.

The relationship between folklore and culture is complex and requires extensive investigation by experts. I have simply suggested some of the ways in which the folklore of the Ramapo Mountain People expresses their culture.

10 RELIGION, FOLK BELIEFS, AND WORLD VIEW

The Mountain People belong to several different religious denominations. But despite their lack of agreement on the specifics of religious belief, the common denominator is Christianity. This Christian world view runs the gamut from the elaborate belief system of the Pentecostal church to the simple Christian belief of an old man from Ringwood who does not attend church but who told me, "There's only three things I believe in—there's a God, there's a Heaven, and there's a Hell."

The ancestors of the Ramapo Mountain People were affiliated with the Dutch Reformed Church. Claes Emanuels and John De Vries II were baptized and married in the New Amsterdam Dutch Reformed Church. In 1686 both were listed as members of that church. When they moved to the Hackensack River Valley, John De Vries II joined the Tappan Dutch Reformed Church, but Claes Emanuels did not. Most of their descendants were not church members, but they continued to be baptized and married in the Dutch Reformed churches at Tappan, New York, Schraalenburgh (Bergenfield), New Jersey, and Clarkstown, New York. Some of the ancestors of the Van Dunk family were baptized by a Lutheran minister, but most were affiliated with the Dutch Reformed Church.

After the migration to the Ramapo Mountains, the Mountain People became affiliated with other denominations. The reasons for this change are not known, although the inaccessibility of the Dutch Reformed churches in the valleys might have been a factor. Some Mountain People now attend one of two Pentecostal churches, in Hillburn or in Mahwah. Others attend a colored Presbyterian church in Hillburn. A few attend the African Methodist Episcopal church in Mahwah and the Episcopal church in Ringwood.

The sizes of these congregations range from about five in the Episcopal church in Ringwood to approximately fifty (including a few outsiders) in the Mahwah Pentecostal church. More Hillburn and Mahwah Mountain People than Ringwood Mountain People attend church regularly. Perhaps this can be explained by the middle-class economic status of those in Hillburn and Mahwah. Most of the Mountain People, however, are not church members. The low percentage of church membership does not mean that the rest of the Mountain People are not religious by nature. It just suggests that the majority are not joiners.

I drove up to Hillburn on a Sunday evening in April 1968. The Pentecostal church was a one-story, white-washed brick structure situated at the crest of a hill at Sixth Street and Chestnut Avenue. In front of the building there was a low stone retaining wall with concrete steps leading up to the church door. On either side of the door were two pointed-arch windows with stained glass. Above the door was a cross formed by the red brick of the wall, and above the gable was a modest square steeple. Neatly trimmed hedges were against the front of the church and in front of them a small sign announcing "Lighthouse Assembly" and the times of the services.

Inside I found beige walls with brown-trimmed wooden pews, and a scarlet carpet in the aisles. In front there was a pulpit with a lectern, with an upright piano on one side and an electric organ on the other. On the wall behind the pulpit was a mural depicting a blue sky with white clouds and a cross with a crown encircling its base. An inscription read "Behold I Come Quickly And My Reward Is With Me. Rev. 22.12."

I arrived early. The only other person in the church was an older man, tall with big bones, boldly defined facial features, straight white hair, and bronze-colored skin. He looked like an Indian, and I later found out he was a mixed-blood Cherokee from North Carolina. His name was Trueheart Solomon or "Brother" Trueheart, in accordance with the Pentecostal custom of calling each other "brother" or "sister." He was a deacon, and he was preparing the church for the evening service. He went into the room behind the pulpit and put on the phonograph a record of chime music, which was amplified through loudspeakers in the church steeple.

While we were talking, we were joined by a short, black man neatly dressed in a suit. Brother Trueheart introduced him as Brother Harold Thompson, a Pentecostal minister who was visiting Hillburn. Brother Harold's first question was if I was a Christian. When I replied that I was not, he made an extended attempt to convert me. He said he didn't know why I had come there that night, but he was sure that it was God who brought me.

The congregation began to arrive. There was little time for introductions, but Brother Trueheart did introduce me to two other people. One was Brother David Rodriguez, a tall handsome young man with Negroid features. I later learned that he was of Cape Verdian ancestry, originally from Massachusetts, now a resident of Hillburn and a deacon in the church. The second person was Brother Trueheart's wife Sister Anna, a short elderly woman with tan-colored skin. She was one of the Mountain People, a licensed Pentecostal preacher now retired, and the founder of the Hillburn church.

The service was about to begin, so I sat in one of the rear pews. There were ten people present. Sister Anna took a seat in the front pew with her husband. Brother David played the organ, and Brother Thompson's wife played the piano. There were two other women present. One was Brother David's mother, and the other was later introduced as Sister Dorothy. There were also three teen-age girls, who sat together.

The service began with the singing of hymns from the Assembly of God hymnal. There was a mixture of styles in the singing. Brother David sang in the nondescript style heard on recordings of hymns showing no regional peculiarities. Sister Anna and the teen-age girls sang in a nasal style that reminded me of southern-white gospel singing.

After the singing, everyone remained standing. Brother David's mother was chosen to "take us before the Lord in prayer." She began praying aloud, and was joined by the others, praying aloud their separate prayers. Some raised either one or both arms in the air with the palms of their hands cupped upward. One could hear certain recurrent refrains: "In the name of Jesus-a," "Praise the Lord," "Thank you, Jesus-a."

Then five members of the congregation stood up one at a time to testify how Jesus was active in their lives. Sister Dorothy's testimony was very emotional. Her delivery resembled the cadences of a preacher. Her pauses were punctuated by an audible inhaling. The pitch and volume of her voice continued to build until she was shouting, and her face was red with emotion. Her testimony lasted about five minutes.

Then Brother Thompson preached. After his sermon, he came down from the pulpit, placed his hands on Sister Anna's head, and blessed her. Following the service people lingered briefly to greet each other and shake hands, after which they departed for home.

During the following months, I attended other services at this church. At one Saturday evening prayer meeting I found five members of the congregation kneeling before the pulpit in prayer. Brother True-heart knelt before one of the pews. On the pulpit was a blackboard on which was written the names of people to be remembered in prayer, including "Sister Anna's two special requests" and "the boys in Viet-nam." During one prayer the request was made for the Lord to save the people on the mountain and the people on the other side of the mountain. Mention was made of Brother Jessie, who was doing mission-ary work on the mountain. Then all stood in a circle, joined hands, and sang a hymn. Brother David invited me to join the circle, and I did.

After the prayer meeting, Brother David invited me across the street to his home. There he told me about the Pentecostal faith and way of life. He said that he does not drink, smoke, dance, nor play cards. Furthermore, he does not go to the movies, although he does occasionally watch television. He said that he disapproves of the loose morality of actors and actresses in general, and especially the way im-morality is marketed in Hollywood. But he said these prohibitions are less important than his positive faith in Jesus as his Saviour.

Brother David said that the Hillburn Pentecostal church used to be affiliated with the largest Pentecostal denomination—the Assemblies of God, founded in 1914—but that the Hillburn church is now inde-pendent. Brother Trueheart Solomon later told me that the Hillburn church disassociated from the Assemblies of God because of what he called the color problem. But Sister Anna told me that when she attended the Zion Bible Institute in East Providence, Rhode Island, they treated her "as if [she] was white." She said, "They let me sleep in their beds and all."

The local Hillburn church has a pastor, two deacons, two trustees, a secretary-treasurer, a Sunday school, a Women's Missionary Council, and the Missionettes (a missionary organization for teen-age girls). Brother David explained that other Pentecostal churches have a Men's Fellowship, but the Hillburn church is too small to support one. There are three degrees of ministers: exhorters (or apprentices), licensed preachers, and ordained ministers. The deacons assist the pastor in administering to the spiritual needs of the congregation, visiting the sick, and serving Holy Communion. The trustees administer to the financial needs and physical upkeep of the church.

The Hillburn Pentecostal church has a Tuesday morning prayer meeting for women, a Wednesday evening Bible study, a Saturday evening prayer service; and on Sunday there is Sunday school and a service in the morning and another service in the evening. Services last from an hour and a half to two hours, depending on how the Spirit moves the congregation.

Brother David told me that people of the Pentecostal faith believe in two sacraments: Holy Communion and adult baptism. He explained that there is also a second baptism in the Holy Ghost in which the Holy Ghost infuses the believer and causes him to "speak in tongues." Speaking in tongues or glossolalia is mentioned in several places in the Bible, but the key reference is in the Book of Acts (2:1–6), wherein is described the Disciples' celebration of the Jewish Feast of Pentecost (*Shavuot*):

And when the day of Pentecost was fully come, they were all with one accord in one place.
And suddenly there came a sound from heaven as a rushing mighty wind, and it filled all the house where they were sitting.
And there appeared unto them cloven tongues like as of fire, and it sat upon each of them.
And they were all filled with the Holy Ghost, and began to speak with other tongues, as the Spirit gave them utterance.

And there were dwelling at Jerusalem Jews, devout men, out of every nation under heaven.

Now when this was noised abroad, the multitude came together, and were confounded, because that every man heard them speak in his own language.

There have been reported incidents of glossolalia throughout the history of Christianity—among the Waldensians, the Jansenists, the Mormons, the Quakers, the Shakers, and in the American camp meeting revivals. In the Pentecostal movement, the "gift of tongues" is accompanied by the "gift of interpretation." After one believer infused by the Holy Ghost speaks in an unknown language, another believer will translate the meaning of the message. I later witnessed speaking in tongues and interpretation in both the Hillburn and the Mahwah Pentecostal churches. To me the sounds suggested nonsense syllables, but to a believer they constitute an unknown language. Believers mention incidents when recognizable languages have been spoken even though the speaker did not know the language.

The Pentecostals also believe in the healing power of God. This belief is based on incidents in the Bible in which Jesus healed the sick. Sometimes, at the end of a service, members of the congregation will go up to the pulpit, where the minister or ministers will lay hands on the person, anoint him with oil, and "in the name of Jesus" the person will be healed. I witnessed this practice in both Hillburn and Mahwah. Often testimonies tell how this ritual or prayer has healed the individual of an ailment.

The best summary of the beliefs of the Pentecostal faith is found in the "Statement of Faith" printed in *The Pentecostal Evangel*, the official periodical of the Assemblies of God.

WE BELIEVE the Bible to be the inspired and only infallible and authoritative Word of God. WE BELIEVE that there is one God, eternally existent in three persons: God the Father, God the Son, and God the Holy Ghost. WE BELIEVE in the deity of our Lord Jesus Christ, in His virgin birth, in His sinless life, in His miracles, in His vicarious and atoning death, in His bodily resurrection, in His ascension to the right hand of the Father, in His personal future return to this earth in power and glory to rule a thousand years. WE BELIEVE in the Blessed Hope, which is the Rapture of the Church at Christ's coming. WE BELIEVE that the only means of being cleansed from sin is through repentance and faith in the precious blood of Christ. WE BELIEVE that regeneration by the Holy Spirit is absolutely essential for personal salvation. WE BELIEVE that the redemptive work of Christ on the cross provides healing of the human body in answer to believing prayer. WE BELIEVE that the baptism of the Holy Spirit, according to Acts 2:4, is given to believers who ask for it. WE BELIEVE in the sanctifying power of the Holy Spirit by whose indwelling the Christian is enabled to live a holy life. WE BELIEVE in the resurrection of both the saved and the lost, the one to everlasting life and the other to everlasting damnation.[1]

In the world view of the Pentecostals the major sociological division is between the saved and the nonsaved. The Pentecostals are an evangelical movement, which means they proselytize to gain converts. The conversion experience is an isolated occurrence in which the individual receives Christ, is saved, and changes his style of life.

I asked John Morgan of Ringwood to describe his conversion.

John Morgan: Well, ah, as far as conversion, that happened about, ah, I'd say three years ago, roughly. I used to be a pretty rough guy once in my life. I did everything—everything that could be done that was wrong. And I went to a church service one night, and suddenly God spoke to my heart, and I gave my heart to God, and it changed my life. That was the time when I used to live in Suffern, and I would go home at night, I wouldn't eat my supper. I wouldn't do anything, unless—until I got—I went in my back room and got on my knees and prayed. Then, ah, I went out and I spoke in another church over in Nyack, and, ah, the Lord was really using me. So—then I got the, ah—I was baptized in water in the Dover Assemblies of God Church. That was a wonderful experience . . .
Cohen: What did it feel like? Did you go into a church? You hear a minister?
John: No. I had—I had been saved at one time before, and I had backslidden, and God spoke to my heart that night, and God was in the meeting. The power of the Holy Ghost was in the meeting so strong that, I think if you didn't get saved that night, you'd never get saved, because the power of the Holy Ghost was so strong in that church . . . I'll tell you, ah, it's a thrilling experience to be saved and to be filled with the Holy Ghost. It's a wonderful experience. But, on the other hand, it's almost as easy to backslide, because if you congregate among sinners, the next thing you know, you're going to be doing the same thing they do, and then you—then you're backsliding. See. And then you'll lose what you've had. But I had that experience. I'm—I'm speaking from experience. I know what happens.

Cohen: I think that maybe some people who might hear this tape don't know what it's like to be in a church when the Holy Ghost is moving. Could you describe that for me?

John: The—when the power of God is moving, it's indescribable. It's indescribable. There is such joy, and I mean overjoy, that it is indescribable. It can't be described. The only one—the only way that it can be known is to experience it oneself. That's the only way.

Cohen: Well, is there singing and dancing?

John: Yes. Now, sometimes—sometimes, ah, the Lord will speak to you, the meeting can be quiet. It doesn't have to be, ah, a shouting meeting or a dancing meeting. The word of God can come forth with such tremendous power that your inner being will just tremble, and you'll be so quiet. I've seen the time when the whole church is just as quiet as could be. There was no outward emotion at all. The people just seemed like the law—or, well, like they say in the world, "on cloud nine." . . .

Cohen: I wonder if you could explain what is meant by the baptism in the Holy Ghost and speaking in tongues?

John: Oh. The speaking in tongues. That is another thing that is indescribable. Because the power of God will come on you, and you'll get—your tongue seems to get so thick that you can't say anything. You're praising God, and praising God, and praising God, and the first thing you know this power hits you, and you—it seems like your tongue gets so thick that you don't speak in the ordinary English language. The next thing you know, a tongue that you don't or no one else in the church knows, except you have someone in there who has the gift of interpretation. Now, the person who has the gift of interpretation will interpret that language. It could be Hebrew. It could come out in Hebrew, it could come out in Chinese, in Japanese. It could come out in a foreign language—any foreign language. And someone who doesn't even know a word in foreign language, the Lord could speak to that person—through that person—and give the interpretation of the message that you bring forth. See. The Bible says that if there is no interpretation of the message, the man only edifies himself, but if there is an interpretation of the message that is brought forth, then he edifies the church . . .

The vocal, emotional style of the Pentecostal church contrasts sharply with the restrained style of Brook Chapel, the colored Presbyterian church in Hillburn located on Sixth Street in "the hollow." It is a white, wood, frame structure with a pitched roof and a modest but graceful steeple. It has small, pointed-arch windows with stained glass. The church is oriented with the gable end toward the road. The entrances are on either side of the building. Wooden stairs lead up to a small porch at either door. While larger than the Lighthouse Assembly, Brook Chapel is considerably smaller than the white Presbyterian church on the other side of Hillburn. Brook Chapel has two rooms, one serving as the chapel and the other as a community room.

I first attended a service at Brook Chapel one Sunday morning in July 1968. I was greeted at the door by Samuel Mann, the principal of the Sunday school, who gave me a printed program. On the outside the program had a color picture with a religious theme. On the inside were the mimeographed order of the service and the announcements for the week. Mr. Mann introduced me to Victor De Freese, the organist. He explained that Brook Chapel was having a joint service with the white Presbyterian church. Reverend Sylvester Van Oort, who normally comes from out of town to conduct services, was on vacation, and in his absence services were being conducted by Reverend Myron Miller of the white Presbyterian church.

There were about forty-five people present in the integrated congregation. I took a seat in a rear pew while Victor De Freese went to the Hammond organ and began to softly play chord progressions. After a few minutes the service began. The congregation rose for the processional hymn. As they sang, a small choir—a few adults and several children in robes—came down the center aisle and stood to the right of the pulpit. They were followed by the minister, who went to the center of the pulpit. After the hymn, the Call to Worship appearing in the program was recited by the minister, and the congregation responded in unison. This was followed by a hymn of adoration, a prayer of confession (also in the program), the responsive reading from the prayer book, and the Gloria Patriae. The congregation sat down.

There was a scripture lesson read by the minister, a choir selection, and the sermon. Then came another hymn, the pastoral prayer, Lord's Prayer, and the offering, for which the congregation stood. They remained standing for a recitation of the Apostle's Creed, which was painted on a large plaque to the left of the pulpit.

I BELIEVE in God the Father Almighty, Maker of heaven and earth:
  And in Jesus Christ His only Son, our Lord; Who was conceived by the Holy Ghost, Born of the Virgin Mary, Suffered under Pontius Pilate,

Was crucified, dead, and buried; He descended into hell; The third day He rose again from the dead; He ascended into heaven, And sitteth on the right hand of God the Father Almighty; From thence He shall come to judge the quick and the dead.

I believe in the Holy Ghost, The Holy Catholic Church; The Communion of Saints; The Forgiveness of sins; The Resurrection of the body; and the Life everlasting. Amen.

The service concluded with a prayer of thanksgiving and the recessional hymn, during which the choir and minister walked down the aisle. The congregation remained standing in meditation after the hymn, while Victor De Freese played chord progressions. When the organ stopped, the congregation quietly greeted each other and walked to the door where Reverend Miller greeted each person as he filed out. The service lasted exactly one hour.

Brook Chapel has the standard organizational structure of Presbyterian churches. Its officers include the pastor, five trustees, two elders, three deacons, a treasurer, and a clerk. The trustees are responsible for the worldly property of the church. The elders are responsible for the spiritual affairs of the church. The elders, the pastor, and the clerk make up the board of session. Brook Chapel also has a Sunday school, choir, and a Missionary Society. The Brook Chapel session is part of the larger institutional structure of the Presbyterian church. The session is part of the presbytery, which is part of the synod, which is part of the general assembly.

The Mount Zion African Methodist Episcopal Zion Church in Mahwah is located on Grove Street just up the hill from the Mahwah Full Gospel Pentecostal Church. It was founded as a Methodist church by the Mountain People in 1857. The building, originally a one-room school house, was donated by H. O. Havemeyer, one of the white farmers in the Ramapo Valley, and moved to its present location from Green Mountain Valley in 1915. In 1904 the Green Mountain Valley church withdrew from the Union Conference of Methodists and joined the black African Methodist Episcopal Zion Conference. As blacks began to attend the church, some of the Mountain People left to join the Full Gospel Pentecostal church down the road.

Today the Mount Zion church has a black pastor from outside the community and a small congregation, mostly black but including some Mountain People. The preaching and singing styles are typical of black churches, and the singing contrasts sharply with the nasal quality of the singing in the Pentecostal churches, which is similar to southern-white fundamentalist denominations.

I attended a Sunday morning worship service in this church one Sunday in April 1968. I met Reverend Robert Perry, who was beginning his second year as pastor. He comes from Bergenfield, New Jersey, each Sunday. He told me that when he started there were only four people in the congregation, but now there were approximately twenty-five. He seemed a bit disappointed he was assigned to such a small congregation, but in his sermon he said while he had dreamed of a large congregation, he had asked to be reappointed to Mount Zion.

There were only two persons I recognized as Mountain People in the service that day. One was the organist, Mrs. Eva Van Dunk from Hillburn. The other was Mrs. Isadore Conklin. The hymnal I was given was donated by a man named De Freese. The rest of the eight people present were blacks.

The church building was very small, and the pews were pushed closely together. The smallness of the building and the smallness of the congregation gave a feeling of intimacy to the service. There was some meager effort at call and response and some hand-clapping on the part of the congregation, but no momentum ever built up. There was a poignancy to this little church that was being abandoned by the Mountain People because of the influx of blacks.

The Episcopal Church of the Good Shepherd, located near the entrance to the Ringwood Mine Area, is actually just a missionary adjunct to the Episcopal church in West Milford, New Jersey. The earlier missionary work of Father A. F. Chillson is now continued by Father Alva Decker. Besides conducting religious services, Father Decker is active in the Community Action Council of Passaic County, the government antipoverty agency. The church building was used as a school for the Project Headstart nursery school run by the CACPC.

Services in the Church of the Good Shepherd are held on Sunday afternoons, after Father Decker presides in the morning at his home church in West Milford. The service I attended was very sparsely attended, only five Mountain People being present. None of them live in the Mine Area. They were Mountain People who had moved out of the Mine Area and live near Ringwood. They came in two cars. When Father Decker arrived he unlocked the building, and we went through the service room into the sanctuary. It was a small crowded sanctuary with an altar in the front. During the service I was struck by the sharp contrast between the formality of the Episcopal ritual and the small surroundings. Father Decker seemed to sense this contrast and conducted the service in a more casual, yet still reverent, manner. I wondered why so few of the Mountain People attended this church. One man in the Mine Area later told me he wouldn't attend this church because the previous minister there had refused to marry him and his wife because it was an interracial union.

Church affiliation tends to integrate some of the Mountain People into the outside society through an institutional structure. The churches are one of the few avenues of contact with outsiders. At the same time, the churches create division within the Mountain People between the church members and those who do not attend church, the saved and the unsaved, as well as between the different denominations. But integration into the outside society has been incomplete because the local congregations in each of these denominations are mostly colored Mountain People. The congregations have resisted merging with white congregations or allowing blacks to attend their churches. Since only a few of the Mountain People are church members, the overall group still manages to resist outside influences.

The folk beliefs * of the Ramapo Mountain People are also part of their basically Christian world view. Folk beliefs generally exist "partially alongside, partially underneath the official levels of religion." [2] Included in the folk beliefs are folk medicine (herb cures, folk remedies, evil eyes), folk religion (witchcraft and the Devil), and folk science (ghost stories, poltergeists, predictions, luck and chance). Some of the younger and more educated Mountain People and also church members consider these traditional folk beliefs to be superstitions. But

* I do not use the term *superstitions* because that term connotes invalidity.

those Mountain People who believe in the folk beliefs see no contra-diction between the folk beliefs and science or religion. The folk beliefs tend to be more common among the lower-class Mountain People in Ringwood than among the middle-class Mountain People in Hillburn and Mahwah.

The traditional knowledge and use of herb cures are still prevalent in Ringwood, but in Hillburn the Mountain People only *remember* their parents and grandparents using these herbs.

John Morgan: I've seen my—I've seen my mother—snow on like this . . . I've seen her put on her old shoes, go up in—go up in the woods, and she'd dig around through the snow 'til she found them roots. She'd come back and she'd make her cough medicine and feed it to us. It always helped us. Yes, sir. I can see her today. How she used to have her pots on the stove—that old left hand [he gestures to show stirring]—she'd [chuckles], yeah.

The American Indians used herbs long before Europeans set foot on America. In 1656 Adriaen Van Der Donck—the first lawyer in New Netherland, and no relation to Augustine Van Donck—wrote about the Indians in New Netherland,

They heal fresh wounds and dangerous bruises in a most wonderful man-ner. They also have remedies for old sores and ulcers, and they also cure venereal affections so readily that many an Italian master who saw it would be ashamed of his profession. All their cures are made with herbs, roots, and leaves (with the powers of which they are acquainted) without making any compounds.[3]

Many of the same herb cures I collected from the Ramapo Mountain People have also been collected from the Delaware Indians.*[4] But this cannot be taken as proof of the alleged Indian ancestry of the Moun-tain People. Because the Indians knew more about the indigenous plants, both Europeans and Africans in America freely borrowed these In-dian herb cures. They were common knowledge in colonial America. The Mountain People themselves do not associate these herb cures with Indian culture.

Certain metals are thought to have therapeutic properties. Some

* A complete list of the herb cures, with a notation of those common to the Delaware Indians, can be found in Appendix B.

of the old-timers in Ringwood used to wear copper bracelets to prevent rheumatism. The American Indians also believed that copper had magical properties, and this might be an Indian survival. Madge Morgan of Ringwood said that rubbing one's eye with a gold ring will cure a stye.

Madge Morgan: Somebody got a stye in the eye? Take a gold ring and rub it. This way, and this way, and then that way. I used to have styes all the time as a child with bad eyes. Used to rub that gold ring over there, this way, two or three times, and that way. I ain't had a stye in my eye in years.

According to Madge's husband John, brass was used to prevent nose bleeds.

John Morgan: Nose bleeds? Today, I don't believe—them days they used to take a piece of brass. Take a brass key—that's all they used to be made out of then—all you could get then—put that on a string and let the kids wear it down the back. Coming around the back of the neck there. That will stop them from having nose bleeds.

Urine and excrement are also considered therapeutic. Gary Lee Oliver of Hillburn mentioned that gargling with urine will cure the quinsy sore throat.

Gary Lee Oliver: And—you're gonna laugh at this. You ever hear of the quinsy sore throat? Alright. I had it. My throat was closed. My grandmother come down and looked at me. I couldn't talk. They tried to give me milk and it would come right back out of my nose. And I had to gargle my throat in my own urine. And that cured it. I've never had it since.

Jimmy De Freese from Ringwood said that gargling with urine was also a cure for the croup. The belief in the curative property of urine has been collected among the Delaware Indians.[5] Chinks Oliver from Hillburn mentioned cow manure as a cure for pneumonia.

Chinks Oliver: Years ago my uncle got cured of pneumonia—bad case—with cow manure. They wrapped his chest up in it, and his back and his chest. They just took a sheet and wrapped him up in it. And in three days, he was breathing right and living again. Yup.

An informant from Ringwood mentioned a poultice of cow manure wrapped in mullein leaf (*Verbascum thapsus*) as a cure for the quinsy sore throat.

Many maladies are cured by transferring them to an animal or an object.

John Morgan: Sore throat. For the quinsy sore throat they used to get a spring toad. Go to the springs, get one of these striped toads. Take that toad. Hold him by the mouth. Let that toad inhale their breath. Take the toad back. Set the toad down by the spring where you got him. You go there in a few days, there'd be nothing left of the toad but just the bones.

John's wife Madge explained how to cure a wart by transference.

Madge Morgan: I'll tell you how I do for warts. I was told this, and it happened good. This ring—this thumbnail was way up in the air with a wart. I used to work down Sloatsburg in the mill. Some of the ladies told me out there. Take an old piece of your dishcloth you wash dishes with, and you wipe that over the warts, wherever you got 'em. Take that out. Put it under a rock. Don't look back. And that's a sure cure. I know it, because I done it on myself. I done it on my girl friend. She had them all over her fingers. Took 'em away.
Cheryine (her granddaughter): Grandma, you did it to me too.
Madge: I done it to her. Took hers away. An old lady told me that.

Frank Milligan spoke about another cure for warts.

Frank Milligan: This I had happen to me so I know it would work, and now I don't know like if I tell you or a woman has to tell you [the magic formula for passing on curative knowledge], I don't know, but, you know, in fact, you don't see many of them anymore, but people used to have a lot of warts. They always said we got them playing with toads. I don't know.

But I know my mother would always say. We would come up with a wart, she'd say, "Now you go down the road"—there were a lot of horses in those days—"and you walk till you find a white horse. When you see a white horse go by, you start to rub that wart, and you just say, 'I wish this wart would go right up that white horse's rectum.' And forget about it. In the morning that wart would be gone." And in the morning [he snaps his fingers], just like that, that wart is gone! Now, I mean, this I had happen so many times. You know, when you do it yourself, you have to believe it.

In some cures the object that caused the injury rather than the wound itself is treated.

Peggy Morgan: Miles Dennison said—he died at the age of ninety-four—and he told us that if the kids ever step on a rusty nail or something, be sure and get the exact nail, and cover it with lard or Crisco or something of that sort, and you put it way up high, and—you know, where nobody can get it or throw it away or anything—and that keeps the foot from becoming infected. And we've done it so many times with these kids around here.
Cohen: That's the nail you put up there?
Peggy: The nail you put up—you know, I don't know why. He never said why, but he always said to do it. Yeah, he said it kept them from getting lock-jaw or getting—becoming infected in any way. And I've done it many times for my boys. It sounds silly, but I don't know. Maybe that helped 'em, maybe it didn't. I don't know.

Ringworm is contained by drawing a circle around the area with a pencil.

John Morgan: Well, now, today—in my day—ah, today, ah—a lot of the doctors tell you get what they call a ringworm. Well, today, most of them 'll tell you, "Well, there's no cure." Well, the way to cure it—now, in my day when they used to get it, they'd take a lead pencil. They'd take a soft lead, and circle that—circle right around that—and that won't spread outside of that pencil mark.
Madge: I know. I had it on my neck once.
John: Yea-up. You get that pencil mark, and she'll die right there.
Allen (their son): They say salt pork is good for that too.

While some of these cures may have been cultural borrowings from the American Indians, many of the folk beliefs are closer to the European tradition of witchcraft than to the American Indian tradition of shamanism.* European witchcraft is a folk religion, a negative

---

* For accounts of the religion and world view of the Delaware Indians, see Richard Adams, *The Ancient Religion of the Delaware Indians* (Washington, D.C.: Law Reporter Printing Co., 1904); Daniel G. Brinton, *The Lenâpe and Their Legends* (New York: AMS Press, 1969, first published in 1884); Frank Speck, *A Study of the Delaware Indian Big House Ceremony* (Harrisburg, Pa.: Pennsylvania Historical Commission, 1931); and Gladys Tantaquideon, *A Study of the Delaware Indian Medicine Practice and Folk Beliefs* (Harrisburg, Pa.: Commonwealth of Pennsylvania Department of Public Instruction and Pennsylvania Historical Commission, 1942).

counterpart to Christianity in which a covenant is made with the Devil rather than God. The European literature of witchcraft is replete with Christian symbols, including witches' Sabbaths, black masses, crucifixes, and so forth.[6] The Bible is used to cast spells and to cure illnesses. It is in this sense that many of the folk remedies of the Ramapo Mountain People are related to Christianity.

A recitation of verses from the Bible is used in a cure known by the Mountain People as "taking the fire [hurt] out of a burn." James Sidney De Groat of Spring Valley, New York, testified to the effectiveness of this cure, which only a few people can perform.

James De Groat: When I was a young man, I worked at American Brakeshoe and Foundry Company in Mahwah, New Jersey. So I was moulding down there—insert moulder—and we were pouring [garbled] hand ladles and I got burnt. And, ah, I came home the best I could, hobbling along. Got home. So in the meantime, a man by the name of Stephen De Groat was a neighbor of mine. He lived right near me, and he passed me up. He asked me what the trouble is, and I told him. So I went on home. I got home the best way I could. [Garbled]

So, anyway, when I got home, all night long I couldn't sleep. The next day in the afternoon my wife went over to this old lady they called Aunt Nance—she wasn't an aunt of ours, but they called her aunt. My wife went over there, and she was telling about it, and so she said, "Well, why don't you ask Steve to come over?" That was her son. And he was the man that passed me on the way going home, so he knew it was burnt 'cause I told him.

So my wife came over back home and told me. I said, "No." I was pretty hurt, you know. I said, "No, I don't want to mess around with it." So I didn't care to have him do it much. But she talked to me, and so finally, I gave in.

And she went back over and told her. So he came over. And he said, "Well, take the bandage off." So my wife did. So he got down on his knees. Right on to the ground. He was in my yard. And, ah, he took his finger and he circled it, and, ah—first one way and then back the other way around, and he kept blowing with the breath of his mouth over it. He did that a few times, and while he was doing it, all the pain left, and I slept like a log. And I guarantee you, I do say that I'll swear by that method that this Steve De Groat did for me.

Cohen: I think you also said something about a man could only tell a woman—

James: Yes, he told my wife that a man could tell a woman—tell her what to do—or a woman could tell a man, but a man could not tell a man and neither could a woman tell a woman. That's right. That's what he told me. So the poor fella's dead and gone, so I don't know. I never learned it.

Another testimony was given by Bob Milligan and his daughter Cynthia from Ringwood.

Bob Milligan: Now, Davie Van Dunk's father, now, he had a gift of pull the fire out of you no matter how bad you were burnt.
Cynthia (his daughter): Yeah.
Bob: Now he could pull fire out of you, and he did it to her, oh, two or three—
Cynthia: It's a little scar now, but it was real big then, you know, while I was real young, and he took the fire right out of it. It didn't bother me after. I didn't burn it. I was scalded real bad.
Bob: I don't care how bad you was burnt, he would—he would make a circle, say words out of the Bible, and blow on it, and when he did it, you would holler, because—
Cynthia: This was a blister from that—
Bob: Yeah. He pull it— pull the fire right out of a burn.
Cynthia: That's right. I got scalded real bad, and he—he took the fire right out of it. When I was about—
Bob: And my [daughter]—Sheila. Oh, it was a poor one to see her. Bernedine. They were burnt with hot grease. The whole pan of hot grease. He pulled the fire right out, and [garbled] He—he is good. And the other brother could stop blood.
Cohen: What was his name?
Bob: Gussie. Gussie could stop blood, and Leroy could pull the fire out. Leroy's still living.
Cynthia: Gussie could pull fire out of you too.
Bob: Yeah. Both of them could.
Cynthia: They both could take the fire out of you.
Bob: Gussie could stop blood too. They were—and their father, see—it was a gift from their father. But he could [only] tell it to a woman, but if he told it to you or I—how to do it—it wouldn't work. Isn't that something? One man can't tell it to another man.
Cynthia: Yeah. 'Cause we, ah—no, he wouldn't tell it to—no, he wouldn't tell it to a woman. 'Cause, you remember, I don't know which one got hurt —was it Sheila got burnt on the hand, and we asked him how to do that and he wouldn't tell us. He said he wouldn't tell nobody how to do it.

When I tried to find out the verses recited from the Bible, I was told that Leroy couldn't tell me because the technique could only be transmitted to a member of the opposite sex. I found a woman in Hillburn who knew how to take the fire out of a burn, but she declined to tell me the verses on the grounds that she would lose the power once she transmitted it to another person. This cure is widespread in Europe and the United States, where it has been collected in Georgia, North Carolina, Washington, D.C., Pennsylvania, Michigan, and Indiana.[7]

Some individuals also possess the ability to stop bleeding. The ailing person need not be present to effect this cure.

John Morgan: Well, I had—I had an uncle. I wouldn't care if you lived in Paterson. You cut yourself bad, and you got word up to him you were bleeding bad and couldn't stop—you could get word up to there or come up there to see him 'bout it, he'd say, "Alright." By the time you'd get home, why, it would stop bleeding. Old fella lives over at Sterling here, guy that cut hisself badly and was bleeding to death, and they send somebody over here, and they found him out—he worked on the farm—he asked about what they wanted and they told him. Wanted to know if he could stop 'em. "Well," he says, "I'll tell you, by the time you get home," he says, "Why, everything will be alright." He could stop blood at any distance—any distance at all, he could stop blood.

When I tried to learn the technique of stopping bleeding, I met the same obstacles I met with taking the fire out of a burn. Evidently the Bible is also used in this cure. Among the Pennsylvania Dutch the Biblical quotation used to stop bleeding is Ezekiel 16:6, "And when I passed by thee, and saw thee polluted in thine own blood, I said unto thee when thou wast in thy blood, [. . .] Live; yea, I said unto thee when thou wast in thy blood, [. . .] Live." The name of the person to be cured is inserted before "live" in the text.[8]

Some of the Mountain People believe that some illnesses are caused by evil eyes, spells cast by malevolent people. A young Hillburn man learned this practice from his grandmother.

Gary Lee Oliver: Like I can give that man a headache for the rest of his life. Get a piece of his hair. Go find a dead tree. Drill a hole in it. Put your hair in it. You'll have a headache from now on.

This theory of illness gives rise to special remedies for the evil eye.

One way to determine who cast the evil eye is to sprinkle mustard seed outside your house.

Frank Milligan: When I was a kid, I overheard how people, you know, could break spells, cast spells, and all this and that. And I've always believed that they were old wives' tales. And my mother said one day, "I'm gonna show you." 'Cause one of the kids was crying and fretting all the time, you know. She believed somebody was trying to put a spell on him. So, she said, "I'll show you who it is."

I said, "Oh, come on, Ma, you can't notice it."

She said, "Well, you watch."

So she went out to the long driveway we had and put mustard seed all the way 'cross the driveway and about fifty feet on each side. "Now," she said, "you watch. Whoever it is, is got to show up, and you watch, they cannot cross that mustard seed."

And sure enough, in a couple of hours this woman came up and stood there, and she kept hollering, "Yoo-hoo. Yoo-hoo. Yoo-hoo."

My mother said, "Don't answer her. Don't answer her," she said, "she got to come into the house."

And finally she walked all the way up—and we had a garden, about two acres—a little farm—so she walked all the way up around it and came down through the back. She said, "I just want to look at your garden."

My mother said, "You see?"

So she stayed a while, and the minute she walked into that house, that kid stopped crying. So my mother told me after, "You watch. When she leaves, she don't dare to walk out that driveway, 'cause she cannot cross that mustard seed."

And when that woman left, she left out the back and down the other way, 'cross the other fields and on up to the road. She would not cross that mustard seed.

Another magical use of mustard seed was explained by Allen Morgan.

Allen Morgan: Well, I'll tell you. One time my wife had a spell on her. Nobody can't tell me she didn't, because she laid in a coma five and a half months. And this certain person didn't come around. I don't mention no names. She didn't come around, didn't come around.

So my aunt told me to put mustard in her shoes. Find one of her shoes. Put mustard in one of her shoes. This was dry mustard. Sprinkle it across the door sill and down the steps. She says, "They will come."

And we did that, and this person came. And after the person came, the person went to see her and looked at her and touched her, and she started to come through. Nobody can tell me no different. This is a—it wouldn't have worked no other way, if I hadn't done what I was told to do. As soon as I see her, I done what she said to do, and that person hadn't been around. I done that. The next day that person was THERE. But she had to go across that mustard. I done that. That's no lie. I don't mention no names, now. When I done that, my wife felt better. She had—she couldn't stand her. She had to go and see her—touch her.

Three cures for the evil eye are mentioned in the following account:

Wally Morgan: Allen's wife—my brother Allen's wife, Barb—I heard her mother said different times and I heard my mother and everyone—if different old people say about people try and cast a spell on you and stuff—they take a lock of your hair and you'd be bothered so. Seem like you was going crazy. They'd say what you do is you remember who that was. You get a picture of 'em. They say you take that and you put it under any waterfall, and that would bring that person to you. It would be on their mind. It would—some way it would get on their mind so strong, they would have to come back to you.

And then she said another thing is: you boil needles in water, she said, and that would drive 'em practically crazy, and they'd have to come to you.

If anybody, you know, tried to cast a spell on you, or something, because there's been times where—I seen a lot of—well, I was young, but you hear these old-timers, if people got sick or, you know, a child got sick or something, they'd have that phrase, "somebody's cast a spell on you."

A kid would wake up, couldn't sleep, and I've seen—well, in our family, daddy or mommy would go out, mostly daddy, he would take burdock and make a necklace and put it around their necks, and then,—I don't know what it did—but eventually they'd stop crying. I don't know what part it played.

Placing a broom across the doorway also is mentioned as a cure.

Barbara Morgan: I remember my mother she was always in a—crippled. She didn't walk in years . . . She had rheumatory arthritis, you know. They said it was that. This person, they said, she had a spell on her which I heard through pins and needles and water and this mustard and everything. And my father laid a broom across the floor, and the minute this person

that had, they claimed, had the spell on her walked across it, she got out of bed and walked. So, I mean, it's good, if you believe in it. I'm not going to tell you, you know, whether it all happened, because I don't know.
John Morgan: I do. I do.
Allen Morgan: Your mother walked again, didn't she?
Barbara: Yes, she walked.
Allen: Alright.
John: I do believe in it.

Brooms are associated with witches in the Anglo-American tradition of folk belief as in Motif G 272.7.2, "Broom across door protects from witch."

Vince Morgan from Mahwah told about using the Bible and coins as remedies against the evil eye.

Vince Morgan: I was about nine or ten years old, and, ah, every night around twelve o'clock I couldn't sleep, you know. These little men, oh, about five or six inches tall with little top hats on 'em, I used to hear 'em coming upstairs, you know. And I couldn't sleep, and they'd get on the bed, and I'd pull the covers over my head, and they'd pull the covers down, and all that stuff. And I was losing weight to beat the band. I was right down [garbled], 'cause I had T.B.

And so my mother she went to my aunt—my great aunt—and told her about it. She said, "Well, somebody got a spell on him." And—you know Aunt Margaret—she said, "I'll find out who it is."

So she give—my aunt told my mother I had to open the Bible to a certain page and put it under my head nights, and wear dimes in the shoes, she said, "and I'll do the rest." She said, "He'll see 'em about three more nights," she said, "and the last night who got that spell on him will be coming right with 'em."

And they sure enough did. That last night they come right upstairs, and I was screaming and hollering, and this lady come in there, sit right on the foot of my bed, and I knowed who she was. And I was screaming and hollering. And my mother came in there. I went—I went in her bed with her and my father and when I went back to bed—she took me there when I went right to sleep—she carried me back in the bed. I would have stayed asleep, you know. And the next night I wasn't bothered with it no more.

It wasn't long after that this lady that had the spell on me she come wanted to know—she got awful sick, and she just wiped the spell right away from me. She didn't last long at all. She died. I can't say no names, but that's the truth.

Destroying a dough effigy of the person who cast the spell can also break the spell.

Allen Morgan: They always say you think somebody got a spell on you, make a dough baby. Put it up on—put it anywhere, I guess, where you can shoot with a gun. Take a buckshot. Shoot through it—
John Morgan: [garbled] chop it. A good chop. Then shoot it, and that person—whoever it is got the spell on to you—that person will feel it—get the effects of it.

Although the belief in witches was at one time widespread among the Ramapo Mountain People and some of the Mountain People still believe in witches, most of the Mountain People are sensitive to the accusation of ignorance that often accompanies admission of this belief. The concept of degrees of belief is applicable here. Some people who tell the stories do not believe in witches. Others partially believe, like a person who says he's not superstitious yet will not walk under a ladder. Still others fully believe.

Cohen: In a lot of places there are people who have evil eyes and things like that—
John Morgan: Oh, yeah.
Madge Morgan: No, I don't believe that. Oh, people said that there used to be witches, everything like that.
John: Well, there is. There is. There *sure* is. There used to be a woman, lived over there in—on the mountain. They used to call her Black Mag. She used to ride the broom. My mother—she asked my mother and my aunt to go over some day for dinner. And my mother—she's dead and gone—but she was a church member, and she wouldn't lie—
Madge: You know that's all coming on tape what you're talking, don't you?
John: I know it. And she said they went to her—well, dinner time come, she said, Mag went to her closet door. The closet was bare. Wasn't a thing in it. So she [garbled] and, ah, "Sit down," she said, and [garbled] sit down a few minutes. She come up with her wood and come back in. "Well," she says, "come in," she says, "for dinner." Ma says when they went in there, "Ah," she says, "what a table that woman had set there." Yeah, she used to come up the mountain, and from there on, they said, she always had a broom. She took the broom up the mountain.

A woman in Hillburn told me that Black Mag would go to the store without any money and return with her basket "laden." The implication was that she acquired the food by means of witchcraft. But a grandson of Black Mag vehemently denies that his grandmother was a witch.

Informant: Just because a woman lived alone—maybe she was a widow or something—who knows?—but they say, "Oh, don't go around her. She's a witch." Like my grandmother—Black Mag they called her. Look I have fought about it . . . What she could do? You know something? She was one of the nicest old women in the—she was a Indian and she had white hair. Her skin was just like mine [dark], but she had sharp features, a sharp nose like, not a wide nose, sharp and she had very fine features . . . Granny we called her . . .
Cohen: Why was it that these stories were told about her?
Informant: Oh, she was a beautiful—she'd come and visit you or anybody and she was always pleasant. It was her looks. She had this white hair, dark complexion, sharp features, and she was little, and she wore the long dresses down that dragged the ground, you know.

Thus there is some indication these stories were told about people who were not self-professed witches. I was unable to locate anyone today who professes to be a witch, even though there are Mountain People who claim to have the power to cure others or to predict the future. But those powers are not classified as witchcraft by the Mountain People.

One function of these witch stories is suggested in the following discussion about another alleged witch.

Wally De Groat: You remember any stories about the woman they used to call Handsome Abbey? She used to ride that broom, was it?
Vince Morgan: Oh, yeah, they *claimed* she did.
Wally: That's what they used to tell us years ago. My mother used to say, "If you don't go to bed, I'm gonna summon Handsome Abbey down to get you kids and take you away." She had told us so many stories about Handsome Abbey that we were afraid of her. They claimed that on certain nights that she could just get up from a chair, get on a broom, and fly out of a window. I've heard a lot of stories about her, but I can't—like—they're stories. That's all.
Vince: She was a nice old lady, you know, but everybody figured she was a witch. They'd say at certain times she would ride around on a broom, they'd say. They'd see her up in the mountains and up through and all that stuff. But I used to go up to her house. She was a nice old lady.

Despite my inability to find any witches, there is evidence that some of the Mountain People used to consult witches. The following account was given by Sam ("Dude") Van Dunk of Livingston Manor, New York.

Sam Van Dunk: Well, I had a cousin. She wanted to tell me something one day, she said, she never told to anybody else. She was like a mother to me. And her husband run away with another woman, and went down South, and his sister-in-law told her to go up and see her sister up in Goshen. She didn't want to go, but she just had to go.

And she went up there, and the woman met her to the door, and didn't ask her no questions or nothing. She said, "You go back home. I know what you come for and," she said, "bring something that your husband used."

And, ah, so she was so scairt, she told me, she knowed that she'd never go up there again, but somehow or other, she had to go back that next day, and she went up there, which is about 80 miles, and the woman met her to the door again, and she says, "Alright, now,"—she hasn't yet opened her purse, but that woman said, "Alright, give me that hankerchief you brought up and ten dollars."

She says, "I can't afford ten dollars."

She said, "I know you'll—you think you can't, but you'll get along without it. You know," she said, "I'm gonna make that woman get married, and the man isn't gonna love her, and I'm gonna make her work the rest of the days of her life, and your husband 'll be home just as fast as the train can bring him."

So he was home in three days.

"Now," she said, "He's going down to the house to see this woman, but the man's gonna order him out, but he don't care nothing 'bout the man, but then the woman's gonna order him out herself."

So then he went back with his wife, and they lived happy after that.

The belief that one can summon another person at a distance was once common among the Mountain People and is still held by some of them. This belief is often associated with witchcraft.

Wally Morgan: Well, I see it around here when I was young. If people they was needed in a hurry and they would—I seen my mother and my father do it and different people—they would turn their back to a stove—in those days we had mostly wood stoves and bought very little coal—people used to go in the woods and use wood all the time—and they'd turn their backs and they throw that salt over their shoulder, and I'll tell you, it would sure hurry them up, and I don't know what part it played with it, but they sure would get there quick. I'll tell you that. I seen it happen. But I was young, but I seen it happen.

A mountain woman who used to live in Mahwah said that another way to summon someone was to cut out a paper figure of that person, put salt on it, and set fire to the edges. When the fire approaches the edges, you say, "Come, [the person's name]. Come, [the person's name]." She said the person will come within fifteen to twenty minutes.

Sam Van Dunk told about an incident in which the person who could summon also had the power of the evil eye.

Sam Van Dunk: When I was a boy, I lived up on the mountain. So me and my brother, Howard, took a walk over to see these people, which was 'bout a mile away from home. And when it got dark, I got a little scairt, and I says to my brother—'cause we had to walk through the woods—"We better go home."

So this woman, which was a white woman, said, "Oh, your father will be after you."

I said, "He doesn't know where we're at."

She said, "Well, he'll be after you."

So just in time for him to walk up the mountain from the shop, he come right on over where we was. In the meantime, that woman went and put some salt on the stove. In about fifteen minutes afterwards, here come my father.

He said, "What are youse boys doing?"

"I didn't know where we was."

"Well, you better get on home."

So she comes over to the house the next morning. She said, "I told you your father would be after you."

I said, "Yeah, but you couldn't do that with me."

And so the next morning, when I woke up, I wasn't hurt, but I couldn't move my legs.

And she said, "How are you, Sam, this morning?"

So my cousin was going to shoot her. And so his sister stopped him. But I was only that way 'bout an hour, and then I got over it. But she just showed me she could do that.

The term *traveling* is not used by the Mountain People, but the phenomenon of a person's mysterious appearance in another place is seen in the following account by John Morgan of Ringwood.

John Morgan: Old Jake Corter he lived up here. He went coon hunting one night. She, she—his mother told me—it was on a Wednesday night—she says, "Jake, there's no use," she says, "you goin' huntin' tonight."

He says, "Why, Ma?"

"It's Wednesday," she says, "an' it's no use goin' huntin' tonight, 'cause," she says, "your dogs will run you crazy," she said, "an' you won't get nothin'."

"Oh," he says, and he laughed it off.

He took his dogs. He went from here on up. The dogs followed him. First thing you know, he said, that dog, he says, struck this track. Oh, he said, it was an awful track. [garbled] Well, he said, he clumb the tree. He got up and he looked up in the top. What you suppose was in the top? There set his mother. His mother set in the top of that tree. She told him, she said, "Jake, I told you there's no huntin' on Wednesday nights." Yes, sir.

Sometimes traveling is combined with the transformation of the person into another creature.

Sam Van Dunk: You talk about these people with [garbled] I had a cousin and he—his name—we used to call him Walker—his name was Walter, but he used to go over around from one side of the mountain to the other to see this girl. And every night he'd come in [garbled] he had to be and he'd say to his pa, he said, "that there black cat crossed my path again."—No, white cat passed across his path.

And he'd go on. The next night he'd come home, "Pa, that white cat walked right in front of me on—in the path."

So, he said, "Why don't you kill it?"

So then he fills his pockets up with stone, and he come home, "I fixed that cat tonight," he says, "Pa, and the next day ol' Jake De Groat couldn't get out of bed." He couldn't get out of bed. That was the cat! That was the cat!

I collected the same motif from a Cherokee Indian in North Carolina, but this story is not a traditional Indian story. It is associated with the European literature on witchcraft.[9]

There is a widely held belief among the Ramapo Mountain People that an infant "born with a veil" (covered with a caul or membrane) will either be able to predict the future or have good luck. The following explanation was given by a mother living in Mahwah.

Mrs. Peggy Morgan: It's like a—it's a skin. It looks like it's clear from a distance, but it's right over the top [of the baby]. I screamed and hollered. I was awake, and I saw her being born and everything, and I screamed, "Oh, what have I done? Why was God punishing me? He gave me a baby without a face!" There was no face on this child. Just like a blank thing.

And the doctor, he was trying to comfort me and he was telling me, "No, the baby's alright. Just wait. The baby's alright." He was going on like this, you know.

So the nurse reached over like this and she got hold of it, and she was going to take it off of her, and the doctor grabbed her right by the hand and said, "Oh, no. Not that way." And he got her from behind her head, and they had her laying across my stomach, and they took it from this way. They took it off. And they tell me that there's a reason for that too. I don't know what it is.

Mrs. Rita Van Dunk (her daughter): Well, they claim if they take it off from the front over the back, it puts the spirits behind you, and if they take it off forward, the spirits are before you, and you can foresee a lot. Now, if that's the case, I shouldn't be able to know nothing.

Peggy: I didn't know anything about a veil. All I know I was screaming that I had been cursed. God had put a curse on me for something I must have done in my life. And then this doctor—this young doctor—this was in 1943 the year she was born in the time of the war—and he begged me for this veil, and he told me that in about two months he had to go overseas, and that his people believed—he was an Italian doctor—they believed that this would bring them a safe journey back and forth, you know. He asked me for it, and I was ignorant to the fact, but if it was going to save somebody's life, by all means, you know. Sure take it . . . But after she was born, then Vince's [her husband] mother told me that I should have kept it, and then that's when she told me all the stuff about him and the veil. But to me—I—it didn't mean anything. I've never even heard about a veil.

An account of a specific prediction that came true was given by Bob Milligan, the brother of Frank Milligan, of Ringwood.

Cohen: Now, also you said that your daughter can—like—last summer you said she was "born under the veil?"
Bob Milligan: Under the veil. Yeah.
Cohen: What does that mean?
Bob: Covered with a veil—a scum. It's a scum of—when the baby is born it—it looks like a veil, like a netting.
Cohen: And what does that mean?
Bob: Ah, people can tell—that anybody that's born with a veil can tell when anybody's going to die. My older sister and my daughter both can do that.
Cohen: You once gave me an example. What was that?

Bob: I guess I can. Ah, Mr. Graham in Pompton Plains he hung hisself—in his own bedroom, and my sister—that's John's [Morgan] step-mother—she told us, she said, "Well," she said, "you know, I saw Mr. Graham hanging over my bed with a rope around his neck."
I said, "Myrtle, that's baloney."
So, sure enough, when she went to work, and she came back, she said, "Didn't I tell you I saw Mr. Graham hang hisself over my bed?"
I said, "Yes."
She said, "Well, it's true. He did."
That's—I could never believe that until she saw it.

The Ramapo Mountains at night can be a spooky place, and stories about ghosts, specters, poltergeists, and mysterious lights are told by the Mountain People. Some of the Mountain People fully believe these stories. Others do not believe in ghosts, but tell the stories anyway. Still others partially believe in them. All of the stories contain traditional folk motifs, such as the ghosts appearing at a specific time, such as midnight or on Halloween.
John Morgan sat one night and talked with his family about the "screech woman" in Ringwood.

John Morgan: I'll tell you what used to be here. I hear him just talk and it just, ah, reminded me of it. Right across in back of this mountain, down, there used to be what they called "a screech woman." A screech woman. And when she screeched, it would raise the hat on your head. But now, Richard says that twelve o'clock at night, now, this thing comes up—up the river—this screech it comes up the river. So she must of changed her course and traveled up that way now. Every night.
Barbara Morgan (daughter-in-law): If she keeps on going that way, she's alright.
John: Brenda's Richie. Yeah.
Wally Morgan (son): He still hears it?
John: Yeah. Aw, he said it'd raise the hat on your head the way she screeched.
Wally: Dogs won't even mess with it.
John: Uh. Huh.

A woman who used to live in Mahwah said that the screech woman appeared every Halloween. She would throw her head back, and "there would be nothing there."
John Morgan talked about another woman ghost.

John Morgan: I hear Terry's place—you know where Terry's place is?— Well, you come up through there when you come to Ringwood. Well, you know that short bend out there. It used to be—I don't know if it were last year, 'cause people don't travel there like they used to—the road is open more. There used to be a woman. At midnight you'd see this woman. She'd have this—like an army uniform on. And you'd pass her, and she'd always had a police dog. That dog stood that high. And she'd have her little—you know these little canes like high tall women have—these pants. She'd dress like that. Yes, sir, boy. Oh. I'm telling you. And I bet you right today. I bet you right today if you take your time and walk slow along these roads and stopped at these places once and a while, you'd hear or see some of these old things.

In the following story the ghosts appeared in the form of two veiled heads.

John Morgan: And I set on my porch one night out there. The moon was going down. I'd say, oh between twelve and one. Set there alone smoking. I set there enjoying myself alone. I like to be alone. Soon something said to me, "Look up back of the house." So I eased my head around, like that, quick, and I looked at that corner of the house there. And there were these two women heads. Had white veils all over them. You could see it from here. Just two heads like my head and hair, looking around the corner. Well, I jumped up quick. I thought somebody was going to have fun with me now. I jumped up quick and run up there. There was nothing to be seen.

The white veils are related to the belief that ghosts usually appear to be white. John Morgan also talked about a white ghost horse.

John Morgan: I'll tell you about [garbled] I did see one night. My father he used to go out twelve o'clock at night with Fred Whitmore. He'd leave —relieve Fred off the hoist there. Moonshine bright as night. And right down at her sister's store—down the road, you go up over—the hard road wasn't in there then—there used to be the dirt road. You had to come up and go right up the street. We stood there talkin', and all at once, her brother says, "Hey, Chet."
     I said, "What?"
     He said, "You hear that horse?" he says, "he's coming down [chuckles] —coming down the line," he says, "I wonder what horse that is."
     Well, we looked and this white thing was that tall, and that was the prettiest white I ever seen in my life. Never seen nothing as white as that.
     So he said—he said to me, he said, "Now we stay on this side, and when that there comes up to us—up this way," he said, "we'd jump on the other side."

Well, that son-of-a-gun got there, before you turn to come up that road. There wasn't a thing to be seen. But it passed by [garbled] and Fred Whitmore right up there by Ross Babcock. They had to get out—they fell out of the track. It was just like a brush of wind passed 'em. They fell—fell out of the track.

Several of the stories deal with ghost dogs. Chinks Oliver from Hillburn talked about one.

Chinks Oliver: Now you know where the lilies grow just above Cranberry Lake? Right. My grandmother was born there. She said one night she was coming from Hillburn, going home. It was dark. And this dog come long side of her and it kept growing, getting bigger and bigger. And she said, after a while her arm was up like that. And this thing was growing like that, but it was going right with her. And she got on that ledge, you know that ledge you cross. She said, "Thank God I'll soon be home." The house was just across the little swale there. She said—When she says, "Thank God I'll soon be home," she said, that thing took off, and, she said, you could hear the trees and everything. And the next day, she said, she looked and saw the print of a cloven hoof. Yeah.

The cloven hoof is often attributed to the Devil in European folk belief.[10] Another version of the ghost dog story was told by Vince Morgan of Mahwah, who heard it from William Mann.

Cohen: And I think it was another story you told me that Bill Mann used to tell about a dog he used to meet when he was coming off the mountain. *Vince Morgan:* Oh, yeah. He told me that story. That was when they had —the golf links wasn't here then. That was all a big field up to the mountain. And he'd be over in Suffern and he'd go across the little bridge down here, and he said he seen this little dog come along side of him. Oh, about ten inches high. And the further he got to the mountain—the closer he got to home, the bigger that dog got. And when he got where the door, the dog was as big as the door was. He went around and around the house 'til he got away from it. Now that's the story he told me. A ghost story, you know. They tell some awful tales, them old jokers.
Wally De Groat: But they swear they're true, every one.

Wally De Groat said his mother also encountered the head of a ghost dog that would accompany her on the way home from work and then disappear.

The following story is told by a man who doesn't believe at all in ghosts, but likes to tell a good story.

Frank Milligan: Like the fellow they call old Grandpop up in Hewitt? Yeah, he come down to the Forge Pond one night, you know, so he told him—now this is a story he told me—he said he went fishing and—so he set down there and, ah, while he was fishing, you know, it started to get dark so he figured, "Well," he said, "I guess I better get going for Hewitt."

So he started, and going over, he said, and when he passed Spook Rock, he, you know, boy—he—well, he was a guy with big long legs—all of sudden, boy, he—well, when he was walking, that would be about a good-sized trot for us—he said, he felt something reach and give a little tug at his coat. He looked back. He didn't see nothing, so he kind of broke into a trot.

Ah, he said, he could go on up—past that Stump Hill, he said, and something reached out and GADUNG! Kind of hard. Ah, he said, he took off a little faster right on out across the flat, down Paterson Hill, he said, and, boy, by that time, he was making pretty good time. And something reached out again, he said, and POOM, POOM! Boy, he said, tugged pretty hard on his coat. Boy, then, he said, he really started to run.

Well, he's going up like that, and he passed the old Hewitt store, and on in through the white gates, and on up home. Well, he said, when he seen the light in the house, he started hollering, "Open the door!"

And old Willy Dink—he had a crippled leg, you know, and he was coming, you know—he had his hand on his knee, you know, and he was limping —that gimpy leg. He said, when he went through the gate, he said, something just reached out and got hold of him—that coat—and stopped him right dead. Well, he said, he just opened his arms up, because he was just pretty near flying then. He opened his arms up, he said, and the coat sailed right off. Right up to the house, and poor Dink was right in front—open—right in front of the door, ready to open it, when he got to the door. He took door, Dink, and everything. Then he grabbed the shotgun, and he told him, "Close the door, for Godsake," he said, "he's after me!"

So they waited. And all night, they set there waiting for him to come in, and he didn't come in. They figured it had to be the Devil. He told Dink, "It's got to be the Devil!"

So daylight come, it got good and bright, well, he got his nerve up, he said, "I'll go down and see." Went down, and there his coat lay by the gate. Picked up his coat, and then when he wrapped the dropline up, he hadn't put the hooks in tight, and the hooks were dragging behind, and every time they hooked in the rock, that's what was pulling on his coat. And the hooks had hooked in the fence, and that's what stopped him, and—but see now, he always thought it was a ghost until he found that just the hooks from the dropline hooked into the fence. Well, he would have sworn it was a ghost had him.

Vince Morgan told a story about a ghost who knew how to dance the buck-and-wing:

Vince Morgan: Ace told me one time—Ace De Groat—he says he come from Suffern and he was playing the mouth organ. He was kind of scairt. It was dark. There was no lights out here then, you know. No roads out here. It was just a foot path.

And he was walking, playing the mouth organ. He hears this dancing in back of him. And he stopped. He stopped playing the music, the dancing stopped. He'd play it again, and the dancing would start up again. He said he tried to see who it was, but he couldn't see no one. So he started playing the music again. He had a flashlight with him. Playing the music again, and he said it was dancing and dancing, dancing. He kept playing. He put the flashlight and shined it back. He didn't see anything. He said and that looked like a shadow. It was a big tall shadow, he said, about eight foot tall. It just danced on out in the woods away from him. It was just like he was dancing on boards, he said. Tap dancing. Buck dancing. Buck-and-wing dancing they call it.

Tales about poltergeists are also told, although that term is not used by the Mountain People.

John Morgan: Well, me and Mousy—I'll tell you this—me and Mousy set here one day. He laid here and I set in the chair, and we heard a noise, and looked at that rocking chair that my son sits in there now. That starts to rock.

And Mousy said, "Daddy, look a here."

I says, "Yes, I see it."

It rocked.

So then we heard a noise. We had glasses up on the shelf over the sink. One of them glasses jumped from the shelf out in the middle of the floor. Set right up, just as if you took your hand and set it down.

And we—that night we set here. We had two televisions there, one in front of the other. And Barb here she had, ah, this Avon stuff. Little bottle of it, set on the back one. [garbled] It jumped from the back one clean over the top of the front one, struck on the middle of the floor and set up there just as keen. Never even quivered or nothing when it hit the floor.

Similar testimony was heard at the Salem witchcraft trials.

John Morgan explained that you can tell whether a place is haunted by wrapping a handkerchief around a knife. If the place is haunted the knife will come out of the handkerchief by itself.

Mysterious lights are also seen in the Ramapos. One hears stories about the Jack o' Lantern, a strange light that appears in the woods. A Hillburn woman said that her mother told her never to follow a Jack o' Lantern, because it would appear in one place, but when you reached there it would be in another place. Soon you would be lost. Similar stories were collected in Ringwood.

There are contemporary equivalents of these sightings.

Wally Morgan: Well, I'll tell you. There's a modern one. I hear a lot of people seen it. Down around the reservoir [Wanaque] you look around [garbled]—you can look across the water, because it's the same road. And you'd see headlights coming at you. You'll never pass that car.

John Morgan: I've seen it. The car will never come to you.

Wally: A lot of people up in there. I've seen it myself . . .

Well, I'll tell you one thing more—more about them that I seen. I really didn't believe it. I did. I'm afraid I had to see it to believe what I saw. Oh, you see these UFOs [Unidentified Flying Objects] there?

Well, me and another fellow we—he took me out to New York State to get some beer and the moon was shining. So coming over the hill back towards this way—Jersey—we thought it was the moon, you know, at first. All of a sudden we see this light, and this white—it was, oh, about seven, · eight times as big as the moon, and it was right off towards Ringwood here. This way from the direction we was coming. It was white and it turned green, then red. I couldn't believe it. All of a sudden, it just dropped right down off the side of the hill. I wanted to get over here in home for I could see—'cause I figured it was here. Right here. And it just disappeared. I never seen no more of it. I never believed nothing like that, but I seen that —that one.

There is a generational difference in the attitudes of the Mountain People toward these sightings. The Morgans, father and son, talked about similar phenomena, but the son had a scientific explanation while the father had none.

John Morgan: I've seen something in my life I know you thought I'd never see if I weren't old enough. And that was when her brother [his wife's] got married. I was working on a stockpile up there at the mines, stocking ore. And up in the north, this green cloud—a little green cloud—started to come close and close, and off towards the east. When it got half way, it got red as blood. As quick as that the whole sky was American flags. The whole sky was American flags. Right in the center there was a big circle. There was that big star setting right in the center of it. And we stopped work and watched them.

Wally Morgan: Well, I'll tell you something I seen. Me and Mousy was coming home from Lois's one night—we used to go down there and play cards. I guess it was about—oh, one-thirty, two o'clock in the morning, and it had stormed but it was cleared off, you know. We had a light rain. And, ah, we're coming up. It was dark. All of a sudden, the place lit up. You didn't even need a—it looked like the moon, but there was no moon. And you know what it was, though? It was the glacier lights. Remember? I came home and told you? At a certain time you can see those glacier lights when the sun hits those big icebergs and stuff. And it lit up the whole sky. That was one big glow.

A magic barrel is the subject of this story told by "Butch" Van Dunk from Hillburn.

Butch Van Dunk: The story goes: Every night around twelve—twelve midnight, a barrel supposed to be full of gold would roll down from the mountain, down a dirt road, and disappear into an old well. And anybody that knowed to run out there and throw an apron or a tablecloth over it they could have it. But as soon as—every time you did it, and, ah—weird people would appear, ah, monsters, big snakes, so you'd have to scream or say something or else—you couldn't have it. It would disappear. It would just go away. And nobody's been able to do it yet. It's still going on. So I understand.

Cohen: You don't remember where you heard that or who told you that story?

Butch: Well, I know it was passed down. My father told me. I know his father told him. It was just passed down. It sounds, you know, ah, kind of weird. But a lot of things happen like that. Even worse stuff.

In the world view of the Mountain People these beliefs are based on a concept of cause and effect that sees no contradiction between folk belief, religion, and science.

Some of the folk beliefs of the Ramapo Mountain People pertain to the occupation of mining, which prior to the closing of the mines in the 1950s was the main employment for the Mountain People in Ringwood. Frank Milligan, who denies that he is superstitious, says that he worked with men in the mine who believed it was bad luck for a woman to enter the mines. "If they saw a woman in the mine, they're gone.

They would get out of there." Folklorist George Korson noted that this is the most common belief in the coal mines of Pennsylvania.[11] Frank Milligan also said that whistling in the mine was considered bad luck. "If you whistled, oh my God, if you ever whistled, you know." It was also believed that the behavior of the mine rats would predict disasters.

Frank Milligan: And if a rat ever showed up in the mine, don't you hurt that rat. Oh, no. No. No.
Russell Mann: When the rats leave, the men leave.
Frank: Yes. Yes. Just like a ship. They would leave it.

Korson stated that this is one of the oldest beliefs in miners' folklore.[12]

Frank's brother Melvin Milligan told me that the thirteenth level of the mines was never worked because, he said, thirteen miners had died on that level. Mel believes that their bodies are still trapped under a rock there. He noted that the mines were closed on Friday the thirteenth.

Notwithstanding some folk remedies and herb cures which may have been borrowed from the American Indians, the religious and folk beliefs of the Ramapo Mountain People reflect a world view that is European in origin. It is basically a Christian world view, not a native American Indian world view. This finding is consistent with the origin of the Ramapo Mountain People. Their ancestors were colored pioneers whose culture was Dutch.

EPILOGUE:
THE AFTERMATH—
INITIAL REACTION TO
A NEW IMAGE

My intention in writing this book did not include social reform. I suspected that the account of the origin of the Jackson Whites was a folk legend. I was prepared to accept the possibility that the legend was based on historical fact. But as the study progressed, it became increasingly obvious that, not only was the legend untrue, it was also the continuing vehicle for the erroneous and derogatory stereotype of the Mountain People. I began to realize that this study involved more than an academic dissertation.

In order to refute the derogatory stereotype and to discourage further use of the name Jackson Whites, I decided to make the results of my research available without waiting for the publication of this book. I gave talks to historical societies, women's clubs, church groups, and groups of the Mountain People. There were articles in local newspapers and in the *New York Times* linking my research with publicity for the self-help housing program in the Mine Area of Ringwood. I appeared with two Mountain People from Ringwood on an educational television program. A copy of my dissertation was made available in a local public library.

I knew that the legend would not die easily. It has had a long oral and written tradition, and it provided the kind of sensational details that outsiders seem to relish hearing about the Mountain People.

I also expected that the Mountain People might be the last to accept their newly documented history. Despite the negative stereotypes in the versions of the legend told by outsiders, the legend, as told by the Mountain People, expressed their self-image of having Indian and white ancestry. On the other hand, I thought that the history of the colored pioneers of the Hackensack River Valley was something about which the Mountain People could be proud. That would, however, require their acceptance of some black ancestry, and I knew that some Mountain People would be upset about that.

When I first began telling the Mountain People about my findings, they listened politely, but I could tell that many did not believe me. That was natural enough. How could I know more about their origins than their own parents and grandparents? But once my research was given publicity in the local press and on television, a change I had not anticipated came about. Whereas I had previously been "Dave" to them, some of the Ringwood Mountain People began calling me "Doc" and "the Professor." They began to take my findings seriously.

Some Mountain People were pleased that the name Jackson Whites and the legend had been refuted. During the question and answer period following the talk I gave to the Mahwah Historical Society, one colored woman stood and said she was proud now to be one of the Ramapo Mountain People.

A woman from Stag Hill told a local newspaper reporter, "I'm glad to read the truth for once. The others who wrote about us just repeated the same old lies . . . The kids are looked down in school because of the lies the others have heard—that's why some of them don't want to finish school."

A man from Stag Hill told the same reporter that teaching the real history of the Ramapo Mountain People in the schools "might help, it might not."

To this the woman retorted: "Maybe they would find it embarrassing at first, but they'll be able to hold their heads up. The Jackson White thing keeps getting brought up so you might as well bring up the truth." [1]

I was contacted by a young colored woman who was attending a nearby state college. She told me she was taking a course in black history in which the black instructor had mentioned the Jackson

Whites, evidently basing his information on E. Franklin Frazier's brief description in *The Negro Family in the United States*. She was understandably upset about the use of the name Jackson Whites; and she invited me, with the approval of the instructor, to visit the class to correct misconceptions about the Ramapo Mountain People. During my talk to the mostly black class about the colored pioneers of the Hackensack River Valley, the young woman sat in the back of the room, appearing to beam with pride.

In time I began to hear rumors that some of the Mountain People were not happy with my study. I learned in Ringwood that some of the Hillburn Mountain People who had read the dissertation in the local public library were upset. Returning to Hillburn, I discovered that some of the Mountain People there were upset that I had grouped the Hillburn people with those in Mahwah and Ringwood. Despite the fact that I could demonstrate their shared ancestry and common culture, the middle-class Mountain People in Hillburn didn't want to be associated with the lower-class Mountain People in Mahwah and Ringwood. One Hillburn woman took strong exception to my using the name Ramapo Mountain People. She insisted that the Hillburn people don't live in the mountains. The term *Mountain People*, she said, gave people the impression that the Hillburn people were hillbillies.

I could understand these objections in terms of a differentiation of the Ramapo Mountain People into the three settlements of Hillburn, Mahwah, and Ringwood, each with its own independent development and degree of economic advancement. I knew that each settlement had dealt with its own problems without any help from the other settlements. This was true of the desegregation of the grammar school and of the election of the first colored trustee in Hillburn, of the dispute about building a new road to Stag Hill in Mahwah, and of the battle for self-help housing in Ringwood. There was no way to resolve this difference between my historical and cultural vision of the Ramapo Mountain People and the self-image of the Hillburn people.

There was a similar problem in dealing with those Mountain People who were members of the fundamentalist Pentecostal churches. In their world view the distinction between saved and unsaved individuals was more important than any other social grouping. Understandably, they didn't want to be associated with unsaved Ramapo Mountain People.

And yet they could not escape the fact that they are so grouped by outside society.

One Hillburn woman was reluctant to talk to me about her impressions of my study because she feared I would use her name. After I assured her I wouldn't, she said that it was good that I had repudiated the name and legend but why did I have to include all that folklore? She felt that the folklore made the Mountain People appear to be superstitious and ignorant. She was especially upset by the tall tales, which she considered outright "lies." She said her coworkers at her place of employment laughed at her and teased her about this folklore. She wanted me to stress the educational attainments of the Mountain People instead of the old-time beliefs and stories.

I knew that the folklore was an important part of the cultural tradition of the Ramapo Mountain People. I was careful not to label the folk beliefs as superstitions because I knew they were part of a world view that was once the world view of most Americans. Folk medicine was an important stage in the development of modern medical knowledge. Also tall tales are not meant to be taken literally; they are jokes, even though they are told with a straight face, and the tale teller will swear they are true. Storytelling is an art fast disappearing, but there are still some great storytellers among the Mountain People. At a time when the mass media are increasingly taking over the socialization of children, folklore represents a continuity of tradition passed down from generation to generation. Yet how could I tell this woman that she should appreciate her own tradition? The desire of the middle-class Mountain People to become like others in American society was paramount.

As I had expected, some of the Hillburn Mountain People were upset that I had proven black ancestry but had found no documentary evidence of early Indian ancestry. While they were pleased that I had refuted the derogatory name Jackson Whites, they didn't want to be told that their self-image was incorrect. As one Hillburn man angrily told me, how would I like it if someone had proven I had black ancestry? This same man was outraged that I had mentioned inbreeding and had used the real surnames of the Mountain People. His features were such that he could easily pass as white. But now everyone knew that his surname was one of those of the Ramapo Mountain People. He then told me two of his personal experiences suggestive of the poignancy of his situation. Once he and his family were using a public swimming pool. Someone asked his name, and when they found out who he was, he and his family were asked to leave. Another time, when working in the house of a white woman, he was allowed to use the refrigerator freely. But when the woman found out his surname, he was asked to bring his own lunch. He told me that he didn't want his children to have to experience what he had experienced. I got the impression that it wasn't so much that he wanted to pass as white; he wanted people to relate to him as an individual.

I knew that I had to use the real surnames of the Mountain People in order to present the genealogical proof of their ancestry. Besides, the surnames of the Mountain People were already widely known. But what could I say to this man? I could have told him that one cannot bury the past, that it would eventually catch up with him and his children. I could have told him that the pattern of marriage within the group has created strong kinship ties at a time when these ties are loosening in the outside society. I could have told him that he should attack the real problem, which was prejudice, not his own ancestry; that he should be proud to be the descendant of colored pioneers. But I felt that I had no right to say these things to him.

When I accompanied Robert Goldstein to the Ramapos to take photographs for this book, numerous Ramapo Mountain People—particularly in Mahwah—perhaps remembering how they have been maligned in print, politely but firmly refused permission to photograph them and the inside of their homes and churches. I tried to convince them that the truth might help set them free from the old canards, but they were adamant.

As if to underscore the validity of their distrust of newspapers and magazines, a few weeks later the Sunday supplement of a Philadelphia newspaper carried an article about them. Although it cited some of the facts of my research, the Mountain People resented the more sensational elements of the story, feeling that once again they had been maligned by outsiders.

Perhaps one day the Ramapo Mountain People and others will no longer repeat or believe the various legends about their origin. But it will take time. For legends and traditional attitudes tend to die slowly, even in the face of facts to the contrary.

APPENDIX A

MOTIFS AND TALE TYPES

Folklore as a medium of oral communication tends to follow certain patterns. Two such patterns are motifs and tale types. Motifs are personages, incidents, actions, or occurrences that tend to reappear in folk tales. Tale types are entire stories, consisting of a number of motifs that tend to reappear in folklore. Folklorists have categorized and numbered these tale types and motifs and have published bibliographies listing where they have been collected. See Antti Aarne and Stith Thompson, *The Types of the Folktales*, 2d revision, Folklore Fellows Communication no. 184 (Helsinki: 1961); Stith Thompson, *Motif-Index of Folk Literature* (Bloomington, Ind.: Indiana University Press, 1956), 6 volumes; and Ernest Baughman, *Type and Motif-Index of the Folktales of England and North America* (The Hague: Mouton and Co., 1966).

An entire school of folklore scholarship, known as the Finnish historic-geographic method, has attempted to use these motifs and tale types to trace the origin and spread of folk traditions. Rather than using this approach, I have viewed folklore in the context of the local culture, emphasizing what their folklore shows about the Ramapo Mountain People. I have included the motif and tale-type numbers in this appendix so that the reader who is interested in seeing where else they have been collected can look them up.

Motifs

A 977.3.1 (a), Devil carrying apron load of stones for building drops them when apron string breaks.

B 112, Treasure-producing serpent's crown

B 765.1, Snake takes tail in mouth and rolls like wheel.

B 765.2, Snake lays aside his crown to bathe.

B 765.6, Snake eats milk and bread with child.

B 765.7, Jointed snake can join its segments when it is broken into pieces.

C 480.1.1, Whistling in mine is tabu.

D 971.1, Magic mustard seed

D 1026.2, Magic cow dung

D 1171.9, Magic barrel (cask)

D 1385.5.1, Copper as defense against ghosts and magic

D 1500.1.23.1, Charm for curing burns or scalds

D 1500.1.37, Urine used in medicine

D 1500.2.4, Magic circle prevents disease.

D 1504.1, Charm stanches blood.

D 1900, Love induced by magic

D 2064.3, Sickness transferred to animal

D 2064.4, Magic sickness because of evil eye

D 2161.2.2, Flow of blood magically stopped

D 2161.4.1, Cure by transferring disease to animal

D 2161.4.2, Disease transferred to object

D 2161.4.8, Cure by putting lock of patient's hair in hole of post or tree, then plugging the hole with wood

D 2161.4.10.1, Wound healed by same spear that caused it

E 423.1.1, Revenant as dog

E 423.1.3.4, Revenant as white horse

E 587.5, Ghosts walk at midnight.

F 456.1.2.1.1, Knocker brings ill luck if one whistles in mine.

F 473.1 (g), Spirits throw furniture and crockery about, often destructively.

F 473.2.1 Empty chair is rocked by invisible spirit.

F 491, Will-o'-the-wisp (Jack O' Lantern) seen over marshy places

F 491.1, Will-o'-the-wisp leads people astray

F 615.0.1, Death of strong man

F 618.1, Strong hero tames ungovernable horse.

F 623, Strong man holds up mountain.

F 624, Mighty lifter

F 624.1, Strong man lifts horse (ox, ass).

F 624.3, Strong hero lifts cart.

F 628.1.2, Strong man kills ox with flat of hand.

G 242.1, Witch flies through air on broomstick.

G 271.2.5, Bible used in exorcism

G 271.4.1 (le), Breaking spell in person by putting bottle of pins by the fire

G 271.4.2 (b), Shooting picture or symbol of witch breaks spell (usually injuring or killing witch).

G 272.7.2, Broom across door protects from witch.

G 303.3.4.5, Devil as a barrel rolls and is impossible to catch.

T 589.4, Birth with veil brings luck.

X 945 (a), Man kills animal with blow of hand.

X 1122.1.2, Lie: hunter salts bullets of great gun so game will not spoil while he walks to get it.

X 1133.2, Man escapes from bear by running for long time from summer to winter.

X 1215.11, Lie: the split dog. Put back together, but back legs point upward.

X 1301.4 (e), Fish is photographed because it is too big to weigh.

X 1301.5 (ha), Scales of big fish are used for shingles, provide new roof for every house in the valley.

X 1321.3.2, Joint snake breaks into forty pieces when man hits it; each piece chases the man.

X 1321.3.3, Blue racer. Snake which can run very fast. Chases victims.

X 1321.4.1 (b), Blue racer chases man over whole state.

X 1322.1 (c), Man thinks big turtle in river is an island, goes to sleep on its back, wakes up miles from starting point.

Tale Types *

No. 1890, The lucky shot: discharge of gun kills the heathcock, which falls on the sprouts of the trees, which kills the bear, and so forth.

No. 1890 A, Shot splits tree limb, bird's feet caught in crack, and other lucky accidents bring much game.

---

* These tale-types are found in Antti Aarne and Stith Thompson, *The Types of the Folktales*, 2d revision, Folklore Fellows Communication no. 184 (Helsinki: 1961).

APPENDIX B

HERB CURES AND FOLK REMEDIES

I collected most of the following herb cures and folk remedies from the family of John and Madge Morgan of Ringwood. Those that are starred (*) also have been collected from the Delaware or Lenni-Lenape Indians, whose ancestors once lived in New Jersey and Pennsylvania, by Gladys Tantaquideon in *A Study of Delaware Indian Medicine and Folk Beliefs* (Harrisburg, Pa.: Commonweath of Pennsylvania Department of Public Instruction and Pennsylvania Historical Commission, 1942).

These starred herb cures and folk remedies may be the only survivals of authentic Indian culture in the culture of the Ramapo Mountain People. But they cannot safely be taken as evidence of Indian ancestry because both European and African settlers in colonial America borrowed many herb cures from the Indians. In those days they were part of the common knowledge.

HERB CURES AND FOLK REMEDIES

Ailment	Remedy: Folk Terminology	Remedy: Scientific Terminology	Preparation
Sore ankle	the white of an egg		Soak the ankle with a rag soaked in egg white.
Arthritis	rattlesnake oil *		
	pine needles		Make a tea out of pine needles; take a whiskey glass full in the morning and night.
Asthma	Wild plumb bark	*Prunus americana*	Scrape down and brew into a tea.

HERB CURES AND FOLK REMEDIES (*Cont.*)

Ailment	Remedy: Folk Terminology	Remedy: Scientific Terminology	Preparation
Sore back	mustard plaster		Take flour and a little bit of dried mustard and water; stir and apply externally.
Bee stings	blueing		Apply externally.
Bleeding	cobwebs		Apply to wound.
Boils	naphtha soap and sugar		Make a poultice and apply to the boil.
Bursitis	rattlesnake oil *		
Breasts (caked when nursing)	mullein leaf *	*Verbascum thapsus*	Warm the leaf and apply to the breast.
Chest cold	skunk's or goose's grease *		Fry on stove and rub on chest like a salve.
	turpentine and lard		Rub on chest.
Colds and the croup	onion syrup		Slice onion, put on stove; then steep in a saucer; take internally with a little sugar.
Colds	Indian cough weed		Brew into a tea and take like cough syrup.
	Isaac fern (?)		Brew into a tea and take internally.
	vinegar vapor		Boil vinegar in a wash basin; throw a towel over your head and breathe the vapor.
Baby's cramps	catnip tea *	*Nepeta cataria*	Brew catnip into a tea and nurse it to the baby in his bottle.
Croup	butter and vinegar		Put a little butter in a spoon with a little vinegar; hold over stove until melted and take internally.
Diarrhea	burnt bread		Make a tea out of burnt bread and drink.

HERB CURES AND FOLK REMEDIES (*Cont.*)

Ailment	Remedy: Folk Terminology	Remedy: Scientific Terminology	Preparation
Earache	sweet oil or tobacco smoke * or breast milk		Pour or blow into the ear.
Sore eye	black ash	*Nephelium semiglaucum*	Cut limb off tree; put end in fire to get juice out; put a drop or two into the eye.
	sassafras juice *	*Sassafras albidum*	Break sassafras and split it open; scrape the inside juice in palm of your hand; add a drop of water and stir with a match stick; apply to eye.
Pink eye	tea bags or tea leaves		Apply tea bag or tea leaves directly to eye.
Festering from a cut	slippery elm	*Ulmus fulva*	
Fever	burvine (?)		Make a tea from the root; acts as a physic.
	dittany	*Cunila mariana*	Brew into a tea and take internally.
	crushed onions		Crush onions and pack them around the ankles.
	snakeroot *	*Aristolochia serpentaria*	Brew into a tea.
	burdock leaf *	*Arctium minus*	Juice from leaf with a drop of sugar taken internally; also apply the leaf itself to the joints of the body.
	peach tree leaves	*Amygdalus persica*	Apply to ankles.
	spicewood tea	*Benzoin benzoin*	Scrape it down with a paring knife; put between two saucers to steep; sweeten and take one spoonful three or four times a day.

HERB CURES AND FOLK REMEDIES (*Cont.*)

Ailment	Remedy: Folk Terminology	Remedy: Scientific Terminology	Preparation
Fever (*Cont.*)	Asafetida	*Ferula asafoetida*	Put in a little sack and hang around the neck.
Grippe or pneumonia	coltsfoot,* prince's pine,* Indian cough weed and molasses	*Petasites palmata* *Chimaphila umbellata*	Mix together and boil on stove until a syrup; take internally.
Impetigo and sores	sulfur and molasses		
Infection	balm of Gilead	*Balsamodendron gileadense*	Make a salve from the buds of the balm of Gilead.
	salt pork or bacon ends		Apply directly to the wound.
Sore joints	witch hazel	*Hamamelis virginiana*	Apply as a liniment.
Back pain from kidneys	pitch pine *	*Pinus rigida*	Roll pine balls into a pill and take internally.
Excessive menstruation	burnt flour		Burn flour and apply to vulva as a powder.
Sore navel on baby	burnt flour		Burn flour and apply to navel as a powder.
Neuralgia	hornets' nest and vinegar		Soak the hornets' nest in warm vinegar and apply directly to the face.
Fallen palate	salt and pepper		Place salt and pepper on a spoon; touch palate with spoon.
Piles	mullein leaf *	*Verbascum thapsus*	Use the leaves instead of toilet paper.
Pneumonia	kerosene		Warm; rub on chest; causes a water blister.
Poison ivy	chestnut leaves	*Castanea dentata*	Rub leaf to get out the juice; apply to the irritation.

HERB CURES AND FOLK REMEDIES (*Cont.*)

Ailment	Remedy: Folk Terminology	Remedy: Scientific Terminology	Preparation
Poison ivy (*Cont.*)	silver leaf ("touch-me-not")	*Impatiens biflora*	Rub leaf on hand to get out the juice; rub juice on the irritation.
Rheuma-tism	snakeroot *	*Aristolochia serpen-taria*	Put in a bottle of whiskey and allow to sit; then drink.
Ringworm	salt pork		Apply externally.
Sprue (babies)	red turnip sprouts and alum root	*Heuchera americana*	Scrape down the turnip and apply with the alum.
Stomach cramp	snakeroot *	*Aristolochia serpen-taria*	Put in a bottle of whiskey and allow to sit; then take a teaspoonful internally.
Stomach pain	calamus root *	*Acorus calamus*	Chew on the root.
	tansy *	*Tanacetum vulgare*	
Sore throat	kerosene and sugar		Gargle with a teaspoon of sugar and kerosene.
	skunk's cabbage root *	*Symplocarpus foeti-dus*	Stew the root and gargle with the juice.
	baked potato plaster		Bake the potato; scoop the insides out and add a little black pepper; apply to throat.
	lemon		Split lemon and apply directly to the throat.
	salt pork, black pep-per, and turpentine		Cover salt pork with black pepper and a little bit of turpentine and apply to sore spot.
	slippery elm	*Ulmus fulva*	Put bark around the neck.
Toothache	onion		Cook onions in fire; put in a rag and apply to the sore.
Worms	tansy *	*Tanacetum vulgare*	Brew into a tea and take internally.

Herb Cures and Folk Remedies (*Cont.*)

Ailment	Remedy: Folk Terminology	Remedy: Scientific Terminology	Preparation
Worms (*Cont.*)	wild cherries	*Prunus*	Scrape down and make a brew; give two teaspoonsful in a glass.
	white oak bark and molasses	*Quercus alba*	
	turpentine and sugar		A couple of drops of turpentine mixed with a little sugar in a spoon; take internally.
	vermifuge		Steep over stove and drink the juice.
	dogwood bark and molasses	*Cornus florida*	Take the white of the dogwood bark and put it in the oven; bake until crispy; roll into a powder and eat with a bit of molasses.

APPENDIX C

A JERSEY DUTCH WORDLIST

In 1910 Professor John Dyneley Prince published an article on the Jersey Dutch dialect in *Dialect Notes* (3, pt. 6 [1910]:459–84). One of his main informants was William De Freece from Ringwood, who spoke what Prince described as the "Negro" variant of the dialect. Prince's article proves that the strange patois mentioned by writers about the Mountain People as early as 1872 was actually Jersey Dutch. It survives in the present-day speech of the Mountain People in such expressions as "I am *feest* of it," meaning in Jersey Dutch, "I am disgusted by it." This survival of some aspects of Dutch culture among the Ramapo Mountain People is in accordance with their genealogical origins.

The following is a list of words and expressions that Prince collected from William De Freece. The words are written in the phonetic notation used by Prince. The list is preceded by a pronunciation key to the notation taken from the article (pp. 461–62).

Pronunciation Key

$a = u$ in English *pull*

$\bar{a} = a$ as in *father*

$\hat{a} = $ A deep close *aw*, as in *awful*, but more constricted

$\ddot{a}$, A vowel commonly heard in this district. It is between *a* in *hat* and *e* in *met*. Common in North Jersey English today.

$\ddot{a}\ddot{a} = $ The prolongation of the above, very flat

$\bar{a}i = \bar{a} + i$, as *i* in *like*

$\ddot{a}\ddot{a}i = \alpha + i$, no English equivalent

$\bar{a}u = $ Ordinary American *ou* in *house*

äu = The Cockney *ou* in *house*

ääu = Prolongation of the above, no English equivalent

b, Not as distinct as in English, often hard to distinguish from *v*. It is like the Spanish medial *b*.

ch, As in English when it occurs, but this sound is usually *tś* (q.v.).

d, As in English. Interchanges with *t*.

e, A short indeterminate vowel something like the *u* in *but*, uttered without opening the mouth very wide

ê = English *ay* in *may*. Not the Holland *ee* which is *ê* + *i*.

eî, Like Holland *ee*, but followed by *î*, upon which the main stress is laid; a very difficult diphthong, often merging into pure *î*.

f = English *f*, interchanges with *v*

g, Like English *g* in *get*, when used. Rare.

h, As in English initial *h*

i, As *i* in *hit*

î, More contracted than *ee* in *meet*

j = Consonantal *y*

k = English *k*

l, Almost the Polish barred *l*, very thick. This *l* does not usually carry an inherent vowel in combination, as in the Holland and Flemish *l*. Thus *twâlf* and not *twâl'f* = Holland *twaalf* "twelve." I find the inherent vowel only in the word *kääl'kûn*, "turkey."

m As in English

n As in English

n = Nasal, as in French *mon*

nn = The nasal followed by *n*

ng As in *sing*

o = A·very short *aw*

ô As English *o* in *Oh*

ö Like *u* in English *fur*

œ The prolongation of the above

œu = *œ* and *ü*, pronounced rapidly together

p As in English

r; r initial and after another consonant, like the ordinary American palatal *r;* final *r* is a strong palatal burr like the Canadian final *r* in *butter*. The Netherland trilled *r* with inherent vowel is never heard . . .

s As in English, interchanges with *z*

ś = The palatized *sh*, like Polish *ś*

t As in English; interchanges with *d*

tś = The palatized *ch*, as in Polish *ć*

u = English *oo* in *foot*

û As English *oo* in *fool*

ü As German *ü* in *Mütze*

ue = The prolongation of the above, as in *vuur* "fire"

v Like English *v*, but not so strong a labial. Difficult at times to distinguish from *b*. Interchanges with *f*.

w As English *w* in *water*. *W* is pronounced thus in South Holland and Flemish today.

x, I use to denote the soft guttural, as in German *Bach*. This sound is never so harsh as in *g*, and before *e*, *i*, it is always palatalized into N. *xj*, as in Flemish.

z As in English, interchanges with *s*

I use the apostrophe to denote and indeterminate short vowel as in the Hebrew *sh'va*.

Words and Expressions Collected from William De Freece by John Dyneley Prince

Ak xân wääx mârge—I am going away tomorrow.

Wän zāl je xân mät māin äut en sxôte—When shall you go out with me and shoot?

Ak häv et sxôn vergêten—I have already forgotten it.

Ak zāl lâik för te onthāne—I should like to remember.

āl de lāng—All along.

äske—Ash-tree (in Holland Dutch, *esschenboom*)

blôte kop—Bald (in Holland Dutch, *bloot* means bare)

bāiebôm—Bee tree

kestänne—Chestnut tree (in Holland Dutch, *kastanjeboom*)

kääukerdif—Chicken hawk (in Holland Dutch, *kuikendief*)

klāin wêxettśe—Chipmunk, literally "little weasel" (in Holland Dutch, *wezelche*)

spränghantje—Grasshopper (in Holland Dutch, *sprinkhaan*)

wêz kāu—Hurry up, literally be quick

ās äk lêv—If I live

hät xât rêgene—It is going to rain.

för it te dûne—In order to do it

kāine blôt kop—A kind of bald

määs—Knife (in Holland Dutch, *mes*)

blât—Leaf (in Holland Dutch, *blad*)

k'nî—Knee (in Holland Dutch, *knie*)

bäästevlês—Meat

xjäält—Money (in Holland Dutch, *geld*)

mönt—Month (in Holland Dutch, *maand*)

môn—Moon (in Holland Dutch, *maan*)

äk wêt nöt—I do not know.

nût—Nut (in Holland Dutch, *noot*)

āike—Oak (in Holland Dutch, *eikenboom*)

wêz mâr stäl—Only be quiet (in Holland Dutch, *maar* = only)

ôver hîr—Over here (in Holland Dutch, *over* = over)

äämer—Pail (in Holland Dutch, *emmer*)

väälthân—Partridge (in Holland Dutch, *veldhoen*)

kläin rûrtśe—A little gun or pistol (in Holland Dutch, *klein roer*)

rolle—Proceed or go along (in Holland Dutch, *rollen*)

râtelslâng—Rattlesnake (in Holland Dutch, *ratelslang*)

sxop—Shovel

än-kôrn—Squirrel (in Holland Dutch, *eekhoorn*)

mâ—Tired

ālle dâx—The whole day (in Holland Dutch, *alle dagen* means every day)

wîzen pêrd äz dāt—Whose horse is that?

xjasterdax—Yesterday (in Holland Dutch, *gisteren*)

wärkt—Work (in Holland Dutch, *werk*)

litt de vîr—Light the fire.

fäängster—Window (in Holland Dutch, *venster*)

ôrêk—Earache (Holland Dutch *oor* plus English ache)

ôxen—Eyes plural (in Holland Dutch, *oog;* plural, *oogen*)

plôt—Foot (in Holland Dutch, *poot,* paw of animal)

vergêten—Forgotten (in Holland Dutch, *vergeten*)

sxôtergâfel—Fork (in Holland Dutch, *schotel* "plate"? plus *gaffel* "fork")

APPENDIX D

POPULATION DISPERSAL OF RAMAPO MOUNTAIN PEOPLE, 1911

Elizabeth S. Kite, the researcher who worked on the unpublished Vineland Training School study of the Ramapo Mountain People entitled "The Jackson Whites: A Study of Racial Degeneracy," compiled an estimate of the population dispersal of the Mountain People circa 1911. Her estimate appears to be based on her own field work in compiling genealogical data rather than on census figures.

I spot-checked her estimates against the manuscript census for 1915 and found her figures roughly accurate for the main settlements of Hillburn and the mountain, Mahwah, Ringwood, and Hewitt. However, she grossly overestimates the number of Mountain People in Orange, New Jersey. I found only one mountain family in Orange in 1915: George and Ida De Groat, colored, residing on Hill Street (New Jersey, State Census: 1915. Essex County). Also her estimate for Newark, N.J., is inaccurate. According to the *Newark Directory: 1910* (Newark: Price and Lee Co., 1910) there were 1 De Freece family, 2 De Groats, 3 Manns, and no Van Dunks then residing in Newark. Kite may have been using a different criterion than surnames to determine who is one of the Mountain People. In any case, her estimates are given because they demonstrate that by 1911 the Mountain People were migrating from the vicinity of their greatest concentration to the farming towns in Orange County, N.Y., the suburban towns in Bergen County, N.J., and the nearby cities of Paterson and Newark. This dispersal as early as 1911 refutes a common misconception that all the Mountain People lived isolated in the Ramapos until recently. The approximate total estimate of 2,611 Mountain People in 1911 includes all those who had moved away from the Ramapos.

I have added an asterisk following names which Kite located in the wrong state—N.J. instead of N.Y. and vice versa.

ESTIMATE OF THE POPULATION DISTRIBUTION
OF THE RACIALLY-MIXED PEOPLE IN 1911

Allendale, N.J.	20	Newark, N.J.	120
Arlington, N.J. *	4	Newburg, N.Y.	15
Blauvelt, N.Y.	20	New Milford, N.Y.	10
Bloomfield, N.J.	5	New Rochelle, N.J. *	12
Bloomingdale, N.J.	20	New York City	25
Blooming Grove, N.Y.	5	Nutley, N.J.	5
Boonton, N.J.	10	North Asbury Park, N.J.	10
Butler, N.J.	5	Oakland, N.J.	10
Carlstadt, N.J.	15	Oradell, N.J.	5
Chester, N.Y.	100	Orange, N.J.	140
Closter, N.J.	10	Park Ridge, N.J.	25
Cresskill, N.Y. *	5	Paterson, N.J.	75
Darlington, N.J.	60	Passaic, N.J.	35
Denville, N.J.	5	Paramus, N.J.	20
Englewood, N.J.	10	Plainfield, N.J.	10
Fishkill, N.Y.	10	Pompton, N.J.	25
Florida, N.Y.	15	Peachburg, N.Y.	5
Glen Ridge, N.J.	5	Ramsey, N.J.	28
Glen Rock, N.Y. *	10	Red Bank, N.J.	5
Goshen, N.Y.	150	Ridgewood, N.J.	15
Greenwood Lake, N.J.	5	Ringwood, N.J.	120
Hackensack, N.J.	20	River Edge, N.J.	20
Harriman, N.Y.	5	Rivervale, N.J.	10
Haskell, N.J.	20	Saddle River, N.J.	25
Hasbrouck Heights, N.J.	5	Sloatsburg, N.Y.	25
Hewitt, N.J.	25	Southfields, N.Y.	15
Hillburn, N.Y. and the		South Orange, N.J.	10
mountain	440	Springfield, N.J.	35
Hillsdale, N.J.	25	Spring Valley, N.Y.	10
Lake, N.Y.	20	Suffern, N.Y.	25
Mahwah, N.J.	130	Tallmans, N.Y.	75
Maplewood, N.J.	5	Waldwick, N.J.	15
McGuinessburg, N.Y.	50	Warwick, N.Y.	20
Midvale, N.J.	15	Washington, N.J.	5
Midland Park, N.J.	5	Washingtonville, N.Y.	15
Middletown, N.Y.	45	West Hoboken, N.J.	10
Millerton, N.Y.	15	West Nyack, N.Y.	25
Monroe, N.J. *	20		
Mt. Holly, N.J.	5	Approximate total estimate	2,611

Source: Vineland Training School, "The Jackson Whites: A Study of Racial Degeneracy," manuscript, Vineland Training School, Vineland, N.J., circa 1911, n.p.

APPENDIX E

SCHOLARLY LITERATURE ON RACIALLY MIXED GROUPS IN THE EASTERN UNITED STATES

In the eastern United States there are more than 200 socially isolated, racially mixed groups—between 75,000 and 100,000 people—who claim Indian ancestry but maintain no tribal affiliations. They have been studied by anthropologists, sociologists, historians, and geneticists. Among the chief problems concerning them have been the origin and identity of these groups. Are they surviving Indian remnants? Are they a separate caste? Or are they primarily descendants of free blacks?

Anthropologists have assumed that these racially mixed groups are surviving remnants of American Indian tribes. In 1889 James Mooney, an anthropologist at the Smithsonian Institution, sent out 1,000 letters requesting information on local Indian tribal and place-names, cultural and archeological remains, and pure- and mixed-blood Indian survivors from Delaware to Georgia. On the basis of this information, he concluded that there was undoubtedly considerable Indian ancestry among blacks in the southern coastal plain region.

In "The Powhatan Confederacy Past and Present," *American Anthropologist*, vol. 9 (1907), Mooney specifically studied the racially mixed people of Tidewater Virginia who considered themselves descendants of the tribes of the Powhatan Confederacy—the Chickahominy, Mattaponi, Nansamond, Nottoway, Pamunkey, Potomac, and Rappahannock Indians. In 1785 Thomas Jefferson had referred to the Mattaponies as having "more negro than Indian blood in them." In 1843 white citizens of King William County, Virginia, had petitioned the state legislature to divide the lands of the Pamunkey Indians on the grounds that the tribe was extinct and those who survived were legally free mulattoes. Mooney concluded that by 1907 the Pamunkey Indians had entirely abandoned their Indian language and customs.

In the 1920s anthropologist Frank Speck of the University of Pennsylvania also studied the racially mixed people of Tidewater Virginia. In *The Rappahannock Indians of Virginia* (New York, 1925) and *Chapters on the Ethnology of the Powhatan Tribes of Virginia* (New York, 1928), Speck argued that the elimination of these people from the ranks of Indians because they were no longer pure-blood Indians would mean that many Indian groups maintaining active tribal traditions in North, Central, and South America also would not be considered Indian. Speck tried to establish the existence of survivals of Indian culture among these alleged descendants of the Powhatan tribes. As examples of their material culture he cited basketry, featherwork, wooden mortars, wood carvings, wooden pipes, and bows and arrows. He also mentioned corn-derived foods in their diet, the custom of head flattening, and the word *ra'rep* (meaning "Indian" as in *rarep* corn) in the vocabulary of the supposed descendants of the Rappahannock Indians.

In *The Nanticoke and Conoy Indians* (Wilmington, 1927), Frank Speck maintained that a racially mixed group residing along the Indian River in Sussex County, Delaware, was a surviving remnant of the Nanticoke Indians. Originally located on the Delmarva Peninsula on the east shore of Chesapeake Bay, most of the Nanticoke Indians had left there by 1748 because of the encroachment of white settlers. They migrated to the north and west and came under the protection of the Iroquois in 1753. When Speck began his field work in 1910, he found most of the surviving Nanticoke Indians were on the Six Nations Reserve in Ontario, Canada. These Canadian Nanticoke still used words from the Nanticoke language, but no language survivals could be found among the alleged remnant in Delaware. The only evidence Speck cited linking the two groups was the surname Street, which was reported in both the Canadian and Delaware groups, but this name had disappeared in Canada by 1927. The most common surnames among the racially mixed people in Delaware (Harmon, Clark, Coursey, Sockum) were not found among the Canadian Nanticokes.

William Harlen Gilbert surveyed several racially mixed groups, which he categorized as "Surviving Indian Groups of the Eastern United States" in the *Smithsonian Institution: Annual Report of the Board of Regents* (1948).

In an essay titled "Indian Cultural Adjustment to European Civilization" printed in *Seventeenth Century America: Essays in Colonial History* (Chapel Hill, 1959), anthropologist Nancy O. Lurie suggested that the Ramps, Melungeons, Brown people, Issues, and other racially mixed groups in the southern Appalachian Mountains might be descendants of the Piedmont tribes of Virginia. In the late seventeenth century, she wrote, these Piedmont tribes were caught between the westward push of whites, the northward migrations of the Carolina tideland tribes, and the southern invasions of the Seneca Indians. Her hypothesis was that this squeeze might have led to their intermixture with blacks, whites, and other Indian tribes.

Sociologists have viewed these racially mixed people as a separate caste. Edward Byron Reuter in *The Mulatto in the United States, Including a Study of the Role of Mixed-Blood Races Throughout the World* (Boston, 1918) and Cedric Dover in *Half Caste* (London, 1937) both maintained that mixed-blood populations around the world generally occupy an intermediate social and cultural status.

In *Race Mixture: Studies in Intermarriage and Miscegenation* (New York, 1931), Reuter argued that racially mixed people develop a distinct personality type. Robert E. Park concurred with this point of view in "Mentality of Racial Hybrids," published in the *American Journal of Sociology*, vol. 36 (1931). Everett V. Stonequist in his book *The Marginal Man: A Study in Personality and Culture Conflict* (New York, 1937) coined the term *marginal man* to identify "the individual, who through migration, education, marriage, or some other influence, leaves one social group or culture without making a satisfactory adjustment to another, finds himself on the margin of each but a member of neither."

In "Personality in a White-Indian-Negro Community," *American Sociological Review*, vol. 4 (1939) Guy B. Johnson used this social-psychological approach to study a triracial group in North Carolina—the Croatans or Lumbees of Robeson County. He asserted that such groups give rise to certain problems of personal adjustment, such as coming to terms with Negroid physical features and the "disorganizing effect of [their] anomalous social position."

E. Franklin Frazier discussed what he termed "racial islands" in a separate chapter of his sociological study of *The Negro Family in the United States* (Chicago, 1939). He maintained that isolated communities of mixed-bloods should be grouped separately from blacks and mulattoes. Whereas mulattoes have generally constituted an upper class among blacks, he wrote, the racial isolates regard themselves as a different race.

Brewton Berry, a sociologist at Ohio State University, concurred with the view that such groups have a separate social status. In *Almost White* (New York, 1963), Berry called them "America's outcasts" and "forgotten men," who "spend their lonely lives in a social limbo—not quite white, not quite Negro, not quite Indian."

Academic historians have tended to overlook small racially mixed groups. In the absence of documented histories, folk legends have developed to explain group origins. For example, the Lumbees or Croatans of North Carolina are said to be the descendants of the Lost Colony of Roanoke, the Melungeons of Tennessee allegedly the descendants of Portuguese pirates, and the Moors of Delaware supposedly the descendants of shipwrecked Spanish sailors. Local historians usually repeat these legends, sometimes labeling them as folklore, often mistaking them for fact.

In *Delaware's Forgotten Folk* (Philadelphia, 1943), C. A. Weslager mentioned several legends about the origins of the Moors and Nanticokes, but he did not conclusively prove or disprove the legends.

In *The Saga of Coe Ridge: A Study in Oral History* (Knoxville, 1970) William Lynwood Montell studied a colony of former slaves in the foothills of the Cumberland Mountains on the Tennessee-Kentucky border. In the absence of written records—the local county records were destroyed during the Civil War and again in fires in 1888 and 1933—Montell used local legends to reconstruct the colony's history. He asserted that folk history expresses the feelings of the people about their past and that local legends are most likely grounded in fact if they have persisted in the same geographical region, if they exist in more than one racial group, or if they are recorded in local histories.

Certainly folk legends convey the attitudes of the people who tell them. But in the absence of documentary proof, one cannot assume that legends are true. The legend about the origin of the Jackson Whites of the Ramapo Mountains fits all of Montell's criteria, yet it is historically untrue.

In general, racially mixed groups claiming Indian ancestry have been subsumed under historical studies of free blacks in pre-Civil War America. In *The Free Negro in Virginia* (Baltimore, 1913) John Russell acknowledged that free blacks included people of Indian and free-black mixed parentage. He showed that some free blacks in Virginia owned property and slaves. His findings about free-black property holders were documented on a state-by-state basis in Carter G. Woodson's *Free Negro Owners of Slaves in the United States in 1830* (Washington, D.C., 1924), James M. Wright's *The Free Negro in Maryland, 1634–1860* (New York, 1921), Luther Porter Jackson's *Free Negro Labor and Property Holding in Virginia, 1830–1860* (New York, 1942), and John Hope Franklin's *The Free Negro in North Carolina, 1790–1860* (Chapel Hill, 1943).

The above historians based their research on public documents, such as state laws, court records, tax lists, and censuses, which reflect the racial classification of the dominant white race. In the nineteenth century manuscript censuses, many of these people with racially mixed ancestry were listed as blacks or mulattoes; in fact, in many states they were *legally* considered blacks.

For example, in *The Free Negro in North Carolina*, John Hope Franklin made no mention by name of any of these racially mixed groups, but they were included in his data. In Robeson County, which Franklin showed had the largest free-black population in the southern part of the state, the majority of the population listed as free blacks in 1830 consisted of people who considered themselves Indian. (This was computed by checking the known surnames of the Lumbees or Croatans against the free-black household heads in the county listed in Carter G. Woodson's *Free Negro Heads of Families in the United States in 1830* [Washington, D.C., 1925].) Nor did Franklin mention the Sampson County Indians (who constituted over half the free-black population in Sampson County in 1830), the Haliwa Indians in Halifax and Warren counties, the Cubans or Person County Indians in Person

County, the Laster Tribe in Perquiman County, and the Machapunga Tribe in Dare and Hyde counties—all racially mixed groups listed as free blacks in the census. While they constituted only a small percentage of the overall free-black population of the state, these racially mixed groups had a separate identity.

There have been a few general historical studies of miscegenation between blacks and Indians that mention these isolated, racially mixed groups. In "The Relations of Indians and Negroes in Massachusetts," *Journal of Negro History*, vol. 5 (1920), Carter G. Woodson used descriptions in primary sources to document the progressive mating with blacks by the Indians of Massachusetts. In "Documentary Evidence of the Relations of Negroes and Indians," *Journal of Negro History*, vol. 14 (1929) James Hugo Johnston cited examples of Indian and black interracial mixing throughout the eastern United States. As examples, he mentioned the Croatans of North Carolina, the Moors of Delaware, and the Melungeons of Tennessee. He concluded that "the Indian has not disappeared from the land, but is now part of the Negro population of the United States." And Kenneth Porter enumerated examples of Indian and black mating over an even larger region in "Relations Between Indians and Negroes Within the Present Limits of the United States," *Journal of Negro History*, vol. 17 (1932). He too cited as examples the Melungeons and the Croatans. However, using these groups as evidence of miscegenation between blacks and Indians only begs the question of their origin.

Previous genealogical studies of these racially mixed groups were more concerned with proving certain now outmoded genetic theories than with ascertaining the origins of the groups. These studies were modeled after Robert L. Dugdale's study of crime, pauperism, disease, and heredity in an upstate New York family titled *The Jukes* (New York, 1877).

Arthur H. Estabrook and Ivan E. McDougle compiled genealogies of a racially mixed group, which they called the Win Tribe, known locally as the Issues of Amherst County, in the Blue Ridge Mountains of Virginia. Their book *Mongrel Virginians: The Win Tribe* (Baltimore, 1926) was published shortly after Virginia passed its "racial integrity" law of 1924 banning marriages between whites and blacks. The text of the law was reprinted in *Mongrel Virginians* as an appendix. Estabrook and McDougle maintained that their book was presented "not as theory or as representing a prejudiced point of view but as a careful summary of the facts of history." They concluded, however, that interracial mating had lowered the intelligence level of the group. This conclusion was based on subjective impressions and rumors gathered in their field work.

The same approach was used by the Vineland Training School of Vineland, New Jersey, in its unpublished study "The Jackson Whites: A Study of Racial Degeneracy" (Vineland Training School files, circa 1911). Henry Herbert Goddard, the director of the Vineland Training School, also used genealogies in *The Kallikak Family* (New York, 1912), a study of the heredity of "feeble-mindedness" in a family from the New Jersey Pine Barrens.

The genealogies on which the above studies were based were all undocumented, and they are especially unreliable concerning early ancestry.

A later generation of scholars has taken a more objective approach to inbreeding. Thomas J. Harte in "Trends in Mate Selection in a Tri-Racial Isolate," *Social Forces*, vol. 37 (1959) and Angelita Q. Yap in *A Study of a Kinship System: Its Structural Principles* (Washington, D.C., 1961) have shown that endogamy (marriage within the group) has been a key factor in maintaining the social solidarity of a racially mixed group known as the Wesorts of southern Maryland.

In "The Little Races," *American Anthropologist*, vol. 74 (1972), Edgar T. Thompson noted that biologists now define race as a breeding population or gene pool. He suggested that racially mixed people who have married within their own group over many generations might validly be considered "little races."

Geneticists are now trying to determine the racial make-up of racially mixed groups. William S. Pollitzer studied the relative frequencies of certain physical traits (skin color, hair type, physical measurements, and so forth) and of certain genetic traits (blood types, hemoglobins, RBC enzymes, and so forth) in selected racially mixed groups in comparison to hypothetical parent populations. In "The Physical Anthropology and Genetics of Marginal People of the Southeastern

United States," *American Anthropologist*, vol. 74 (1972), Pollitzer reported that the Indian ancestry differs from group to group. He estimated that the admixture in the ancestry of the Lumbee Indians of North Carolina was 42 percent white, 48 percent black, and 10 percent Indian. For the Haliwa Indians of North Carolina he estimated that the admixture was 33 percent white, 53 percent black, and 14 percent Indian. But he estimated that the Melungeons of Tennessee have 86 percent white ancestry, 14 percent black ancestry, and *no* Indian ancestry, despite their claims to the contrary. As useful as this genetic study is to understanding the present racial make-up of these groups, it does not fully answer the question of their origin, because some of this racial admixture may have occurred recently.

The closest any previous researcher has come to documenting the actual origins of these racially mixed enclaves in the eastern United States is the geographic-distribution study made by historical geographer Edward Price. He reported his findings in his Ph.D. dissertation "Mixed Blood Populations of Eastern United States as to Origins, Localizations, and Persistence" (Berkeley, 1950) and in his article "A Geographic Analysis of White-Negro-Indian Racial Mixture in Eastern United States," *Annals of the Association of American Geographers*, vol. 43 (1953). By studying the manuscript federal censuses for the nineteenth century, Price found that most of the ancestors of these racially mixed groups were listed as free blacks and mulattoes. They appeared to have arrived at their present locations at the time of pioneer settlement. But this finding is too general to be of real use.

In view of the fact that all these groups have legends about their origin that are so important to their group identity, it is odd that no one has previously used documented genealogies to test the historical validity of these legends.

It remains to be seen whether genealogical data are available for other racially mixed groups in the eastern United States. It is my belief that only by combining documented genealogical research with research from other disciplines can the origin and identity of these groups be reliably established.

NOTES

Chapter 1   *The Origin of the Jackson Whites*

1. John C. Storms, *The Origin of the Jackson-Whites of the Ramapo Mountains* (Park Ridge, N.J.: Printed by the author, 1936), p. 3. Storms issued a 2d ed. in 1945, a rev. 2d ed. in 1953, and an enl., illus. ed. in 1958.

2. Ibid., pp. 4–5.

3. Ibid., pp. 6–8.

4. Ibid., pp. 8–11.

5. Ibid., pp. 13–15.

6. Ibid., p. 13.

7. Ibid., pp. 15–16.

8. Charles H. Kaufman, "An Ethnomusicological Survey Among the People of the Ramapo Mountains," *New York Folklore Quarterly* 23 (March 1967):3–43; ibid., (June 1967): 109–31; Miles M. Merwin, "The Jackson Whites," *Rutgers Alumni Monthly* 42, no. 8 (July 1963):21–36; Constance Crawford, "Jackson Whites," (M.A. thesis, School of Education, New York University, 1940); Linda Stamato, "The Jackson-Whites of the Ramapo Mountains," (M.A. thesis, Seton Hall University, 1968).

9. Anthony F. C. Wallace, *The Modal Personality Structure of the Tuscarora Indians* . . . , Smithsonian Institution, Bureau of American Ethnology Bulletin no. 150 (Washington, D.C., 1952), p. 15.

10. Edward J. Lowell, *The Hessians and Other German Auxiliaries of Great Britain in the Revolutionary War* (New York: Harper & Brothers, 1884), pp. 300, 213n.

11. Ibid., pp. 285–86.

12. G. C. Coster, *Hessian Soldiers in the American Revolution: Records of Their Marriages and Baptisms of Their Children in America, Performed by Rev. G. C. Coster, 1776–1783*, trans. Marie Dickoré (Cincinnati: C. J. Krehbiel Co., 1959).

13. Max von Eelking, "A List of the Officers of the Hessian Corps Serving Under Generals Howe, Clinton, and Carleton, 1776–1783," in *The German Allied Troops in the North American War of Independence, 1776–1783*, trans. J. C. Rosengarten (Albany, N.Y.: Joel Munsell's Sons, 1893), pp. 281–351.

14. *New Jersey Archives*, 1st ser. vols. 11, 12, 19, 20, 24–29 *Newspaper Extracts*, ed. William Nelson (Paterson, N.J.: Press Printing & Publishing Co., 1894, 1895, 1897, 1898, 1902–17), 2d. ser., vols. 1–5 *Newspaper Extracts*, eds. William Stryker, Francis Lee, Austin Scott, and William Nelson (Trenton, N.J.: John L. Murphy Publishing Co., 1901–17).

15. William Hugh Jansen, "The Esoteric-Exoteric Factor in Folklore," in *The Study of Folklore*, ed. Alan Dundes (Englewood Cliffs, N.J.: Prentice-Hall, 1965), pp. 43–51.

16. "A Community of Outcasts," *Appleton's Journal of Literature, Science, and Art* 7, no. 156 (Saturday, Mar. 23, 1872):325.

17. David Cole, ed., *History of Rockland County, New York* . . . (New York: J. B. Beers & Co., 1884), p. 266.

18. J. M. Van Valen, *History of Bergen County, New Jersey* (New York: New Jersey Publishing & Engraving Co., 1900), pp. 181–82.

19. Arthur S. Tompkins, ed., *Historical Record to the Close of the Nineteenth Century of Rockland County, New York* (Nyack, N.Y.: Van Deusen & Joyce, 1902), p. 552.

20. William Nelson, "Annual Report of the Corresponding Secretary for 1906/7," *Proceedings of the New Jersey Historical Society*, 5 (October 1907):120.

21. Frank Speck, "Jackson Whites," *Southern Workman* 40, no. 2 (February 1911):104.

22. Vineland Training School, "The Jackson Whites: A Study of Racial Degeneracy," (Manuscript, Vineland, N.J., circa 1911), n.p.

23. Raymond H. Torrey, et al., *New York Walk Book*, American Geographical Society Outing Series no. 2 (New York, 1923), p. 90.

24. Ibid.

25. Lee Benson, *The Concept of Jacksonian Democracy: New York as a Test Case* (New York: Atheneum, 1964, first published in 1961), pp. 301–4.

26. Henry C. Beck, *Fare to Midlands* (New York: E. P. Dutton & Co., 1939), pp. 73–74; reprinted as *The Jersey Midlands* (New Brunswick: Rutgers University Press, 1963).

27. Ibid., pp. 74–75.

28. Constance Crawford, "Jackson Whites," pp. 47–48.

29. Ibid.

30. E. Franklin Frazier, *The Negro Family in the United States*, rev. and abridged ed. (Chicago: University of Chicago Press, 1966, first published in 1939), p. 173.

31. Vineland Training School, "The Jackson Whites," n.p.

32. *Rockland County Journal* 28 (Saturday, Feb. 9, 1878):4. I am indebted to Professor Carl Nordstrom of Brooklyn College for this reference.

33. Speck, p. 105.

34. Vineland Training School, "Jackson Whites," n.p.

35. Edward Thomas Price, Jr., "Mixed-Blood Populations of Eastern United States as to Origins, Localizations, and Persistence," (Ph.D. dissertation, Department of Geography, University of California, Berkeley, 1950), pp. 111, 259.

36. Vineland Training School, "Jackson Whites," n.p.

Chapter 2   *Colored Pioneers in New Amsterdam and the Hackensack River Valley*

1. William Stuart, "Negro Slavery in New Jersey and New York," *Americana Illustrated* 16, no. 4 (October 1922):348.

2. Ibid., p. 349.

3. E. B. O'Callaghan, ed., *Calendar of Historical Manuscripts in the Office of the Secretary of State, Albany, New York*, pt. 1, *Dutch Manuscripts, 1630–1664* (Albany, N.Y.: Weed, Parsons & Co., 1865–66), p. 87.

4. Isaac Newton Phelps Stokes, *The Iconography of Manhattan Island, 1498–1909* (New York: Robert H. Dodd, 1922), 4:97.

5. Alexander C. Flick, ed., *History of the State of New York* (New York: Columbia University Press, 1933–37), 1:342.

6. Jasper Danckaerts, *Journal of Jasper Danckaerts*, eds. James B. Bartlett and J. Franklin Jameson (New York, 1913), reprinted in *The History of the United States*, vol. 1, *1600–1876 Source Readings*, eds. Neil Harris, David J. Rothman, and Stephan Thernstrom (New York: Holt, Rinehart, & Winston, 1969), p. 60.

7. O'Callaghan, *Calendar*, pt. 1, p. 328.

8. E. B. O'Callaghan, ed., *The Register of New Netherlands, 1626 to 1674* (Albany, N.Y.: J. Munsell, 1865), pp. 11, 14.

9. James Grant Wilson, ed., *The Memorial History of the City of New York* (New York: New York History Co., 1892), 1:214.

10. O'Callaghan, *Calendar*, pt. 1, p. 104.

11. Stokes, *Iconography*, 4:111–12.

12. "Records of the Reformed Dutch Church in New Amsterdam and New York," *Collections of the New York Genealogical and Biographical Society*, vol. 2 (1901), *Baptisms, 1639–1730*, p. 23.

13. Stokes, *Iconography*, 4:111–12.

14. "Records of the Reformed Dutch Church in New Amsterdam and New York," vol. 1 (1890), *Marriages, 1639–1801*, p. 46.

15. Taken from a list of members of the New York Dutch Reformed Church in Wilson, *Memorial History of New York*, 1:452.

16. Genealogical Notebooks, Budke Collection MSS, New York Public Library.

17. "Records of the Reformed Dutch Church in New Amsterdam and New York," 2:26.

18. Ibid., p. 11.

19. Genealogical Notebooks, no. 2, Budke Collection MSS, New York Public Library.

20. "Records of the Reformed Dutch Church in New Amsterdam and New York," 1:47.

21. Ibid., vol. 2, *Baptisms, 1639–1730*, pp. 142, 147, 158, 169, 184.

22. New York State Historian, *Third Annual Report of the State Historian of the State of New York: 1897* (Albany, N.Y.: Wynkoop Hollenbeck Crawford Co., 1898), p. 442.

23. George H. Budke, "The History of the Tappan Patent," *The Rockland Record . . .* , ed. George H. Budke (Nyack, N.Y.:Rockland County Society of the State of New York, 1931), 2:35–42.

24. Ibid., pp. 42–43.

25. Ibid., p. 43.

26. Ibid., pp. 35, 43.

27. Genealogical Notebooks, Budke Collection MSS, New York Public Library.

28. "Census of Orange County, . . . 1702," *The Rockland Record . . .* , 2:72.

29. "Census of Orange County, 1712," ibid., 2:22–23.

30. Budke, "The History of the Tappan Patent," p. 43.

31. Orange County, N.Y., Deeds, bk. 1, pp. 17–18.

32. Ibid., pp. 42–44.

33. Ibid., pp. 62–63.

34. Ibid., pp. 93–95.

35. Ibid., pp. 140–42.

36. Ibid., pp. 145–46.

37. Ibid., pp. 147–48.

38. Ibid., pp. 88–90.

39. Ibid., pp. 324–25.

40. Ibid., pp. 322–23.

41. Ibid., pp. 181–83.

42. Ibid., pp. 183–86.

43. "Records of the Dutch Reformed Church in New Amsterdam and New York," 1:182.

44. Records of the Clarkstown Reformed Church, Budke Collection MSS, New York Public Library, fol. 49.

45. Tax Assessment List, Clarkstown, New York, 1787, Budke Collection MSS, New York Public Library, fol. 52.

46. Jackson Turner Main, *The Social Structure of Revolutionary America* (Princeton, N.J.: Princeton University Press, 1965), p. 27.

47. Budke, "The Tappan Patent," p. 43.

48. Orange County, N.Y., Deeds, bk. 1, pp. 159–60.

49. Ibid., pp. 79–81.

50. Ibid., pp. 106–8.

51. Ibid., pp. 109–11.

52. "Records of the Reformed Dutch Churches at Hackensack and Schraalenburgh, New Jersey," *Collections of the Holland Society of New York*, vol. 1, pt. 2 (1891), p. 49.

53. "Baptisms at Tappan from October 25, 1694 to January 10, 1816," in David Cole, *History of Rockland County, New York* (New York: J. B. Beers & Co., 1884), p. 11.

54. "A Muster Roll of the Men Raised and Passed in the County of Orange for Capt. Howel's Company, May 19, 1760," in *Muster Rolls of the New York Provincial Troops, 1755–1764* (New York: New-York Historical Society, 1892), p. 332.

55. "Records of the Reformed Dutch Churches at Hackensack and Schraalenburgh, New Jersey," vol. 1, pt. 2 (1891), p. 50.

56. Ibid., 1:48.

57. "Baptisms at Tappan," p. 9.

58. Ibid., p. 6.

59. "Records of the Reformed Dutch Churches at Hackensack and Schraalenburgh, New Jersey," vol. 1, pt. 2, p. 46.

60. Orange County, N.Y., Deeds, bk. 1, p. 283.

61. Main, pp. 25–26.

62. Genealogical Notebook, Budke Collection MSS, New York Public Library, fol. 50.

63. "Baptisms at Tappan," p. 24.

64. New Jersey State Archives, Wills, New Jersey State Library, Trenton, Lib. 33, File 2335B, p. 156.

65. "Records of the Reformed Dutch Churches of Hackensack and Schraalen-burgh, New Jersey," vol. 1, pt. 2, p. 53.

66. Ibid., vol. 1, pt. 1, pp. 230, 232.

67. Abstracts of the Records of the Surrogates Office of Manhattan, Budke Collection MSS, New York Public Library, Lib. 29, fol. 95.

68. U.S., Bureau of the Census, *Heads of Families . . . 1790. New York* (Washington, D.C., 1908), p. 142.

69. U.S., Bureau of the Census, Second Census of the United States: 1800, New York (manuscript), p. 102.

70. *Muster Rolls of the New York Provincial Troops,* pp. 334, 404, 460.

71. Quoted in James Hugo Johnston, "Documentary Evidence of the Relations of Negroes and Indians," *Journal of Negro History* 14, no. 1 (January 1929):27.

72. The name Mary Jane Defries appeared on a list of Delaware Indians on a reservation in Kansas in 1866 who decided to become American citizens. Her age was given as twenty-four, and she was a family head with two children. ("List of Delawares on Reservation in Kansas Who Decided to Become American Citizens," John G. Pratt Papers, microfilm roll no. 5, compiled circa 1866, quoted in *The Delaware Indians: A History,* by C. A. Weslager [New Brunswick: Rutgers University Press, 1972], p. 516.)

Chapter 3 *The Migration to the Ramapo Mountains*

1. "An Act for Regulating of Slaves, Passed March 11, 1713–14," *Acts of the General Assembly of the Province of New Jersey . . .* ed. Samuel Allinson (Burlington, N.J.: Isaac Collins, 1776), p. 20.

2. "An Act Respecting Slaves, 14 March 1798," *Laws of the State of New Jersey,* comp. William Paterson (New Brunswick, N.J.: Abraham Blauvelt, 1800), pp. 312–13.

3. Bergen County, N.J., Deeds, Book S, p. 170.

4. Ibid., Book R, p. 428.

5. Ibid., Book V2, p. 463.

6. Ibid., Book S, p. 176.

7. Records of the Rockland County Clerk's Office, Historical Miscellanies, vol. 2, Budke Collection MSS, New York Public Library.

8. "Federal Census of 1800 for Orange County, New York," *New York Genealogical and Biographical Record,* vol. 64, no. 1 (January 1933), p. 62.

9. U.S., Bureau of the Census, Fifth Census of the United States: 1830. New Jersey (manuscript), n.p.

10. Bergen County, N.J., Deeds, Book U, p. 153.

11. Ibid., Book V2, p. 103.

12. Ibid., Book I4, p. 257.

13. U.S., Bureau of the Census, Seventh Census of the United States: 1850. New Jersey (manuscript), n.p.

14. Wills and Inventories, New Jersey State Archives, New Jersey State Library, fol. 5568 B.

15. U.S., Bureau of the Census, Third Census of the United States: 1810. New York (manuscript), n.p.

16. U.S., Bureau of the Census, Fourth Census of the United States: 1820. New York (manuscript), n.p.

17. List of Employees in John Suffern's Ledger, in James Ransom, *Vanishing Ironworks of the Ramapos* (New Brunswick, N.J.: Rutgers University Press, 1966), p. 218.

18. U.S., Bureau of the Census, Seventh Census of the United States: 1850. New Jersey (manuscript), n.p.

19. Bergen County, N.J., Deeds, Book W5, p. 282.

20. Ibid., p. 284.

21. Ibid., Book B6, p. 211.

22. Carter Godwin Woodson, *Free Negro Heads of Families in the United States in 1830* (Washington, D.C.: Association for the Study of Negro Life and History, 1925), pp. 75, 105.

23. Herbert S. Ackerman and Arthur J. Goff, comp., "Records of the Zion Lutheran Churches of Saddle River and Ramapo, New Jersey," (Ridgewood, N.J.: typescript, 1943), n.p.

24. Saxby V. Penfold, *Romantic Suffern* (Tallman, N.Y.: Rockland County Historical Committee, 1955), p. 4.

25. "Marriages in the Reformed Dutch Church, New York City," *New York Genealogical and Biographical Record*, vol. 70, no. 1 (January 1939), p. 39.

26. Penfold, p. 46.

27. U.S., Bureau of the Census, *Heads of Families at the First Census of the United States . . .* (Washington, D.C., 1908), p. 140.

28. Rockland County, N.Y., Wills, Book C, p. 329.

29. Herbert S. Ackerman and Arthur J. Goff, comp., "Records of the Ramapo Reformed Dutch Church and of the Ramapo Lutheran Church," (Ridgewood, N.J.: typescript, 1944), p. 85.

30. Ibid., p. 77.

31. Vineland Training School, "The Jackson Whites: A Study of Racial Degeneracy," (Vineland, N.J.: manuscript, c. 1911), n.p.

32. U.S., Bureau of the Census, Sixth Census of the United States: 1840. New Jersey (manuscript), n.p.

33. U.S., Bureau of the Census, Seventh Census of the United States: 1850. New York (manuscript), n.p.

34. Payroll for the Ringwood furnace, Nov. 30, 1869, manuscript in the possession of Lewis West, Midvale, N.J.

35. John Y. Dater, "The Growth of Mahwah," in John Y. Dater and Chester A. Smeltzer, *The Birth of Ramsey and the Growth of Ramsey* (Ramsey, N.J.: Ramsey Journal Press, 1949), p. 174.

36. "Inventory of Andrew Hopper, late of the township of Franklin made the 25th day of November, 1813," Bergen County, N.J., Records of Inventories, Liber B, p. 248.

37. Irving Stoddard Kull, "Slavery in New Jersey," *Americana Illustrated* 24 (October 1930):464.

38. From Mrs. E. Oakes-Smith, *The Salamander*, quoted in Willard L. De Yoe, "Hopper House and Valley Rd. History Ends With Anecdotes, Legends, Notes About Period," *Ramsey Journal* (Thursday, Aug. 15, 1957), p. 9.

39. New Jersey, State Census for New Jersey: 1865. Bergen County (manuscript), n.p.

40. U.S., Bureau of the Census, Tenth Census of the United States: 1880. New Jersey (manuscript), n.p.

41. "Records of the Ramapo Reformed Dutch Church," p. 22.

42. Ibid.

43. "Records of the Ramapo Presbyterian Church, Hillburn, New York," manuscript in the church's manse, n.p., n.d.

44. John C. Storms, The Origin of the Jackson-Whites of the Ramapo Mountains (Park Ridge, N.J.: Privately printed, 1936), pp. 16–17.

45. Bergen County, N.J., Deeds, Book Z6, p. 597.

46. "Records of the Ramapo Reformed Church," p. 21.

47. U.S., Bureau of the Census, Ninth Census of the United States: 1870. New Jersey (manuscript), p. 62.

48. New Jersey, State Census of New Jersey: 1865. Passaic County (manuscript), n.p.

49. U.S., Bureau of the Census, Tenth Census of the United States: 1880. New Jersey (manuscript), p. 44.

50. Records of the Ramapo Presbyterian Church, n.p.

51. New York, Bureau of the Census, State Census of New York: 1855. Rockland County (manuscript), pp. 173–76.

52. Bergen County, N.J., Deeds, Book C7, p. 529.

53. Ibid., Book A7, p. 70.

54. Ibid., Book U4, p. 152.

55. New York, Bureau of the Census, State Census of New York: 1855. Rockland County (manuscript), pp. 77–80.

56. U.S., Bureau of the Census, Seventh Census of the United States: 1850. New Jersey (manuscript), n.p.

57. Bergen County, N.J., Deeds, Book Z6, p. 597.

58. U.S., Bureau of the Census, Seventh Census of the United States: 1850. New Jersey (manuscript), n.p.

59. Bergen County, N.J., Deeds, Book C5, p. 535.

60. Ibid., Book D6, pp. 258, 261.

61. U.S., Bureau of the Census, Seventh Census of the United States: 1850. New Jersey (manuscript), n.p.

62. Bergen County, N.J., Deeds, Book M6, p. 257.

63. Ransom, pp. 11–12.

64. "A Community of Outcasts," Appleton's Journal of Literature, Science, and Art 7, no. 156 (Saturday, Mar. 23, 1872):327–28.

65. U.S., Bureau of the Census, Tenth Census of the United States: 1880. New Jersey. New York (manuscript), n.p.

66. New York, Bureau of the Census, State Census of New York: 1915. Rockland County (manuscript), n.p.; New Jersey, State Census of New Jersey: 1915. Bergen County. Passaic County (manuscript), n.p.

67. New Jersey, Adjutant General's Office, Record of Officers and Men of New Jersey in the Civil War, 1861–1865 (Trenton, N.J.: John L. Murphy, 1876), 2:987, 1510, 1209, 1503; 1:574, 1567, 1566.

68. List in J. Bogert Suffern, "Town of Ramapo," in Historical Record to the Close of the Nineteenth Century of Rockland County, ed. Arthur S. Tompkins (Nyack, N.Y.: Van Deusen & Joyce, 1902), p. 533.

Chapter 4   *Mahwah*

1. Donald W. Becker, *Indian Place-Names in New Jersey* (Cedar Grove, N.J.: Phillips-Campbell Publishing Co., 1964), pp. 31–32.

2. Willard L. De Yoe, "Ramapo Valley History Begins in This Issue," *Ramsey Journal* (Thursday, July 4, 1957), p. 5.

3. Saxby V. Penfold, *Romantic Suffern* (Tallman, N.Y.: Rockland County Historical Committee, 1955), p. 33.

4. Willard L. De Yoe, "Another Installment Given in History of Bergen's Original Subdivision, the Ramapo Tract," *Ramsey Journal,* Thursday, July 30, 1959, p. 12; Edward Franklin Pierson, *The Ramapo Pass,* ed. H. Pierson Mapes (Ramapo, N.Y.: Privately printed, 1955, written in 1915), pp. vii, 31.

5. Penfold, pp. 33–34.

6. Ibid.

7. Quoted in Pierson, p. 40.

8. Ibid.

9. *Mahwah: Portrait of a Town* (Mahwah, N.J.: Mahwah Chamber of Commerce, 1960), p. 12.

10. "Road from 15 M. Stone, near Suffran's to Fort Lee, Hackensack, Haverstraw, etc.," by Captain John W. Watkins, Erskine-DeWitt map no. 26, New-York Historical Society, August 1778.

11. "Roads from Ringwood to Pompton Plains and From Pompton Plains to Sufferns," by Robert Erskine, Erskine-DeWitt map no. 42, New-York Historical Society, 1778.

12. Bergen County, N.J., Deeds, Book U, p. 153.

13. Ibid., Book V2, p. 103.

14. Carter Godwin Woodson, *Free Negro Heads of Families in the United States in 1830* (Washington, D.C.: Association for the Study of Negro Life and History, 1925), p. 75.

15. John Y. Dater, "The Growth of Mahwah," in Charles A. Smeltzer and John Y. Dater, *The Birth of Ramsey and the Growth of Ramsey* (Ramsey, N.J.: Ramsey Journal Press, 1949), p. 143.

16. Ibid., pp. 163–74.

17. Ibid., pp. 155–57.

18. Ibid., pp. 144–45.

19. *Mahwah: Portrait of a Town,* pp. 28, 13–14.

20. Bergen County, N.J., Deeds, Book 729, p. 330.

21. Ibid., Book 1239, p. 563; Book 1259, p. 28; Book 1314, p. 76; Book 1498, p. 172; Book 1666, p. 80.

22. Ibid., Book 1859, p. 226.

23. Ibid., Book 2328, p. 622; Book 2383, p. 468; Book 2392, p. 108; Book 2468, p. 418; Book 2514, p. 37.

24. *Bergen Evening Record* (Hackensack, N.J.), Oct. 23, 1956, p. 21.

25. Ibid., May 13, 1957, p. 17.

26. Ibid., June 20, 1957, p. 29.

27. Ibid., July 16, 1957, p. 17.

28. Ibid., July 24, 1957, p. 29.

29. Ibid.

30. Ibid., Aug. 1, 1957, p. 1.

31. Ibid., Aug. 2, 1957, p. 1.

32. Ibid., Aug. 5, 1957, p. 2.
33. Ibid., Aug. 10, 1957, p. 1.
34. Ibid., Sept. 18, 1957, p. 1.
35. Ibid., Oct. 15, 1957, p. 21.
36. Ibid., Oct. 22, 1957, p. 19.
37. Ibid.
38. Ibid., Oct. 25, 1957, p. 25.
39. Ibid.
40. Ibid., Nov. 2, 1957, p. 1.
41. Ibid., Nov. 27, 1957, p. 1.
42. Ibid., Nov. 23, 1957, p. 12.
43. Ibid., Nov. 26, 1957, p. 21.
44. Ibid., Nov. 27, 1957, p. 1.
45. *Ramsey Journal,* Nov. 28, 1957, p. 8.
46. *Bergen Evening Record* (Hackensack, N.J.), Nov. 25, 1957, p. 29.
47. Ibid., Dec. 3, 1957, p. 5.
48. Ibid., Dec. 7, 1957, p. 2.
49. Ibid., Dec. 6, 1957, p. 29.
50. Ibid., Dec. 9, 1957, p. 25.
51. Ibid., Dec. 27, 1957, p. 17.
52. Ibid.

Chapter 5 *Ringwood*

1. The account of the Ringwood iron industry is based on James M. Ransom, *Vanishing Ironworks of the Ramapos* (New Brunswick, N.J.: Rutgers University Press, 1966); Theodore W. Kury, "Historical Geography of the Iron Industry in the New York-New Jersey Highlands, 1700–1900," (Ph.D. dissertation, Department of Geography, Louisiana State University, 1968); Albert H. Heusser, *George Washington's Map Maker: A Biography of Robert Erskine,* ed. Hubert G. Schmidt (New Brunswick, N.J.: Rutgers University Press, 1966, first published in 1928); Allan Nevins, *Abram S. Hewitt: With Some Account of Peter Cooper* (New York: Harper & Brothers, 1935).

2. This account is based on *Ringwood: Golden Jubilee, 1918–1968* (Ringwood, N.J.: Ringwood Golden Jubilee, Inc., 1968).

3. U.S., Bureau of the Census, *Censuses of the United States: 1930. 1940. 1950. 1960. 1970. New Jersey. Population.* (Washington, D.C., 1932, 1943, 1952, 1963, 1973).

4. Report of Findings of Progress Development Grant, Community Action Council of Passaic County, Hewitt, N.J., 1967 (in the files of the CACPC office).

5. T. R. Reid, Ford Motor Company, Dearborn, Michigan, to Andrew F. Marshall, Mar. 29, 1971 (in the files of HOW-TO, Inc., Hewitt, N.J.).

6. *Suburban Trends* (Bloomingdale, N.J.), Oct. 3, 1971, p. 10.

7. Ibid., Oct. 4, 1970, p. 35.

8. *New York Times,* Mar. 8, 1971, p. 37.

9. *Argus* (West Milford, N.J.), Mar. 10, 1971, p. 10.

10. Ibid.

11. *Bulletin* (Ringwood, N.J.), Mar. 25, 1971, p. 2.

12. *Suburban Trends,* Apr. 14, 1971, p. 9.

13. Ibid., Mar. 29, 1972, p. 28.

14. Ibid., July 9, 1972, p. 1.
15. Ibid., Aug. 6, 1972, pp. 1, 2.
16. Ibid.
17. *Argus*, Aug. 6, 1972, p. 7.

Chapter 6 *Hillburn*

1. The information on the founding of Hillburn is based on J. Bogart Suffern, "Town of Ramapo," in *Historical Record to the Close of the Nineteenth Century of Rockland County, New York*, ed. Arthur S. Tompkins (Nyack, N.Y.: Van Deusen & Joyce, 1902), pp. 537–40; Saxby V. Penfold, *Romantic Suffern* (Tallman, N.Y.: Rockland County Historical Committee, 1955), pp. 79–81; Edward Franklin Pierson, *The Ramapo Pass*, ed. H. Pierson Mapes (Ramapo, N.Y.: privately printed, 1955, written in 1915).

2. New York, Bureau of the Census, State Census of New York: 1875. Rockland County (manuscript), n.p.

3. Rockland County, N.Y., Deeds, Book 124, p. 619.

4. Ibid., Book 128, p. 134.

5. Ibid., Book 143, p. 33.

6. Ibid., Book 163, p. 387.

7. Ibid., Book 166, p. 381.

8. Suffern, "Town of Ramapo," pp. 524–25, 536–40; Penfold, pp. 79–81.

9. Compiled from U.S., Bureau of the Census, *Eighteenth Census of the United States: 1960. New Jersey. Population.* (Washington, D.C., 1963).

10. Ibid.

11. Computed from Township of Mahwah, Tax List. 1972 (on file in the Bergen County Tax Board, Bergen County Courthouse, Hackensack, N.J.).

12. Computed from Town of Ramapo, Tax List. 1972 (on file in the Town of Ramapo Tax Board, Rockland County, N.Y.).

13. "Brief School History of Rockland County," manuscript in the Suffern Public Library, 1941, n.p. (mimeographed).

14. *P.M. Daily*, vol. 4, no. 71 (Sept. 9, 1943), p. 10; ibid., no. 75 (Sept. 14, 1943), p. 12; NAACP *Bulletin*, vol. 2, no. 9 (October 1943), p. 10.

15. *Nyack Journal News*, vol. 54, no. 106 (Sept. 9, 1943), p. 1.

16. Ibid.

17. Ibid., no. 107 (Sept. 10, 1943), p. 1.

18. Ibid., no. 109 (Sept. 13, 1943), pp. 1–2.

19. *P.M. Daily*, vol. 4, no. 75 (Sept. 14, 1943), p. 12.

20. *Nyack Journal News*, vol. 54, no. 110 (Sept. 14, 1943), p. 1.

21. Ibid., no. 123 (Sept. 29, 1943), p. 1.

22. Ibid., no. 134 (Oct. 12, 1943), p. 1.

23. Ibid., no. 139 (Oct. 18, 1943), p. 1; *New York Times*, vol. 13, no. 31314 (Oct. 19, 1943), p. 21; *P.M. Daily*, vol. 4, no. 105 (Oct. 19, 1943), p. 11.

24. *Nyack Journal News*, vol. 54, no. 138 (Oct. 16, 1943), p. 4.

25. Ibid.

26. Ibid., no. 141 (Oct. 20, 1943), p. 4.

27. Ibid., no. 140 (Oct. 19, 1943), p. 1.

28. Ibid., no. 112 (Sept. 16, 1943), p. 1.

29. Ibid., no. 114 (Sept. 18, 1943), p. 1.

30. Ibid., no. 122 (Sept. 28, 1943), p. 1.

31. "Church History and Buyer's Guide, Including Cook Book of Favorite Recipes" (Hillburn, N.Y.: Ramapo Presbyterian Church, n.d.), n.p.

32. New York, Bureau of the Census, Census of the State of New York: 1875. Rockland County (manuscript), n.p.

33. New York, Bureau of the Census, Census of the State of New York: 1915. Rockland County (manuscript).

34. U.S. Bureau of the Census, *Fifteenth Census of the United States: 1930. Population. New York* (Washington, D.C., 1932).

35. Compiled from U.S. Bureau of the Census, *Censuses of the United States. Population. New York. 1880–1970.* (Washington, D.C., 1883, 1894, 1895, 1897, 1901–2, 1913, 1923, 1932, 1943, 1952, 1963, 1973).

36. Rockland County, Bureau of Elections, Party Enrollment Lists, District 5 (Hillburn), 1914 to present.

37. *Nyack Journal News*, vol. 57, no. 268 (Mar. 19, 1947), p. 1.

38. Hillburn, N.Y., Village Board Minutes, March 1960, n.p.

39. Ibid., March 1968, n.p.

Chapter 7 *Race*

1. Brewton Berry, *Almost White* (New York: Macmillan, 1963), pp. 15–16, 40.

2. Richard A. Goldsby, *Race and Races* (New York: Macmillan, 1971), p. 21.

3. W. Lloyd Warner made this distinction between the sociological and biological definitions of race in his introduction to Allison Davis, Burleigh B. Gardner, and Mary R. Gardner, *Deep South: A Socal Anthropological Study of Caste and Class* (Chicago: Phoenix Books, University of Chicago Press, 1964, first published in 1941), pp. 7–8.

4. Edgar T. Thompson, "The Little Races," *American Anthropologist* 74, no. 5 (October 1972): 1295–1306.

5. Constance Crawford, "Jackson Whites" (M.A. thesis, School of Education, New York University, 1940), p. 75.

6. This epithet has been collected in reference to the Redbones, a racially mixed group in western Louisiana, by Edward Thomas Price, Jr., "Mixed-Blood Populations of Eastern United States as to Origins, Localizations, and Persistence," (Ph.D. dissertation, Department of Geography, University of California, Berkeley, 1950), p. 11. Brewton Berry notes the use of *yellow hammers* to refer to another group. Berry, p. 40.

7. This term was also collected in 1968 by Linda Stamato, "The Jackson-Whites of the Ramapo Mountains," (M.A. thesis, Seton Hall University, 1968), p. 39.

8. E. Franklin Frazier, *The Negro Family in the United States,* rev. & abridged ed. (Chicago: University of Chicago Press, 1966, first published in 1939), pp. 173–74.

9. From a program for the church service, dated Jan. 25, 1970, the A.M.E. Zion Church, celebrating its 113th anniversary. The source of the information in the program was Mrs. Isadora Conklin.

Chapter 8　*Family and Kinship*

1. "A Community of Outcasts," *Appleton's Journal of Literature, Science, and Art* 7 (Mar. 23, 1872): 325.

2. George Weller, "The Jackson Whites," *New Yorker* 14 (Sept. 17, 1938): 29, 30.

3. George Peter Murdock, *Social Structure* (New York: Macmillan Co., 1960), p. 1.

4. Ibid., pp. 1–2.

5. Arthur W. Calhoun, *A Social History of the American Family* (Cleveland: Arthur H. Clark Co., 1917), 1:176.

6. George H. Budke, "The History of the Tappan Patent," *Rockland Record*, ed. George H. Budke (Nyack, N.Y.: Rockland County Society of the State of New York, 1931), 2:43.

7. Their names appear as the grantors on a 1715 deed in which they sold 20 morgen of land to Jacob Vleeraboom, Orange County, N.Y., Deeds, bk. 1, pp. 140–42.

8. New Jersey, State Archives, Wills, Lib. 33, File 2335 B, p. 156.

9. Compiled from marriage records of neighboring churches during the period 1818 to 1898 in which the age of one or both of the individuals was listed. There were 34 males and 36 females in the sample.

10. Compiled from federal and state manuscript censuses for the nineteenth century.

11. Compiled from U.S., Bureau of the Census, Tenth Census of the United States: 1880. New York. New Jersey (manuscript).

12. Compiled from New York, State Census of New York: 1915. Rockland County (manuscript).

13. Compiled from U.S., Bureau of the Census, *Eighteenth Census of the United States: 1960. New York. New Jersey. Population.* (Washingotn, D.C., 1963).

14. Anti-Poverty Survey, Community Action Council of Passaic County, Hewitt, N.J., 1966–67 (in the files of the CACPC).

15. Murdock, p. 92.

16. Elmora Matthews, *Neighbor and Kin: Life in a Tennessee Ridge Community* (Nashville: Vanderbilt University Press, 1965), pp. xxiii–xxiv.

17. This data was computed from genealogical charts compiled from informants among the Mountain People and previous genealogical studies, including Vineland Training School, "The Jackson Whites: A Study in Social Degeneracy," (manuscript, Vineland Training School, c. 1911); Dorothy Osborn, "Family of Cora Haring and Margeret Abdullah," manuscript in the Eugenics Record Office Files, Dwight Institute for Human Genetics, University of Minnesota, 1917.

18. Matthews, pp. 35–41.

19. Spencer T. Snedecor and William K. Harryman, "Surgical Problems in Hereditary Polydactylism and Syndactylism," *Journal of the New Jersey Medical Society* 37, no. 9 (September 1940): 443–49.

20. George Weller, "The Jackson Whites," *New Yorker* 14, no. 31 (Sept. 17, 1938): 29.

21. Town of Ramapo, N.Y., Tax List, 1972 (on file in the Town of Ramapo Tax Board, Rockland County, N.Y.)

Chapter 9 *Folklore as an Expression of the Culture*

1. Folklorist Dan Ben-Amos defined folklore as "artistic communication in small groups." Dan Ben-Amos, "Toward a Definition of Folklore in Context," *Journal of American Folklore* 84, no. 331 (January-March 1971): 13.

2. Folklorist Jan Harold Brunvand defined folklore as "those materials in culture that circulate traditionally among the members of any group in different versions, whether in oral form or by means of customary example." Jan Harold Brunvand, *The Study of American Folklore: An Introduction* (New York: W. W. Norton & Co., 1968), p. 5.

3. Folklorists have categorized and numbered these tale types and motifs and compiled bibliographies listing where they have been collected. See Antti Aarne and Stith Thompson, *The Types of the Folktales*, 2d revision, Folklore Fellows Communication no. 184 (Helsinki: Folklore Fellows, 1961); Ernest Baughman, *Type and Motif-Index of the Folktales of England and North America* (The Hague: Mouton, 1966); and Stith Thompson, *Motif-Index of Folk Literature* (Bloomington: Indiana University Press, 1956), 6 vols.

4. European folklorist Carl Wilhelm von Sydow termed these local versions of folktales *oicotypes*. Carl Wilhelm von Sydow, *Selected Papers on Folklore*, ed. Laurits Bodker (Copenhagen: Rosenkilde & Bagger, 1948), pp. 50–51.

5. Compiled from U.S., Bureau of the Census, Census of the United States: 1850. 1880. New York. New Jersey (manuscript); and New Jersey, State Census of New Jersey: 1915. Bergen County. Passaic County (manuscript).

6. Charles Kaufman, "An Ethnomusicological Survey Among the People of the Ramapo Mountains," *New York Folklore Quarterly* 23, no. 2 (June 1967): 121–22.

7. Anne Lutz, "The Ballad of the Butcher Boy in the Ramapo Mountains," *New York Folklore Quarterly* 3, no. 1 (Spring 1947): 30–33.

8. Kaufman, pp. 125–26.

9. Julian Pilling, "Buck and Wing: Notes on Lancashire Clog Dancing," *English Dance and Song* 23, no. 1 (January 1959): 25–26; Patricia Tracey, "More About Clog Dancing: The East Lancashire Tradition," ibid., no. 2 (April 1959): 39–40; Edward B. Marks, *They All Sang* (New York: Viking Press, 1934), p. 65; W. G. Raffe, *Dictionary of the Dance* (New York: A. S. Barnes & Co., 1964), p. 79.

10. "A Community of Outcasts," *Appleton's Journal of Literature, Science, and Art* 7, no. 156 (Saturday, Mar. 23, 1872): 325–26.

11. John Dyneley Prince, "The Jersey Dutch Dialect," *Dialect Notes* 3, pt. 6 (1910): 459–84.

12. Ibid., p. 460.

13. Ibid., p. 459.

14. Ibid., p. 467.

15. J. H. Combs, "Old, Early, and Elizabethan English in the Southern Mountains," *Dialect Notes* 4 (1913–17): 283–97.

16. Professor Raven McDavid, Department of English, University of Chicago to David Cohen, Dec. 19, 1969.

17. Donald W. Becker, *Indian Place Names in New Jersey* (Cedar Grove, N.J.: Phillips-Campbell, 1964), pp. 68, 18–19, 31–32, 83–84.

18. James B. H. Storms, *A Jersey Dutch Vocabulary*, n.p.; Edward Franklin Pierson, *The Ramapo Pass*, ed. H. Pierson Mapes (Ramapo, N.Y.: Privately printed, 1955), p. 4.

19. James Ransom, *Vanishing Ironworks of the Ramapos* (New Brunswick, N.J.: Rutgers University Press, 1966), pp. 319–30.

20. Thompson, *Motif-Index*, Motif B 765.6.

21. Ibid., Motif B 765.6; Baughman, *Motif-Index*, Motif X 1321.3.2.

22. Baughman, *Motif-Index*, Motif X 1215.11.

23. Richard Dorson, *American Folklore* (Chicago: University of Chicago Press, 1959), p. 44.

24. Baughman, Motif X 1133.2.

25. Daniel G. Brinton, *The Lenape and Their Legends* . . . (New York: Ams Press, 1969, first published in 1885), pp. 179–83.

26. Baughman, Motif X 1322.1 (c).

27. Aarne and Thompson, no. 1890 A.

28. Baughman, Motifs X 1301.4 (e); X 1301.5 (ha).

29. Thompson, *Motif-Index*, Motifs F 624.3; F 624.1.

30. Richard Dorson, *Buying the Wind* (Chicago: University of Chicago Press, 1964), p. 53.

31. Vineland Training School, "The Jackson Whites; A Study of Racial Degeneracy" (Vineland, N.J., manuscript, c. 1911), n.p.

Chapter 10   *Religion, Folk Beliefs, and World View*

1. *Pentecostal Evangel*, no. 2847 (Dec. 1, 1968), p. 4.

2. Don Yoder, "Official Religion versus Folk Religion," *Pennsylvania Folklife* 15, no. 11 (Winter 1965–66): 38.

3. Adriaen Van Der Donck, *A Description of the New Netherlands*, ed. Thomas F. O'Donnell (Syracuse: Syracuse University Press, 1968, first published in 1656), p. 95.

4. Gladys Tantaquideon, *A Study of Delaware Indian Medicine and Folk Beliefs* (Harrisburg, Pa.: Commonwealth of Pennsylvania Department of Public Instruction and the Pennsylvania Historical Commission, 1942).

5. Ibid., p. 34.

6. See, George Lyman Kittredge, *Witchcraft in Old and New England* (New York: Atheneum, 1972, first published in 1929); M. A. Murray, *The Witch-Cult in Western Europe* (Oxford: Oxford University Press, 1962, first published in 1921).

7. Charles Edward Burgin, "The Extraction of Pain From Burns," *North Carolina Folklore* 8 (July 1960): 17; *Frank C. Brown Collection of North Carolina Folklore* (Durham, N.C.: Duke University Press, 1952–61), 6:138.

8. Yoder, p. 45n.

9. Kittredge, p. 177.

10. Murray, pp. 29 ff.

11. George Korson, *Coal Dust on the Fiddle* (Philadelphia: University of Pennsylvania Press, 1943), p. 201.

12. Ibid., pp. 205–6.

Epilogue   *The Aftermath—Initial Reaction to a New Image*

1. *Herald News* (Ridgewood, N.J.), May 20, 1971, p. A-2.

BIBLIOGRAPHY

Primary Sources

Manuscripts and Manuscript Collections

Bergen County Court House, Hackensack, N.J.:
  Black Births in Bergen County, 1804–1844.
  Deeds.
  Manumission of Slaves, Liber A.
  Tax Assessment List, Township of Mahwah, 1972.
  Wills and Inventories.
Bergen County Historical Society, Johnson Free Library, Hackensack, N.J.:
  New York and New Jersey Cemeteries. Compiled by Herbert S. Acker-
    man and Arthur J. Goff, 1947.
  Paramus Reformed Dutch Church Records, Marriages 1799–1900, Bap-
    tisms 1851–1900. Compiled by Herbert S. Ackerman and Arthur J.
    Goff, 1944.
  Pascack Dutch Reformed Church Records and Cemetery. Compiled by
    Herbert S. Ackerman and Arthur J. Goff, 1946.
  Records of the Ramapo Reformed Dutch Church and of the Ramapo
    Lutheran Church. Compiled by Herbert S. Ackerman and Arthur
    J. Goff, 1944.
  Records of the Zion Lutheran Churches of Saddle River and Ramapo,
    N.J. Compiled by Herbert S. Ackerman and Arthur J. Goff, 1943.
  Saddle River Dutch Reformed Church and Cemetery. Compiled by
    Herbert S. Ackerman and Arthur J. Goff, 1944.
  Tombstone Inscriptions, Bergen County. Compiled by Rev. Edward
    Kelder, 3 vols.
Community Action Council of Passaic County, Hewitt, N.J.:
  Report of Findings of Progress Development Grant, 1967.
  Survey conducted from December 1966 to March 1967 of the Ringwood
    Mine Area.
Eugenics Records Office Files, Dwight Institute of Human Genetics, Uni-
versity of Minnesota, Minneapolis, Minn.:

Osborn, Dorothy, Pedigree of Van Donk-De Grote Albino Family.
Hillburn Village Hall, Hillburn, N.Y.:
    Village Board Minutes.
New Jersey Historical Society, Newark, N.J.:
    New Jersey Boundary Papers, 1769. 2 vols.
    New York and New Jersey Boundary ca. 1748–1753, 2 vols.
    Discovery, Grants, and Settlements of New Jersey ca. 1606–1700.
New Jersey State Archives, State Library, Trenton, N.J.:
    State Census for New Jersey: 1855. Bergen and Passaic Counties.
    State Census for New Jersey: 1865. Bergen and Passaic Counties.
    State Census for New Jersey: 1915. Bergen and Passaic Counties.
    Wills and Inventories.
New-York Historical Society, Map Section, New York City:
    Road from 15 M. Stone, near Suffran's to Fort Lee, Hackensack, Haver-
        straw, etc., by Captain John W. Watkins, Erskine-DeWitt map no. 26.
    Roads from Ringwood to Pompton Plains and from Pompton Plans to
        Sufferns, by Robert Erskine, Erskine-DeWitt map no. 42.
New York Public Library, Manuscript Section, Budke Collection, New
York City, N.Y.:
    Abstracts of Deeds recorded in Liber A in the Office of the Clerk of
        Rockland County, N.Y. (1798–1808), fol. BC-66.
    Assessment Rolls for the Town of Clarkstown, Rockland County, N.Y.,
        for the Years 1841 and 1842, fol. BC-24.
    Assessment Rolls—Real and Personal Estates in the Town of Orange,
        County of Rockland, N.Y., for the Years 1796, 1807, 1808, 1817, 1820,
        1821, 1826, 1827, 1829, 1832, 1837, fol. BC-47.
    Calendar of Wills and Letters of Administration Pertaining to Estates in
        Rockland County, N.Y., to the End of the Year 1850, fol. BC-68.
    Clarkstown, N.Y., Tax Assessment List, 1787, fol. BC-52.
    Genealogical Notebook, 3 vols., fol. BC-58m, 59, 60.
    Grand Jury List, Rockland County, N.Y., 1827, 1828, 1830, fol. BC-22.
    Historical Manuscripts, vol. A-E, Wills, Deeds, Mortgages, Church
        Records, Bills of Sale, Estate Inventories, 1666–1898, fol. 72–74, 34–35.
    Marriage Records of the Reformed Dutch Churches of Tappan and
        Clarkstown, Rockland County, N.Y., 1694–1831. Compiled by David
        Cole and Walter Kenneth Griffin, fol. BC-50.
    Original Assessment Rolls for the Town of Clarkstown, Rockland
        County, N.Y., for the Years 1848, 1850, 1851, 1852, 1853, 1854, fol.
        BC-25.
    Original Assessment Rolls for the Town of Clarkstown, Rockland
        County, N.Y., for the Years 1855, 1856, 1857, fol. BC-26.
    Original Assessment Rolls for the Town of Clarkstown, Rockland County,
        N.Y., for the Years 1858, 1859, 1860, 1861, 1862, 1863, 1864, 1865. 8
        vols., fol. BC-13–20.

Papers Relating to the New York and New Jersey Boundary, 1686–1775; 1924, fol. BC-29.

Patents Granted for the Lands in the Present County of Rockland, N.Y., fol. BC-67.

Records of the Clarkstown Reformed Church (Rockland County, N.Y.), also the Baptismal Records of the Ramapo Evangelical Lutheran Church. Translated from Dutch by George H. Budke, fol. BC-49.

Records of the Greenbush Presbyterian Church at Blauvelt, Rockland County, N.Y., Marriages, Baptisms and Membership from the Origination of the Church in 1812 to the Close of 1850, fol. BC-61.

Records of the New Hempstead Presbyterian Church, Known Locally as the English Church; 1919, fol. BC-65.

Records of the Reformed Dutch Church of West New Hempstead, commonly called the Brick Church, also the Kakiat Reformed Dutch Church, fol. BC-64.

Records of the Tappan Reformed Church. Baptisms, 1816–1870; Marriages, 1831–1870, fol. 48.

Suffern, Andrew. Account Book, 1795–1804, fol. BC-4.

———. Account Book–Ledger B, fol. BC-6.

Suffern, John. Account Book–Haverstraw General Store, fol. BC-8.

Supervisors of the Poor, Account Book, 1793–1819, also 1847–1867. Clarkstown, N.Y., fol. BC-7.

Tombstone Inscriptions, fol. 37–45.

Rockland County Court House, New City, N.Y.:

Deeds.

Party Enrollment Lists.

New York State Census for Rockland County: 1855.

New York State Census for Rockland County: 1865.

New York State Census for Rockland County: 1875.

New York State Census for Rockland County: 1892.

New York State Census for Rockland County: 1905.

New York State Census for Rockland County: 1915.

Wills and Inventories.

Rutgers University Library, Special Collections, New Brunswick, N.J.:

Kite, Elizabeth. Manuscript Research Notes on the Jackson Whites, box 5.

———. Compilation of the Jackson White Rose family, box 5.

———. Correspondence Relating to Research on the Jackson Whites, box 5.

Vineland Training School, The Jackson Whites: A Study of Racial Degeneracy. Vineland, N.J., c. 1911. Microfilm.

Town of Ramapo, N.Y. Tax List. 1972. Hillburn.

United States, Bureau of the Census:

Second Census of the United States: 1800. New York: Rockland County.
  Orange County.
Third Census of the United States: 1810. New York: Rockland County.
  Orange County.
Fourth Census of the United States: 1820. New York: Rockland County.
  Orange County.
Fifth Census of the United States: 1830. New York: Rockland County.
  Orange County. New Jersey: Bergen County. Passaic County.
Sixth Census of the United States: 1840. New York: Rockland County.
  New Jersey: Passaic County. Bergen County.
Seventh Census of the United States: 1850. New York: Rockland County.
  New Jersey: Bergen County. Passaic County.
Eighth Census of the United States: 1860. New York: Rockland County.
  New Jersey: Bergen County. Passaic County.
Ninth Census of the United States: 1870. New York: Rockland County.
Tenth Census of the United States: 1880. New York: Rockland County.
  New Jersey: Bergen County. Passaic County.
West, Lewis, private collection, Midvale, N.J.:
  Account of the General Store at the Long Pond Furnace, 1866.
  Long Pond Ironworks, Account Books, 1866–69.
  Monthly Paylists of the Ringwood Ironworks.
  Payroll for the Greenwood Lake Ice House, August 9, 1879.
  Payrolls for the Ringwood Furnace, 1869.
  Store Sales for the Copper and Hewitt Company Store, August 1879.

Books

Banta, Theodore. *A Frisian Family: The Banta Genealogy.* New York:
  n.p., 1893.
Baptisms at Clarkstown from August 13, 1749, to December 28, 1794,
  History of Rockland County, New York. Edited by David Cole. New
  York: J. B. Beers & Co., 1884.
Baptisms at Tappan from October 25, 1694 to January 10, 1816, *History of
  Rockland County, New York.* Edited by David Cole. New York: J. B.
  Beers & Co., 1884.
Bergen County, N.J., Board of Justices and Chosen Freeholders. *Minutes of
  the Justices and Freeholders of Bergen County, New Jersey, 1715–1795.*
  North Hackensack, N.J.: Bergen County Historical Society, 1924.
Coster, G. C. *Hessian Soldiers in the American Revolution: Records of their
  Marriages and Baptisms of their Children in America, performed by Rev.
  G. C. Coster, 1776–1783, Chaplain of 2 Hessian Regiments.* Translated by
  Marie Dickoré. Cincinnati, Ohio: C. J. Krehbiel Co., 1959.
Danckaerts, Jasper. *Journal of Jasper Danckaerts.* Edited by James B. Bart-
  lett and J. Franklin Jameson. New York: 1913, reprinted in *The History*

of the United States. vol. 1. 1600–1876. Source Readings, eds. Neil Harris, David J. Rothman, and Stephan Thernstrom. New York: Holt, Rinehart & Winston, 1969.

Donck, Adriaen Van Der. A Description of the New Netherlands. Edited by Thomas F. O'Donnell. Syracuse, N.Y.: Syracuse University Press, 1968. First published in 1656.

Eelking, Max von. The German Allied Troops in the North American War of Independence, 1776–1783. Translated and abridged from the German by J. C. Rosengarten. Albany, N.Y.: Joel Munsell's Sons, 1893.

Longworth, David. Longworth's American Almanac, New York Register and City Directory. New York: David Longworth, 1805–26.

Meyers, Carol M. Early New York State Census Records, 1663–1772. 2d ed. Gardena, Calif.: RAM Publishers, 1965.

Muster Rolls of New York Provincial Troops, 1755–1764. New York: New-York Historical Society, 1892.

New Jersey. Acts of the General Assembly of the Province of New Jersey. Edited by Samuel Allinson. Burlington, N.J.: Isaac Collins, 1776.

————. Laws of the State of New Jersey. Compiled by William Paterson. New Brunswick, N.J.: Abraham Blauvelt, 1800.

————. Adjutant General's Office. Official Register of the Officers and Men of New Jersey in the Revolutionary War. Trenton, N.J.: William T. Nicholson & Co., 1872. 2 vols.

————. Record of Officers and Men of New Jersey in the Civil War, 1861–1865. Trenton, N.J.: John L. Murphy, 1876.

New Jersey and the Negro: A Bibliography, 1715–1966. Trenton, N.J.: New Jersey Library Association, 1967.

New Jersey Archives. 1st ser. vols. 11, 12, 19, 20, 24–29 Newspaper Extracts, ed. William Nelson, Paterson, N.J.: Press Printing & Publishing Co., 1894, 1895, 1897, 1898, 1902–17; vol. 22 Marriage Records. ed. William Nelson, Paterson, N.J.: The Press Printing & Publishing Co., 1900; vols. 23, 30–39 Abstracts of Wills, eds. William Nelson, Elmer T. Hutchinson, and A. Van Doren Honeyman, Newark & Sommerville, N.J.: New Jersey Law Journal & Unionist-Gazette Association, 1918–44; 2d sers. vols. 1–5 Newspaper Extracts, eds. William Stryker, Francis Lee, Austin Scott, & William Nelson, Trenton, N.J.: John L. Murphy Publishing Co., 1901–17.

New York, Secretary of State. Calendar of N.Y. Colonial Manuscripts Indorsed Land Papers in the Office of the Secretary of State of New York, 1643–1803. Albany, N.Y.: Weed, Parsons & Co., 1864.

New York State Historian. Third Annual Report of the State Historian of the State of New York, 1897. Albany & New York: Wynkoop Hallenbeck Crawford Co., 1898.

Newark Directory: 1910. Newark: Price & Lee Co., 1910.

Niebyl, Elizabeth Hale. A Program for Housing in the Township of Mahwah, New Jersey: A Survey of Selected Areas and Recommendations for *the Removal of Substandard Conditions.* Mahwah, N.J.: Volunteer Committee Concerned with the People of the Ramapos, Inc., 1955.

O'Callaghan, E. B., ed. *Calendar of Historical Manuscripts in the Office of the Secretary of State, Albany, New York.* Pt. 1, *Dutch Manuscripts, 1630–1664.* Albany, N.Y.: Weed, Parsons & Co., 1865.

———. *The Documentary History of the State of New York.* Albany, N.Y.: Weed, Parsons & Co., 1849. vols. 1–4.

———. *Documents Relative to the Colonial History of the State of New York.* Albany, N.Y.: Weed, Parsons & Co., 1861.

———. *The Register of New Netherlands, 1626 to 1674.* Albany, N.Y.: J. Munsell, 1865.

Stokes, Isaac Newton Phelps. *The Iconography of Manhattan Island, 1498–1909.* New York: Robert H. Dodd, 1922. 6 vols.

United States, Bureau of the Census. *Heads of Families at the First Census of the United States Taken in the Year 1790. New York.* Washington, D.C.: Government Printing Office, 1908.

———. *Tenth Census of the United States: 1880. New York. New Jersey. Population.* Washington, D.C.: Government Printing Office, 1883.

———. *Eleventh Census of the United States: 1890. New York. New Jersey. Population.* Washington, D.C.: Government Printing Office, 1894, 1895, 1897.

———. *Twelfth Census of the United States: 1900. New York. New Jersey. Population.* Washington, D.C.: Government Printing Office, 1901–2.

———. *Thirteenth Census of the United States: 1910. New York. New Jersey. Population.* Washington, D.C.: Government Printing Office, 1913.

———. *Fourteenth Census of the United States: 1920. New York. New Jersey. Population.* Washington, D.C.: Government Printing Office, 1923.

———. *Fifteenth Census of the United States: 1930. New York. New Jersey. Population.* Washington, D.C.: Government Printing Office, 1932.

———. *Sixteenth Census of the United States: 1940. New York. New Jersey. Population.* Washington, D.C.: Government Printing Office, 1943.

———. *Seventeenth Census of the United States: 1950. New York. New Jersey. Population.* Washington, D.C.: Government Printing Office, 1952.

———. *Eighteenth Census of the United States: 1960. New York. New Jersey. Population. Housing.* Washington, D.C.: Government Printing Office, 1963.

———. *Nineteenth Census of the United States: 1970. New York. New Jersey. Population.* Washington, D.C.: Government Printing Office, 1973.

Van Laer, Arnold John Ferdinand, ed. *Documents Relating to New Netherlands, 1624–1626, in the Huntington Library.* San Marino, Calif.: Huntington Library, 1924.

Vries, David Peterson de. *Voyages from Holland to America, A.D. 1632 to 1644.* Translated by Henry C. Murphy. New York: Billin & Bros., 1853.

Westervelt, Frances A., comp. *Bergen County, New Jersey, Marriage Rec-*

ords Copied from the Entries as Originally Made at the Court House by the Ministers and Justices of the Peace of the County. New York: Lewis Historical Publishing Co., 1929.

Woodson, Carter Godwin. *Free Negro Heads of Families in the United States in 1830.* Washington, D.C.: Association for the Study of Negro Life and History, 1925.

Periodicals

Baptisms in the Lutheran Church, New York City, From 1725, *New York Genealogical and Biographical Record* 97 (1966): 92–105, 163–70, 223–30.

Census of Orange County, New York, Based on the True Account of the Inhabitants Returned by Dirck Storm, Clerk of the County, June 16, 1702, *The Rockland Record, Being the Proceedings and Historical Collections of the Rockland County Society of the State of New York, Inc., for the Years 1931 and 1932.* Vol. 2 (1931): 65–79.

Census of Orange County, 1712; ibid., Vol. 2 (1931): 22–23.

Federal Census of 1800 for Orange County, New York, *New York Genealogical and Biographical Record,* 64 (January 1933): 62.

Flatbush Dutch Church Records, *Yearbook of the Holland Society of New York.* New York: Holland Society of New York, 1898.

Hoffman, William J.: An Armory of American Families of Dutch Descent, *New York Genealogical and Biographical Record* 19 (July 1938): 224–26.

Marriages in the Reformed Dutch Church, New York City, *New York Genealogical and Biographical Record,* 70 (January 1939): 39.

Marriages in the Village of Bergen in New Jersey beginning 1665, *Yearbook of the Holland Society of New York.* New York: Holland Society of New York, 1914. Vol. 2, *Bergen Book,* pp. 57–85.

Records of the Reformed Dutch Church in New Amsterdam and New York. *Collections of the New York Genealogical and Biographical Society.* Vol. 1 (1890) *Marriages, 1639–1801;* Vol. 2 (1901) *Baptisms, 1639–1739;* Vol. 3 (1902) *Baptisms, 1731–1800.*

Records of the Reformed Dutch Churches of Hackensack and Schraalenburgh, New Jersey, *Collections of the Holland Society,* vol. 1 (1891), pt. 1, *Hackensack;* pt. 2, *Schraalenburgh.*

Some Early Records of the Lutheran Church, New York, *Yearbook of the Holland Society of New York.* New York: Holland Society of New York, 1903.

Newspapers

Argus (West Milford, N.J.)
Bergen Evening Record (Hackensack, N.J.)
Bulletin (Ringwood, N.J.)

Herald News (Ridgewood, N.J.)
New York Times (New York City, N.Y.)
Nyack Journal News (Nyack, N.Y.)
P.M. Daily (New York City, N.Y.)
Ramsey Journal (Ramsey, N.J.)
Rockland County Journal (Nyack, N.Y.)

Secondary Sources

Unpublished Materials

Baird, Doris. The Jackson Whites and Their Culture. Original essay in Suffern Library, Suffern, N.Y., n.d.

Baker, Tunis. The Jackson Whites. Term paper, Paterson (N.J.) Normal College, n.d.

Brief School History of Rockland County, New York. A study prepared by the pupils, teachers, and friends of the Rockland County Public Schools, 1941. Mimeographed.

Cornell, H.; Deluca, P.; and Ziegler, M. Sociological Study of the Jackson Whites. Manuscript in Pascack (New Jersey) Historical Society, n.d.

Crawford, Constance. Jackson Whites. M.A. thesis, School of Education, New York University, 1940.

Finn, Rev. John W. A Ramapo Treasure Hunt. Address to Bergen County Historical Society, Hackensack, N.J., Oct. 21, 1965. Copy in Ridgewood (New Jersey) Public Library.

Goldstein, Kenneth S. A Guide for Field Workers in Folklore. Ph.D. dissertation, Department of Folklore, University of Pennsylvania, 1963.

Hadlock, Nancy. The Jackson Whites of the Ramapo Mountains. Report in Ridgewood (New Jersey) Public Library, c. post-1940s.

Kaufman, Marie L. Public Health Nursing Among the Jackson Whites. Unpublished essay on file in Suffern Public Library, Suffern, N.Y., 1951.

Kury, Theodore W. Historical Geography of the Iron Industry in the New York-New Jersey Highlands, 1700-1900. Ph.D. dissertation, Department of Geography, Louisiana State University, 1968.

Machol, E. A. The Ramapo Mountain People: A Problem of Acceptance. Thesis on file in the Suffern Public Library, Suffern, N.Y., 1966.

Merwin, Miles M. The Jackson Whites. B.A. thesis, Rutgers University, New Brunswick, N.J., 1963.

Moskowitz, Miriam. The Educational Problem of the People of the Ramapos. Master's thesis, Jersey City State College, 1968.

Newark, N.J., Public Library. The Jackson Whites: References to Books, Documents, and Magazines, October 1941.

Nordstorm, Carl A. A Finding List of Bibliographical Materials Relating to Rockland County, New York. Compiled for the Tappan Zee Historical Society, Orangeburg, N.Y., and the Office of the County Superintendent of Schools, New City, N.Y., 1959.

Price, Edward Thomas, Jr. Mixed-Blood Populations of Eastern United States as to Origins, Localizations, and Persistence. Ph.D. dissertation, Department of Geography, University of California, Berkeley, 1950.
Ramapo Presbyterian Church. Church History and Buyer's Guide Including Cook Book of Favorite Recipes. Hillburn, N.Y.: Ramapo Presbyterian Church, n.d. Pamphlet.
Stamato, Linda. The Jackson-Whites of the Ramapo Mountains. M.A. thesis, Seton Hall University, 1968.

Books

Aarne, Antti. *Types of the Folktale; Classification and Bibliography.* Trans. and ed. by Stith Thompson. 2d edition. Helsinki: Suomalainen Tiedeakatemia Academia Scientiarum Fennica, 1961.
Abbott, Wilbur. *New York in the American Revolution.* New York: Charles Scribner's Sons, 1929.
American Society of Genealogists. *Genealogical Research Methods and Sources.* Washington, D.C.: American Society of Genealogists, 1960.
Arensberg, Conrad M., and Kimball, Solon T. *Culture and Community.* New York: Harcourt, Brace, & World, 1965.
Baughman, Ernest Warren. *Type and Motif—Index of the Folktales of England and North America.* The Hague: Mouton & Co., 1966.
Beals, Ralph L., and Hoijer, Harry. *An Introduction to Anthropology.* New York: Macmillan, 1959.
Beck, Henry C. *Fare to Midlands.* New York: E. P. Dutton & Co., 1939; reprinted as *The Jersey Midlands.* New Brunswick, N.J.: Rutgers University Press, 1963.
Becker, Donald William. *Indian Place-Names in New Jersey.* Cedar Grove, New Jersey: Phillips-Campbell Publishing Co., 1964.
Bedell, Cornelia. *Now and Then and Long Ago in Rockland County.* Suffern, N.Y.: privately printed, 1941.
Benson, Lee. *The Concept of Jacksonian Democracy: New York as a Test Case.* New York: Atheneum, 1964, first published in 1961.
Berry, Brewton. *Almost White.* New York: Macmillan Co., 1963.
Boulding, Kenneth E. *The Image; Knowledge in Life and Society.* Ann Arbor: University of Michigan Press, 1956.
Brinton, Daniel Garrison. *The Lenâpe and Their Legends* . . . Philadelphia: D. G. Brinton, 1885.
Brunvand, Jan Harold. *The Study of American Folklore; An Introduction.* New York: W. W. Norton & Co., 1968.
Calhoun, Arthur Wallace. *A Social History of the American Family from Colonial Times to the Present.* 3 vols. Cleveland: Arthur H. Clark Co., 1917.
Clayton, William Woodford, and Nelson, William. *History of Bergen and Passaic Counties, New Jersey* . . . Philadelphia: Everts and Peck, 1882.

Cole, David, ed. *History of Rockland County, New York* . . . New York: J. B. Beers & Co., 1884.

Combination Atlas of Rockland County, New York. Philadelphia: F. A. Davis & Co., 1876.

Cooley, Henry Scofield. *A Study of Slavery in New Jersey.* Johns Hopkins University Studies in History and Political Science. Baltimore: Johns Hopkins University Press, 1896.

Cross, Dorothy, et al. *Archaeology of New Jersey.* 2 vols. Trenton: Archaeological Society of New Jersey, 1941, 1956.

Davis, Allison, and Dollard, John. *Children of Bondage: The Personality Development of Negro Youth in the Urban South.* Washington, D.C.: American Council on Education, 1940.

Davis, Allison; Gardner, Burleigh B.; and Gardner, Mary R. *Deep South: A Social Anthropological Study of Caste and Class.* Abridged ed. Chicago and London: Phoenix Books, University of Chicago Press, 1965. First published in 1941.

Demos, John. *A Little Commonwealth: Family Life in Plymouth Colony.* New York: Galaxy Books, Oxford University Press, 1970.

Dollard, John. *Caste and Class in a Southern Town.* 3d ed. Garden City, N.Y.: Doubleday Anchor Books, 1957. First published in 1937.

Dorson, Richard. *American Folklore.* Chicago: University of Chicago Press, 1959.

———. *Bloodstoppers and Bearwalkers.* Cambridge, Mass.: Harvard University Press, 1952.

———. *Buying the Wind.* Chicago: University of Chicago Press, 1964.

Dover, Cedric. *Half-Caste.* London: Martin Secker & Warburg, 1937.

Durie, Howard I., *The Kakiat Patent.* Pearl River, N.J.: Star Press, 1970.

Emerson, Josephine. The Jackson Whites, *In the Hudson Highlands.* Edited by Solvitur Ambulando. New York: Appalachian Mountain Club, 1945.

Flick, Alexander C., ed. *History of the State of New York.* Vol. 1. New York: Columbia University Press, 1933–37.

Foster, Laurence. *Negro-Indian Relationships in the Southeast.* Philadelphia: University of Pennsylvania Press, 1935.

Frank C. Brown Collection of North Carolina Folklore, The. Edited by Newman Ivy White. 7 vols. Durham, N.C.: Duke University Press, 1952–61.

Franklin, John Hope. *The Free Negro in North Carolina, 1790–1860.* Chapel Hill: University of North Carolina Press, 1943.

Frazier, E. Franklin. *The Free Negro Family: A Study of Family Origins Before the Civil War.* Nashville, Tenn.: Fisk University Press, 1932.

———. *The Negro Family in the United States.* Rev. and abridged ed. Chicago: University of Chicago Press, 1966, first published in 1939.

Goldsby, Richard A. *Race and Races.* New York: Macmillan, 1971.

Green, Frank Bertangue. *The History of Rockland County.* New York: A. S. Barnes & Co., 1886.

Greven, Philip J., Jr. *Four Generations: Population, Land, and Family in Colonial Andover, Massachusetts.* Ithaca, N.Y.: Cornell University Press, 1970.

Goode, William. *The Family.* Englewood Cliffs, N.J.: Prentice-Hall, 1964.

Guss, A. A. Early view of the Pennsylvania interior; the Juniata and Tuscarora Indians and explorations of the Indian traders, in *A History of . . . the Susquehanna and Juniata Valleys.* . . . Edited by Franklin Ellis and A. N. Hungerford. Vol. 1. Philadelphia: Everts, Peck, & Richards, 1886.

Halpert, Herbert, ed. *Christmas Mumming in Newfoundland.* Toronto: University of Toronto Press, 1969.

Harrington, Mark Raymond. *Dickon Among the Lenape Indians.* Philadelphia: John C. Winston, Co., 1938. Now distributed as *Indians of New Jersey.* New Brunswick, N.J.: Rutgers University Press, 1963.

Harvey, Cornelius Burnham, ed. *Genealogical History of Hudson and Bergen Counties, New Jersey.* New York: New Jersey Genealogical Publishing Co., 1900.

Heusser, Albert H. *George Washington's Map Maker: A Biography of Robert Erskine.* Edited by Hubert G. Schmidt. New Brunswick, N.J.: Rutgers University Press, 1966, first published in 1928.

Hewitt, Edward R. *Ringwood Manor, the Home of the Hewitts.* Trenton, N.J.: Trenton Printing Co., 1946.

Hewitt, J. N. B. Tuscarora, *Handbook of American Indians North of Mexico.* Edited by Frederick Webb Hodge. Smithsonian Institution. Bureau of American Ethnology Bulletin 30 Washington, D.C., 1912, pp. 842–53.

Homans, George. *The Human Group.* New York: Harcourt, Brace, & Co., 1950.

Hudson, Sue F. *Background of Ho-Ho-Kus History.* Ho-Ho-Kus, N.J., Woman's Club, 1953.

Jackson, Luther Porter. *Free Negro Labor and Property Holding in Virginia, 1830–1860.* New York: D. Appleton-Century Co., 1942.

Jansen, William Hugh. The Esoteric-Exoteric Factor in Folklore, in *The Study of Folklore,* edited by Alan Dundes. Englewood Cliffs, N.J.: Prentice-Hall, 1965, pp. 43–51.

Johnson, Elias. *Legends, Traditions and Laws of the Iroquois or Six Nations and History of the Tuscarora Indians.* Lockport, N.Y.: Union Printing & Publishing Co., 1881.

Kenyon, Theda. *Something Gleamed.* New York: Julian Messner, 1948.

Kittredge, George Lyman. *Witchcraft in Old and New England.* New York: Atheneum, 1972, first published in 1929.

Korson, George. *Black Rock: Mining Folklore of the Pennsylvania Dutch.* Baltimore, 1960.

————. *Coal Dust on the Fiddle*. Philadelphia: University of Pennsylvania Press, 1943.

Krummel, Henry B. Geography of New Jersey, in *Archaeology of New Jersey* by Dorothy Cross. Vol. 1. Trenton, N.J.: Archaeological Society of New Jersey and the New Jersey State Museum, 1941.

Lacerda, Jean Baptiste de. The Metis, or half-breeds of Brazil, in *Papers on Inter-Racial Problems*. Edited by G. Spiller. London: P. S. King & Son; Boston: World's Peace Foundation, 1911.

Leiby, Adrian C. *The Early Dutch and Swedish Settlers of New Jersey*. New Jersey Historical Series. Princeton, N.J.: D. Van Nostrand Co., Inc., 1964. Now distributed by Rutgers University Press, New Brunswick, N.J.

————. *The Revolutionary War in the Hackensack Valley; The Jersey Dutch and the Neutral Ground, 1775–1783*. New Brunswick, N.J.: Rutgers University Press, 1962.

Livingston, Rosa [Ackerman]. *Turkey Feathers, Tales of Old Bergen County*. 1st ed. Little Falls, N.J.: Phillip-Campbell Press, 1963.

Lossing, Benson J. *The Pictorial Field-Book of the Revolution*. 2 vols. New York: Harper & Brothers, 1855.

Lowell, Edward J. *The Hessians and Other German Auxiliaries of Great Britain in the Revolutionary War*. New York: Harper & Brothers, 1884.

Lowie, Robert. *Social Organization*. New York: Rinehart, 1948.

Mahwah, New Jersey, Chamber of Commerce. *Mahwah: Portrait of a Town*. Mahwah, N.J.: Chamber of Commerce, 1960.

Main, Jackson Turner. *The Social Structure of Revolutionary America*. Princeton, N.J.: Princeton University Press, 1965.

Marks, Edward B. *They All Sang*. New York: Viking Press, 1934.

Matthews, Elmora Messer. *Neighbor and Kin: Life in a Tennessee Ridge Community*. Nashville, Tenn.: Vanderbilt University Press, 1965.

Morgan, Edmund. *Virginians at Home: Family Life in the Eighteenth Century*. Charlottesville, Va.: Dominion Books, University of Virginia Press, 1952.

Morner, Magnus. *Race Mixture in the History of Latin America*. Boston: Little, Brown, & Company, 1967.

Morris, Ira K. *Morris's Memorial History of Staten Island, New York*. 2 vols. West New Brighton, Staten Island: Published by the Author, 1900.

Murdock, George Peter. *Social Structure*. New York: Macmillan Co., 1960.

———— et al. *Outlines of Cultural Materials*. 4th rev. ed. New Haven: Human Relations Area Files, Inc., 1961.

Murray, M. A. *The Witch-Cult in Western Europe*. Oxford: Oxford Paperbacks, Clarendon Press, 1962, first published in 1921.

Nevins, Allan. *Abram S. Hewitt, with Some Account of Peter Cooper*. New York: Harper & Brothers, 1935.

New Jersey Library Association. *New Jersey and the Negro: A Bibliography, 1715–1966*. Trenton: New Jersey Library Association, 1967.

Newcomb, William W. The culture and acculturation of the Delaware Indians, in *Anthropological Papers, Museum of Anthropology, University of Michigan*, no. 10. Ann Arbor: University of Michigan Press, 1956.

Partridge, Eric. *A Dictionary of Slang and Unconventional English* . . . 5th ed. New York: Macmillan Co., 1966.

————. *A Dictionary of the Underworld* . . . London: Routledge & Kegan Paul, 1949.

Penfold, Saxby Vouler. *Romantic Suffern: The History of Suffern, New York, from the Earliest Times to the Incorporation of the Village in 1896.* Tallman, New York: Rockland County Historical Committee, 1955.

Peterson, A. Everett. Population and industry, in *History of the State of New York.* Edited by Alexander C. Flick, vol. 1, *Wigwam and Bouwerie.* New York: Columbia University Press, 1933.

Pierson, Edward Franklin. *The Ramapo Pass, Including the Village of Ramapo Works, Founded by the Pierson Brothers in 1795, Josiah Gilbert, Jeremiah Hulsey, and Isaac Pierson and Other Historical Particulars.* Edited by H. Pierson Mapes. Ramapo, N.Y.: privately printed, 1955, written in 1915.

Pomfret, John E. *The Province of East New Jersey, 1609–1702: The Rebellious Proprietary.* Princeton: Princeton University Press, 1962.

Raffe, W. G. *Dictionary of the Dance.* New York: A. S. Barnes & Co., 1964.

Ransom, James M. *Vanishing Ironworks of the Ramapos: The Story of the Forges, Furnaces, and Mines of the New Jersey-New York Border Area.* New Brunswick, N.J.: Rutgers University Press, 1966.

Redfield, Robert. *The Little Community and Peasant Society and Culture.* Chicago: University of Chicago Press, 1956.

Reina, Ruben. *The Law of the Saints, A Pokoman Pueblo and Its Community Culture.* New York: Bobbs-Merrill Co., 1966.

Reuter, E. B. *The Mulatto in the United States, Including a Study of the Role of Mixed-Blood Races Throughout the World.* New York: Negro University Press, 1969, first published in 1918.

————. *Race Mixture; Studies in Intermarriage and Miscegenation.* New York: Whittlesey House, McGraw-Hill, 1931.

Ringwood: Golden Jubilee, 1918–1968. Ringwood, N.J.: Ringwood Golden Jubilee, Inc., 1968.

Roome, William. *The Early Days and Early Surveys of East New Jersey.* Morristown, N.J.: Jerseyman Steam Press, 1883.

Russell, John H. *The Free Negro in Virginia, 1619–1865.* Johns Hopkins University Studies in Historical and Political Science. New York: Negro Universities Press, 1969, first published in 1913.

Sawyer, Sister Claire Marie, O.S.F. *Some Aspects of the Fertility of a Tri-Racial Isolate.* Washington: Catholic University of America, 1961.

Schrabisch, Max. *Aboriginal Rock Shelters and Other Archaeological Notes of Wyoming Valley and Vicinity.* Reprint from *Proceedings and Collec-*

tions of the Wyoming Historical and Geological Society, vol. 19. Wilkes-Barre, Pa.: E. B. Yordy Co., 1926.

Shapiro, H. L. The mixed-blood Indian, in *The Changing Indian.* Edited by Oliver La Farge. Norman, Ok.: University of Oklahoma Press, 1942.

Skinner, Alanson B. *The Indians of Greater New York.* Cedar Rapids, Ia.: Torch Press, 1915.

———, and Schrabisch, Max. *A Preliminary Report of the Archaeological Survey of the State of New Jersey.* Bulletin 9. Trenton: Geological Survey of New Jersey, 1913.

Smeltzer, Chester A., and Dater, John V. *The Birth and Growth of Ramsey and Mahwah.* Ramsey, N.J.: Ramsey Journal, 1949.

Speck, Frank Gouldsmith. *A Study of the Delaware Indian Big House Ceremony* . . . Harrisburg: Pennsylvania Historical Commission, 1931.

Stephenson, John B. *Shiloh: A Mountain Community.* Lexington, Kentucky: University of Kentucky Press, 1968.

Stimpson, George W. Who are the Jackson Whites? in *Things Worth Knowing.* New York: A. L. Burt Co., 1932, pp. 377–78.

Stonequist, Everett V. *The Marginal Man: A Study in Personality and Culture Conflict.* New York: Russell and Russell, 1961, first published in 1937.

———. Race mixture and the mulatto, in *Race Relations and the Race Problem* . . . Edited by Edgar T. Thompson. New York: Greenwood Press, 1968, pp. 246–70.

Storms, James B. H. *A Jersey Dutch Vocabulary.* Park Ridge, N.J.: Pascack Historical Society, 1964.

Storms, John C. *Origin of the Jackson-Whites of the Ramapo Mountains.* Park Ridge, N.J., 1936, reprinted 1945, 1953, 1958.

Sydow, Carl Wilhelm von. *Selected Papers on Folklore.* Edited by Laurits Bodker. Copenhagen: Rosenkilde & Bagger, 1948.

Tantaquideon, Gladys. *A Study of Delaware Indian Medicine Practice and Folk Beliefs.* Harrisburg: Commonwealth of Pennsylvania, Department of Public Instruction, Pennsylvania Historical Commission, 1942.

Terhune, Albert Payson. *Treasure.* New York and London: Harper & Brothers, 1926.

Terry, Walter. *The Dance in America.* New York: Harper & Brothers, 1956.

Thompson, Edgar Tristram, ed. *Race Relations and the Race Problem: A Definition and an Analysis.* New York: Greenwood Press, 1968.

Thompson, Stith. *The Folktale.* New York: Dryden Press, 1946.

———. *Motif-Index of Folk Literature.* 6 vols. Bloomington: Indiana University Press, 1956.

Tompkins, Arthur S., ed. *Historical Record of the Close of the Nineteenth Century of Rockland County, New York.* Nyack, N.Y.: Van Deusen & Joyce, 1902.

Torrey, Raymond H.; Place, Frank; and Dickinson, Robert L. *New York*

Walk Book. American Geographical Society Outing Series no. 2. New York: American Geographical Society, 1923.

United States, Department of Labor, Office of Policy Planning and Research. The Negro family: the case for national action (by Daniel Patrick Moynihan), 1965, in *The Moynihan Report and the Politics of Controversy.* Edited by Lee Rainwater and William L. Yancey. Cambridge, Mass.: Massachusetts Institute of Technology Press, 1967, pp. 41–124.

United States, Work Projects Administration. *Indian Site Survey of New Jersey, March 16, 1936–June 30, 1938.* Trenton: New Jersey State Museum, 1938.

Van Loon, Lawrence Gwyn. *Crumbs from an Old Dutch Closet: The Dutch Dialect of Old New York.* The Hague: M. Nijhoff, 1938.

Van Valen, J. M. *History of Bergen County, New Jersey.* New York: New Jersey Publishing & Engraving Co., 1900.

Wallace, Anthony F. C. *The Modal Personality Structure of the Tuscarora Indians, as Revealed by the Rorschach Test.* Smithsonian Institution, Bureau of American Ethnology Bulletin no. 150. Washington, D.C.: 1952.

Weller, George. The Jackson Whites, in *A New Jersey Reader.* Foreword by Henry Charlton Beck. New Brunswick, N.J.: Rutgers University Press, 1961.

Wentworth, Harold. *American Dialect Dictionary.* New York: Thomas Y. Crowell Co., 1944.

Wertenbaker, Thomas Jefferson. *The Founding of American Civilization. The Middle Colonies.* New York: Charles Scribner's Sons, 1938.

Weslager, C. A. *Delaware's Forgotten Folk: The Story of the Moors and Nanticokes.* Philadelphia: University of Pennsylvania Press, 1943.

———. *The Delaware Indians: A History.* New Brunswick, N.J.: Rutgers University Press, 1972.

Westervelt, Frances A. *History of Bergen County, New Jersey, 1630–1923.* 3 vols. New York: Lewis Historical Publishing Co., 1923.

Widmer, Kemble. *The Geology and Geography of New Jersey.* The New Jersey Historical Series, volume 19. Princeton, New Jersey: D. Van Nostrand Co., 1964.

Williams, William Carlos. *Paterson.* New York: New Directions Publishing Co., 1963, first published in 1946.

———. To Elsie, in *Chief Modern Poets of England and America,* edited by Gerald De Witt Sanders, et al. 4th ed. Vol. 2, *The American Poets.* New York: Macmillan Co., 1929.

Wilson, James Grant, ed. *The Memorial History of the City of New York from its First Settlement to the Year 1892.* New York: New York History Co., 1892.

Yap, Angelita Q. *A Study of a Kinship System: Its Structural Principles.* Washington: Catholic University of America, 1961.

Periodicals

Beale, Calvin L. American tri-racial isolates, *Eugenics Quarterly* 4 (December 1957): 187–96.

Ben-Amos, Dan. Toward a Definition of Folklore in Context, *Journal of American Folklore* 84 (January-March 1971): 3–15.

Berger, Meyer. Hill Folk at the City's Portals—Only "Forty-five Minutes From Broadway" Dwell Primitive People Whose Lives Are Still Untouched by the Turbulent Stream of the Metropolis, *New York Times Magazine* (March 24, 1935): 13, 22.

Budke, George H. The History of the Tappan Patent, in *The Rockland Record; Being the Proceedings and Historical Collections of the Rockland County Society of the State of New York Inc. for the Years 1931 and 1932.* Vol. 2. Nyack, N.Y.: Rockland County Society of the State of New York, 1931.

Burgin, Charles E. The Extraction of Pain from Burns, *North Carolina Folklore* 8 (July 1960): 17.

Burnett, Swan M. A note on the Melungeons, *American Anthropologist* 2 (October 1889): 347–49.

Chanler, David. The Jackson Whites: An American episode, *Crisis* 45 (May 1939): 138.

Combs, L. H. Old, early, and Elizabethan English in the southern mountains, *Dialect Notes* 4 (1913–17): 283–97.

Community of outcasts, A. *Appleton's Journal of Literature, Science, and Art* 7 (Saturday, Mar. 23, 1872): 324–29.

Connolly, James C. Slavery in colonial New Jersey and the causes operating against its extension, *Proceedings of the New Jersey Historical Society* 14 (April 1929): 181–202.

De Yoe, Willard L. Ramapo Valley History Begins in This Issue, *Ramsey Journal* (Ramsey, New Jersey), July 4, 1957, pp. 1, 5.

———. Second Chapter of Ramapo Valley History Given, *Ramsey Journal*, July 11, 1957, pp. 7, 9.

———. Hopper House History Is Continued, *Ramsey Journal*, July 18, 1957, pp. 7, 10.

———. History of Hopper House and Ramapo Valley Continues, *Ramsey Journal*, July 25, 1957, p. 7.

———. History of Hopper House and Valley Road During Revolutionary Times is Continued with Story of Lafayette and French Army, *Ramsey Journal*, Aug. 1, 1957, p. 7.

———. Victorious End of Revolution Recounted in Part of History of Hopper House, Valley Road, *Ramsey Journal*, Aug. 8, 1957, p. 5.

———. Hopper House and Valley Road History Ends with Anecdotes, Legends, Notes About Period, *Ramsey Journal*, Aug. 15, 1957, pp. 9, 12.

Demos, John. Notes on life in Plymouth Colony, *William and Mary Quarterly* 22 (April 1965): 264–86.

Dunlap, A. R., and Weslager, C. A. Trends in the naming of tri-racial mixed blood groups in the eastern United States, *American Speech* 22 (April 1947): 81–87.

Foster, George M. What is folk culture? *American Anthropologist* 55 (April–June 1953): 159–73.

Gardner, D. H. The emancipation of slaves in New Jersey, *Proceedings of the New Jersey Historical Society* 9 (January 1924): 1–21.

Gilbert, William Harlen, Jr. Memorandum concerning the characteristics of the larger mixed-blood racial islands of the eastern United States, *Social Forces* 24 (May 1946): 438–47.

Greene, Frances E. The tobacco road of the North, *American Mercury* 53 (July 1941): 15–22.

Greven, Philip J., Jr. Family structure in seventeenth-century Andover, Massachusetts, *William and Mary Quarterly* 23 (April 1966): 234–56.

Hand, Wayland D. The folklore, customs, and traditions of the Butte miner, *California Folklore Quarterly* 5 (1946): 153–78.

Harris, Mark. America's oldest interracial community, *Negro Digest* 6 (July 1948): 21–24.

Harte, Thomas J. Trends in mate selection in a tri-racial isolate, *Social Forces* 37 (March 1959): 215–21.

Homans, George C., and Schneider, David M. Kinship Terminology and the American kinship system, *American Anthropologist* 57 (December 1955): 1194–1208.

Honeyman, Abraham Van Doren. Early trials of Negroes in Bergen County, *Proceedings of the New Jersey Historical Society* 10 (1925): 357.

Johnson, Guy B. Personality in a White-Indian-Negro community, *American Sociological Review* 4 (August 1939): 516–23.

Johnston, James Hugo. Documentary evidence of the relations of Negroes and Indians, *Journal of Negro History* 14 (January 1929): 21–43.

Kaufman, Charles H. An ethnomusicological survey among the people of the Ramapo Mountains, *New York Folklore Quarterly* 23 (March 1967): 3–43; ibid. (June 1967): 109–31.

Kull, Irving Stoddard. Slavery in New Jersey, *Americana Illustrated* 24 (October 1930): 443–72.

Linn, William Alexander. Slavery in Bergen County, N.J., *Papers and Proceedings of the Bergen County Historical Society* 4 (1907–8): 23–40.

Lockridge, Kenneth. Land, Population and the Evolution of New England Society, 1630–1790, *Past and Present* 39 (April 1968): 62–80.

Lucas, E. H. The role of folklore in the discovery and rediscovery of plant drugs, *Centennial Review of Arts and Science* 3 (Spring 1959): 173–88.

Lutz, Anne. The ballad of the butcher boy in the Ramapo Mountains, *New York Folklore Quarterly* 3 (Spring 1947): 28–35.
———. The ballad of "Brave Pudding and the Spy" in the Ramapo Valley, *New York Folklore Quarterly* 10 (1954): 279–84.
McKinley, Albert E. English and Dutch Towns of New Netherlands, *American Historical Review* 6 (1900): 1–18.
Merwin, Miles M. The Jackson Whites, *Rutgers Alumni Monthly* 42 (July 1963): 21–36.
Milling, Chapman J. Is the serpent tale an Indian survival? *Southern Folklore Quarterly* 1 (March 1937): 43–55.
Miner, H. The folk-urban continuum, *American Sociological Review* 17 (October 1952): 529–37.
Mintz, Sidney W. The folk-urban continuum and the rural proletarian community, *American Journal of Sociology* 59 (September 1953): 136–43.
———. On Redfield and Foster (brief communications), *American Anthropologist* 56 (February 1954): 87–92.
Morgan, Edwin Vernon. Slavery in New York, *Half-Moon Series* 2 (January 1898).
N.A.A.C.P. Bulletin 2 (October 1943): 10.
Nelson, William. Annual report of the corresponding secretary for 1906–07, *Proceedings of the New Jersey Historical Society* 5 (October 1907): 120.
Northrup, A. Judd. Slavery in New York: A historical sketch, *New York State Library Bulletin. History* 6 (May 1900): 243–313.
Odum, Howard W. Folk sociology as a subject field for the historical study of total human society and the empirical study of group behavior, *Social Forces* 31 (March 1953): 193–223.
Park, Robert E. Mentality of racial hybrids, *American Journal of Sociology*, 36 (January 1931): 534–55.
Pilling, Julian. Buck and wing: Notes on Lancashire clog dancing, *English Dance and Song* 23 (January 1959): 25–27.
———. Description of clog dance taught by Joss Robinson, Yorkshire, *English Dance and Song* 23 (June 1959): 85.
Price, Edward T. A geographic analysis of White-Indian-Negro racial mixtures in the eastern United States, *Annals of the Association of American Geographers* 43 (June 1953): 138–55.
Prince, John Dyneley. The Jersey Dutch dialect, *Dialect Notes* 3 (1910): 459–84.
Ramapo Memories, Magazine of History 4 (September 1906): 139–44.
Rankin, Edward S. The Ramapo Tract, *Proceedings of the New Jersey Historical Society* 50 (1932): 375–94.
Redfield, Robert. The folk society, *American Journal of Sociology* 52 (January 1947): 293–308.
———. The natural history of the folk society, *Social Forces* 31 (March 1953): 224–28.

Rogers, James C. Taking out fire, *North Carolina Folklore* 16 (May 1968): 46–52.

Skinner, Alanson. A primitive new race in the very heart of civilization: The "Jackson Whites," *American Examiner* (1911). In the files of the Eugenics Records Office, Dwight Institute for Human Genetics, University of Minnesota.

Snedecor, Spencer T., and Harryman, William K. Surgical Problems in Hereditary Polydactylism and Syndactylism, *Journal of the New Jersey Medical Society* 37 (September 1940): 443–49.

Speck, Frank. Jackson Whites, *Southern Workman* 40, no. 2 (February 1911): 104–7.

Splitter, Henry Winfred. Miner's luck, *Western Folklore* 40 (1956): 229–46.

Stuart, William. Negro slavery in New Jersey and New York, *Americana Illustrated* 16 (October 1922): 347–67.

Thompson, Edgar T. The Little Races, *American Anthropologist* 74 (October 1972): 1295–1306.

Torrey, Raymond H. Peter Hasenclever: A pre-revolutionary iron-master, *New York State Historical Association Proceedings* 34 (1936): 306–15.

Tracy, Patricia. More about clog dancing: The East Lancashire tradition, *English Dance and Song* 23 (April 1959): 39–41.

Wallace, Anthony F. C. The Tuscarora, sixth nation of the Iroquois confederacy, in *Proceedings of the American Philosophical Society*, 93 (May, 1949): 159–65.

Warner, W. Lloyd. American caste and class, *American Journal of Sociology* 42 (September 1936): 234–39.

Weller, George. The Jackson Whites, *New Yorker* 14 (Sept. 17, 1938): 29–39.

Westervelt, Frances A. Hackensack Township, Bergen County . . . Facts and figures from 800 mss, the gift of Abraham R. Collins. *Papers and Proceedings of the Bergen County Historical Society* 11 (1915/16): 14–91.

Who are the Jackson Whites? *Pathfinder* (Sept. 5, 1931): 20.

Woodson, Carter G. Free Negro owners of slaves in the United States in 1830, *Journal of Negro History* 9 (January 1924): 41–85.

——. The relations of Negroes and Indians in Massachusetts, *Journal of Negro History* 5 (January 1920): 45–57.

Yoder, Don. Official Religion versus Folk Religion, *Pennsylvania Folklife* 15 (Winter 1965–66): 36–52.

INDEX